Talking, writing and learning 8–13

SCHOOLS COUNCIL WORKING PAPER 59

Talking, writing and learning 8–13

the report of the Schools Council
English in the Middle Years of
Schooling Project, Goldsmiths' College
University of London

Margaret Mallett
and Bernard Newsome

Foreword by JAMES BRITTON

Evans/Methuen Educational

First published 1977 for the Schools Council
by Evans Brothers Limited
Montague House, Russell Square, London WC1B 5BX
and Methuen Educational
11 New Fetter Lane, London EC4P 4EE

ISBN 0 423 89910 4

Printed in Great Britain by
Richard Clay (The Chaucer Press) Ltd
Bungay, Suffolk

Contents

Foreword

I would hazard a guess that few of the reports the Schools Council has produced will have so long a history as this one. All the more reason, for my part, to welcome its publication at last; and perhaps some excuse for me, in writing this foreword, to take a brief look at its history. But it will be history as remembered events, not a slice of what some sociologists have called 'documentary reality' (which proves, I suspect, a poor ghost that cannot survive long after we have filed away our agenda papers).

To begin (as tedious writers do) at the beginning; in October 1965, having served six years on the Secondary School Examinations Council English Panel, I found myself at the first meeting of the 'nucleus English Panel' of the Schools Council, under the chairmanship of Percy Wilson. One of the earliest papers to appear on the agenda was a draft that had been prepared for internal circulation but was later to be published as Schools Council Working Paper No. 3, *English: a Programme for Research and Development in English Teaching* (HMSO, 1965). Members of the English Inspectorate and the SSEC English Panel had, if my record serves me aright, taken some part in drafting the document in the winter of 1964/65. The Schools Council's initial manifesto had identified three priority areas for research and development, and one of these was the teaching of English. What the document set out to do was to map the area of existing and needed research and propose a national organization for dissemination and development. By the time the English panel met, a small ad hoc and short-lived body called the Consultative Committee on Communication had worked on the document and recommended the commissioning of five projects intended to form an interrelated nucleus of research into language development. Thus, by the time the document appeared as Working Paper No. 3, the English Panel had given its approval, and things were moving: 'The Council has already authorised the commissioning of the major research project in the field of communications . . . The aim here is to build up a picture of the development of a child's powers of communication and the relative contribution made by different learning media to it' (page 16). The climate in which these early meetings of the panel and the consultative committee were carried on was an exhilarating one. Inevitably, the size of the budget compared very unfavourably with the scope of the proposed undertakings, but hopes were high for the sort of funding that might be forthcoming in the future.

Among the five projects established to form 'the nucleus' was the Written Language of 11–18 Year Olds Project (1966–71) that I directed at the University of London Institute of Education. The project was commissioned to look at the development of writing abilities in the secondary-school years; a brief outline of its objectives, as recorded at the time, makes the particular point that a study would be made of 'the relationship of "personal" to "impersonal" uses of the written language'.

It seems, looking back, that in the area of English work in schools, the founding of the Schools Council ushered in a very productive period. From a number of dissociated activities, reflecting a variety of approaches, something like a concerted effort and a coherent policy began to emerge. The National Association for the Teaching of English, formed in 1963, was closely associated with the Council's work through the English Panel. Existing research projects (notably the Nuffield Programme in Linguistics and English Teaching (1964–67), directed by Professor M. A. K. Halliday, which was taken over by the Schools Council in 1967) and new projects as they were launched were encouraged towards a greater measure of co-operation and cross-fertilization. Also a new chapter in international exchanges began with the Anglo-American Seminar at Dartmouth in 1966 and the Squire–Applebee study of English High Schools, launched in December of the same year. Meanwhile, the development of the new CSE syllabuses was bringing teachers into closer consultation, a proceeding in which the Council played an active role.

In due course the nucleus English Panel was extended, made representative and became the English Subject Committee. Its first years were marked by a proliferation of sub-committees which led a surprisingly active existence. Among them was a Secondary English Sub-committee, and a Primary one; after deliberating for some eighteen months they felt the need to work as a joint sub-committee and this they continued to do for a further eighteen months, at which point, in November 1968, the English in the Middle Years Working Party came into existence. In January 1970 this working party produced for internal circulation a sixteen-page document on English in the middle years of schooling. In the main this is a rationale, a theoretical statement of objectives at this stage. It draws upon the thinking of the Written Language of 11–18 Year Olds Project and shows how the distinction between 'personal' and 'impersonal' writing has evolved into a set of three main function categories for writing, 'transactional', 'expressive' and 'poetic'. The document survived to become one of the starting-points for the project reported in the present volume.

A crowning achievement of the Primary English Sub-committee had been to bring into being a two-year project, Language Development in the Primary Schools, directed by the late Connie Rosen at Goldsmiths' College. Its purpose was to seek out examples of successful practice and examine them in the light of 'theoretical understanding which is becoming available from current projects'. It ran from 1969 to 1971. (See *The Language of Primary School Children* by Connie and Harold Rosen, published by Penguin Education in 1973.) When in 1969 Professor Alec Ross put forward a proposal for a small team to prepare advice on the teaching of English for the project he was directing on the middle years curriculum (Middle Years of Schooling Project, 1968–72), the matter was referred to the English Committee, now under the chairmanship of John Dixon. After some negotiation, the Middle Years Working Party of the English Committee detailed a scheme by which the new undertaking could meet Professor Ross's needs, benefit from their own deliberations, and be closely associated with Connie Rosen's project and the Schools Council Writing Research Unit at the Institute of Education, University of London.

As a result, in September 1970 a two-year project, English in the Middle Years of Schooling, was established under the directorship of Bernard Newsome, who had for four years been a full-time research officer in the Writing Research Unit. His teaching experience had been in secondary schools. Margaret Mallett, an experienced primary-school teacher, was appointed as research officer for the team. For the first term the project was located at the London Institute of Education, for the remainder of the time at Goldsmiths' College, London.

Thus many strands intertwined to produce this enterprise, though it may be difficult for a newcomer to the scene to perceive any pattern. The strands continued to intertwine in a very active way throughout the deliberations of the project's Consultative Committee: I doubt if the Schools Council meeting rooms have housed a livelier or more stimulating set of meetings. In the summer of 1972, when the project ended, Bernard Newsome returned home to Melbourne after an absence of many years. A great deal of valuable material had been gathered and the outline of the report had been sketched out, but much remained to be done before it could be ready for publication.

Everyone who has been concerned with the project will be grateful to Margaret Mallett for taking over the task of presenting the report for publication, and to the Schools Council staff for their persistence and their expert editorial support; while at the same time they will want to acknowledge the irreplaceable value of Bernard Newsome's original contribution.

It has often been noted that one of our typical responses to stress is to reduce the number of dimensions we are prepared to take into account in arriving at a judgement. We cannot today breathe the air of the 1960s and we do our work as teachers in an atmosphere of less confidence and fainter encouragement than we did then. Pressures, economic and other, are more and more sharply felt; and there are signs that our response to this situation includes a narrowing of our educational perspectives. For this reason I believe the contribution of this report may be more timely today than it would have been when the funding ceased in 1972; that it provides a corrective more urgently needed today than then. A reader cannot fail to be struck by the breadth of views and sympathies that these two observers take into the classrooms that provided their data; and while they consistently look beyond the 'how' to the 'why', there is nothing doctrinaire in their judgements and no simple orthodoxy emerges. As follow-up reading to the Bullock Report (for reasons both favourable and unfavourable to that report), I can recommend nothing better to anyone concerned with language and learning in the middle years of schooling.

JAMES BRITTON

Acknowledgements

Bernard Newsome, whose teaching experience has been at secondary level, directed the English in the Middle Years of Schooling Project while I, a primary-school teacher, was research officer keeping a special eye on the younger pupils. In practice both members of the team worked with the whole age-range. Alison Varley was our secretary, and as she had taught English before joining the project her help went further than administration.

Bernard Newsome and I worked on Chapter I together (I wrote the first eight contexts, Bernard Newsome the last four) and we planned the other chapters before his return to Australia. He wrote the first half of Chapter III, 'Talking to learn', and an introduction and the section on the work of two able writers for Chapter IV, 'Writing'. I based Chapter II on a paper he wrote for a Schools Council consultative committee. I also wrote the second part of Chapter III, the rest of the chapter on writing, and the final chapter. Since it was I who acted on the recommendations of the Council's committees in producing the report, the final responsibility for the report is mine.

Without the help of a number of people the report could not have reached publication. We owe much to the pupils, teachers and headteachers whose authorities allowed us to visit and work in their schools. The schools are listed at the end of the report. There were some teachers whose help for various reasons went beyond allowing us to observe them and use their material and here we thank Carol Barden, Pennie Blackie, Tom Carr, Silas Harvey, Jim Holland, Elizabeth Cartland, Tom Gannon, Heather Lyons, Peter Medway, Sam McCready, Tom McCutcheon, Tom Stabler, Rosemary Straker, Janet Watson and James and Gwen Wratten for their distinctive part in the development of our thinking.

I am grateful for the guiding hand of Professor James Britton and his constant reassurance and encouragement. My colleague at Goldsmiths' College, Jo Kelly, commented most helpfully on the final section of the chapter on writing which deals with the handling of technical aspects.

Geraldine Murray, another colleague, made some insightful general comments and helped me to improve Chapter III. I also benefited from the wisdom of my friend Angela Williams of Breton Hall College of Education in pulling together the section on writing across the curriculum in Chapter IV.

Our consultative committee provided a particularly wide range of classroom and research experience on which we drew during the course of the project. Tom McCutcheon and Jim Holland made a special contribution. They collected a rich range of material – tapes of talk and samples of writing in Northern Ireland.

Members of both the Schools Council English Committee and the English Research and Development Working Party proffered much constructive advice, and Patrick Creber made some important comments on the section on story-telling and poem-making in Chapter IV.

Del Goddard, Chairman of the Schools Council Steering Committee B Publications Sub-committee commented helpfully on the final chapter.

I was fortunate indeed in the help I had from the final editor of the report in the Council's Publications Section. I acknowledge also the help of other members of the Schools Council, not least the two curriculum officers concerned.

There are certain problems for mothers of very young children in tackling work of this nature and my grateful thanks are given to my mother-in-law, Joyce Mallett, for caring for Katie and Anna on many occasions. Above all it has been my husband David who, not only by sharing responsibility for children and chores but also by listening to developing ideas and commenting on first drafts as an intelligent layman, has helped me see this report through.

MARGARET MALLETT

Introduction

This report aims to get teachers thinking about the priorities in a language programme for pupils in the middle years of schooling. The emphasis is on the potential of talking and writing for learning although, as illustrated in the contexts in Chapter I, all four language processes – talking, listening, writing and reading – often run together. Helping pupils to use language with facility, flexibility and satisfaction should not be the responsibility of the English teacher alone, and the role of language in all lessons is considered.

Is there, none the less, a special area in which the English teacher operates, an area not easily integrated with other subjects? We are sure there is and argue the case for preserving a space for exploring the concerns of the developing individual, matters not tied to any particular theme or topic. At the heart of English teaching lie the thoughts, feelings, preoccupations and developing ideas of the pupils and we must start from these. The conventions of spelling and punctuation need to be mastered and there is a wealth of literature to explore, but skills and books are the servants and not the masters of the informed English programme.

Teaching is often rather a solitary occupation; teachers do not always know what is happening in other classrooms, even in the same school. We consider ourselves fortunate indeed to have had the opportunity to observe and talk to so many imaginative teachers and their pupils throughout England and Northern Ireland during the project. Much depends on the capacity of individual teachers to bring insight and sensitivity to the selection of material for a particular group and to the careful organization of each teaching/learning situation. We share here some of the best of what we saw, and without being prescriptive in a narrow sense we try to comment helpfully on the organization of the learning programme. What these pupils and teachers do together tells us much more about 'promising' practice than, for example, the fact that a school operates an integrated studies programme, or that a primary or middle school is open-plan.

Even the best practice can benefit from theoretical knowledge about the role of language in learning and we refer to the work of Vygotsky, Piaget, Bruner, Kelly, Langer, Harding and Britton. The message came through clearly, in talking to teachers in the schools and teachers' centres where so many of our ideas were developed, that theory is most helpful when it is yoked to classroom practice. We have taken cognisance of this in our discussion of particular issues.

Guide to the report

The first chapter presents an anthology indicating the range of language work encountered over the two-year project. We describe enterprises, topics, integrated programmes and shorter-term episodes in some detail. Transcripts do, of course, cut us off from the immediacy of the human voice and we were not always able to capture enough of the talk and chatter. We hope, however, that we have been able to give some indication of how these teachers and pupils work together and the many and complicated factors connected with successful practice. Some of the contexts are a common feature of many schools. They are included because we see our task as reinforcing what is tried and tested and found to be sound, as well as pointing to what is less familiar but worth attempting (for example, the rarely encountered improvisation work exemplified in Context 6). The contexts are the life-blood of the report and we refer back to them many times; subsequent chapters deal with the issues arising here.

The difficulty many pupils experience in dealing with systematic learning was evident in much that we saw. 'Starting from the pupils' frameworks' has become a cliché, but how far is this actually practised, and how many of us really understand its implications for day-to-day practice? In Chapter II we examine the problems pupils face in bridging the gap between personal experience and school learning.

In Chapter III we study spoken language and its special contribution to learning, and look at the implications of different teaching styles for pupil understanding. We consider the important place of 'spectator-role' talk and improvised drama in the learning programme.

We turn next, in Chapter IV, to writing. Facing the hard fact that for many pupils this is for the most part a meaningless chore, we consider how teachers can devise a programme in which pupils can see the value and relevance of their writing. The accent is on expressive writing, writing to learn, and we look at ways in which we can help pupils make progress in writing across the curriculum, using both personal and impersonal forms of language, and enjoy writing their own poems and stories. We comment on the place of spelling and punctuation and end the chapter with an analysis, in terms of function, of the writing of pupils at extreme ends of our age-range.

Finally, in Chapter V we set out what seems to have emerged from the inquiry and describe the progress of six schools in solving problems in the curriculum.

The schools

Some local authorities have come to see the age-span from eight to thirteen as a distinct one, during which pupils bridge the gap between the infant stage, when they first meet the formal demands of school, and the secondary stage with its more differentiated curriculum. Middle schools were, therefore, of special interest to us but we were not, and are not, committed to any particular kind of organization. (In the last chapter we indicate the advantages and disadvantages of different patterns.) We observed pupils in the upper primary school and the lower secondary school, as well as those of all ages in middle schools.

Our brief was to look at 'promising' practice which in general we took to indicate situations in which pupils were faced with a wide range of opportunities for activities of different kinds reflected in a rich variety of language work. The work of the project team covered as far as possible the following variables: primary schools following an integrated day and those with a more subject-centred curriculum; secondary and middle schools which integrate English with other subjects and those where English appears as a discrete unit on the timetable; city, village and rural schools, schools with different kinds of intake and those working under special pressures (for example, inner-city schools).

How were the schools which we were to visit, re-visit, work and observe in selected? We wrote to all the directors of education in England asking for a short list of schools with particular strengths and for permission to contact them. The National Association for the Teaching of English and its primary sub-committee helped us, sending lists of schools we could usefully visit, and many people in education known to us personally directed us towards schools specially concerned with language work. During the first term we made many visits and finally trimmed our list to about forty schools (including six in Belfast) having decided we could more usefully look in detail at a relatively small number of schools rather than at a greater number more superficially.

During the first visit an information sheet would be completed with the help of headteacher and staff. This proved a good point of reference, a reminder of the details when we received tapes and writing. A folder was assembled on each school and by the end of the project most bulged with writing and examples of transcribed talk and drama. By the second term we had collected a range of interesting material and were able to send out a guide to interested schools on making collections of work for the project. Our interest was in the ordinary work of the schools; there was no intervention programme and our visits did not alter the normal course of the school day.

The children

What is the nature of the journey taken between the years eight to thirteen? Are these years a distinct period in that we can make some generalizations about the things achieved? What is the role of the school in development in these years? We explore these themes in different ways in this report.

We believe that teachers have the power to harness the will to learn in a way that neither parents nor peer group can achieve; yet we must not underestimate the importance to children of their homes and neighbourhood, their family and friends. Their feelings and thoughts, their perspective on the world articulated in their language, is where to begin, but not where to end. The challenge for teachers is to use what pupils bring to the learning situation to engineer their progress. They also need to build into the programme opportunities for individuals as well as presenting a common core of learning for all the pupils.

What are pupils like at different points in this age-range? Can we make any tentative generalizations, while remaining aware of the enormous range of individual differences? In Chapter IV we learn something about the worlds of two children through their writing. Cathy's preoccupations differ from Kerry's partly, of course, because they are different people but also because of the age-gap. The introspection and soul-searching of some of

Cathy's writing is a function of her age, just as Kerry's work reflects some of the special vitality of the younger child.

In the early contexts in Chapter I we find younger children delighting in the physical environment and making progress in exploring their world; we note them showing an enthusiasm for animals and their care, making collections of shells and such like, enjoying craft and art work, indeed all practical work, and chatting about everything they have done and seen. But what is the extent and what are the limitations of their mental operations? Piaget observes that few pre-adolescents are able to test out a hypothesis by systematic consideration of all the possibilities. This does not mean, how-ever, that they cannot think through problems, particularly those with a practical basis and reflect on all that they encounter. Indeed in Kelly's terms[1] we are continually building up expectations about the world and modifying them in the light of further experience. This is a way of looking at the learning process which is entirely compatible with Piaget's well-known 'adaptation' model in which the learner is constantly forging new syntheses out of old and new information.

While, as we have already said, there is no doubt that the world of objects is exciting and important to younger children, it is simply not true to say that they cannot also deal with things in the imagination. Their poems and stories show that they can conjecture about possibilities and create other self-consistent worlds. We believe Piaget's concept of 'decentring',[2] the increasing capacity to see the world from different perspectives, to under-stand the viewpoints of others, is a useful one in looking at development from eight to thirteen. It permeates all aspects of development and the fact that in general an eight-year-old is at an earlier stage along this continuum than the thirteen-year-old has implications for his personal relationships and his intellectual operations, but we are not sure whether the younger child's thinking and feeling is qualitatively different. We have found that quite young children are capable of considerable sympathetic insight where, for example, the plight of pets or siblings is concerned. On the other hand people – parents, teachers and peers – are significant in a different way at eight and thirteen. Perhaps it is in the more subtle areas of personal relationships that the young child's lack of experience of life is evident. The Freudians believe that 'latency', the pre-adolescent period, is a less fraught time because the individual is free from both the emotional vulnerability of the pre-school years and the intense feelings about social and sexual matters which accompany adolescence.[3] We take the point but we have noticed that junior schoolchildren are easily upset by any uncertainty at home or by difficulties in making friends in school.

By the age of thirteen the hypothesis-making which we have already pinpointed as a way of learning from the earliest stages, centres more comfortably than before on things not directly encountered. The individual becomes increasingly able to deal with the abstract as well as the concrete, with the general as well as the specific. For the majority, however, this kind of progress takes a long time (see Context 12 in Chapter I). We can help, says Bruner,[4] by not inhibiting 'the shrewd guess, the fertile hypothesis', even if these are not quite correct. In Chapter III we describe the approaches of some teachers in fostering in their pupils this growing capacity to understand and formulate ideas. We feel sure that it is above all through talking and writing with an 'expressive' function, in that it reflects the learner's perspective, his needs and thoughts, that pupils in this age-range move into new frameworks, become able to organize new syntheses. In personal relationships the thirteen-year-old seems more aware than younger children of what other people might be thinking, particularly about himself, and this can be inhibiting. Adults, he notes, are making judgements about him, and in turn he no longer accepts their authority without question. Perhaps of paramount importance is the opinion of the peer group, his status in their judgement outweighs that of any adult – parent or teacher. (See the extract from fourteen-year-old Cathy's diary on pages 196–7 and compare with nine-year-old Kerry's piece on 'The visit', page 190.)

Just living in the world, relating to others, coming to know what their feelings and reactions are and what they expect of us, is the background to development. The school has the difficult task of keeping pace with and extending this development.

References and notes

1. GEORGE A. KELLY, *A Theory of Personality* (Norton, New York, 1963).
2. JEAN PIAGET, *Language and Thought of the Child* (Routledge & Kegan Paul, 3rd edn, 1959). See p. 45 for a discussion of the characteristics of egocentrism.
3. See ERIK H. ERIKSON, *Childhood and Society* (Norton, New York, 1950),

chapter 7, for an insightful account of the individual's predicament at eight stages from infancy to old age.

4. J. S. BRUNER, *The Process of Education* (Vintage Books, Random House, New York, 1960).

1. Contexts

GROUP 1   BEING ALIVE IN THE WORLD

The two contexts in this group show children exploring at first hand the world of things and people. In each example the teacher clearly recognizes that the environment outside the school is a fruitful setting for the learning activities of young children – activities which draw upon what children already know and give them sufficient challenge in the way of new experience.

Context 1, 'Two outings to a park', shows the school taking immediate advantage of seasonal features in the locality. Delay of a day might mean an opportunity missed. Context 2, 'A study of Craster village', ventures into a new environment. It was unfamiliar in that the children did not know at first hand either the people and their way of life, or the objects, buildings and setting of the area. They did not, however, come to the study ignorant either of what it is like to live in a community or of what it is to do a specialized job.

In Context 1 planning was minimal, the immediate whim of the children infusing the outing with enough purpose. The second context did have some built-in objectives. Preparations were put in hand to organize a morning's work; they planned a visit to a kipper factory and a guided tour of a castle. The teacher suggested what might usefully be noted and helped the children prepare sets of questions to aid them in their encounters with the villagers. It was not envisaged that the children should put aside what they themselves saw as interesting and significant in trying to be faithful to ideas put forward at the planning stage. Children were encouraged to give a personal view in work arising out of the field trip.

The absence of specific objectives does not mean that teacher and pupils lacked direction and commitment. Perhaps the central point of such excursions is to be found in the many ways children respond to what confronts them, and the ways in which they share their individual impulses and reactions. The gap between living and learning is narrow here and whatever new learning occurs, sanctions the ordinary way of approaching events and encourages faithfulness to one's own experience and knowledge. When individuals are not under the stress of having to grapple with some one else's framework – whether they are approaching a familiar environment in an unusual state, as in Context 1, or venturing further afield in exploring the environment, as in Context 2 – they gain confidence in their capacity to make sense of what they encounter.

Context 1 Taking advantage of chance events – two outings to a park

The school was in a small village (intake ninety), with children of professional people, skilled and semi-skilled factory workers and farm labourers. The class was of mixed-ability nine- to eleven-year-olds (with a few children not yet nine). (See Chapter V, pages 230–3.)

This school has a concern to be responsive to its natural environment, and teachers are often willing to rearrange the planned work when a special opportunity arises. The first outing to the park was on a summer afternoon, so sunny that the outdoors was nothing less than a powerful magnet. The second outing happened because the children came into school chattering about the morning hoar frost, the first that year, and how it had transformed the countryside. Neither teacher nor children had any procedure set down; they moved into the park together and then split into small groups, sometimes with the teacher, sometimes with their friends, and examined and talked about the things of interest which they found.

The summer outing

The children spent about an hour in the park. There was no pressure on them to observe things systematically, or to record observations to use in later work. They were free just to talk in their self-chosen groups about what they came across in their walk.

The kind of talk they engaged in is predictable. As groups came upon something of interest they felt under no compulsion to describe it, or relate their observations systematically to formal bodies of knowledge. Rather they related them to their personal knowledge and histories. They would share their experiences related to what they had found. It seems fairly typical of this age-group that they should do this by a rapid accummulation of bold claims, like this group which found a caterpillar:

PUPIL 1 It's a moth caterpillar, isn't it?

PUPIL 2 I've got some green ones at home.

PUPIL 3 Do you know, I've never seen one that colour before.

PUPIL 1 (*picking it up*) They always curl up when you pick them up.

PUPIL 2 I keep them you know – in the caterpillar season, we have hundreds climbing about on our walls.

PUPIL 3 We have hairy ones – yeah, and them tiger ones and those, only much bigger than those.

PUPIL 2 We kept some in bowls – and we separated the big ones 'cos they ate more than the little ones. They ate all the lettuce.

PUPIL 1 I had one of those and it mated.

This way of talking contrasts with what happens when a child has a whole incident to tell, when the rapid interchange is replaced by extended narrative. Typically, such stories draw upon powerful experiences. The girl who found a spider, nine-year-old Rosemary, entered the conversation with an autobiographical anecdote:

> When my cousin was sleeping with me – we was in my room asleep and in the night a spider come up the bottom of the bed and crawled over me and my cousin. It climbed up the wall and fell down on my cousin's face and she says 'Get off, you spider' and then it climbs down to the bottom of the bed. Then I said, 'Jen, Jen' and then she woke up . . . So then she started moving and the spider ran up – and she threw the blankets over it. We jumped out of bed – but we couldn't find the spider because the blanket was on it. We were scared in case the spider ran out of the blanket. So we took some blankets downstairs and took some blankets off my sister's bed and she came with us downstairs.
>
> In the morning my dad says 'What the 'ell are you doing down 'ere?' So we said 'There was a big spider in our bed last night!'

An eavesdropper to both of the above conversations would almost certainly know what had provoked the talk. Children's talk can, however, move very rapidly away from the starting-point, and the end of the conversation have no connexion at all with what initiated it, although each part of the conversation is related to what went before. One girl made a collection of feathers. Showing a large one to the group, she observed, 'You can use this as a pen'. From this the group moved very rapidly to a discussion of their television watching habits, moving from history plays in which quill pens were used to something as far from the original observation as horror films:

PUPIL 1 You can use this as a pen.
PUPIL 2 Yes, that's what people did do with long feathers at one time.
PUPIL 1 Yes, I was just saying that.
PUPIL 2 Yes, like Queen Elizabeth I.
PUPIL 1 I was watching Queen Elizabeth and um 'Enry VIII. They were the same. 'Enry VIII used these.
PUPIL 3 Did he?
PUPIL 4 Do you watch horror films?
PUPIL 2 I watch Kong King.
PUPIL 1 King Kong!
PUPIL 2 Dr Jekyll and Mr Hyde, and er . . . the Curse of the Werewolf.
PUPIL 4 I watch that one . . .
PUPIL 2 And Frankenstein.
PUPIL 1 Yes I watch some of them and I has my nightie on before I goes to bed and then I watches it.

These snippets of talk characterize children's ways of approaching the environment when they have no specific objectives, and there is no pressure to fulfil defined classroom purposes. When the teacher joined in the conversation (composition of the groups altered continually; in the hour's excursion most children exchanged some words with the teacher) she took up the role of an adult companion, willing to be interested in all the children wished to say to her. In so far as she asked questions, these had more to do with understanding what the child wished to bring to her attention than with attempting to extend the children's knowledge. Through talk like this the children come to see their teacher as a person concerned with their interests. The contribution this makes to the social bond between pupil and teacher should not be underestimated.

TEACHER Where were you standing when you saw your sunbeam?
PUPIL 1 By some trees.
TEACHER What did you do?
PUPIL 1 Tried to touch it – we got nearer – then it kind of like runs away.
TEACHER What happened when you put your hand out?
PUPIL 1 It was windy against it . . .
PUPIL 2 Oh like a shadow – like trying to catch your shadow – if you move forward, it goes.
TEACHER The sunbeam didn't come and touch you?
PUPIL 1 No.
PUPIL 2 If you put your hand out sometimes it will come and touch it.

While this talk does not significantly increase the children's knowledge about caterpillars, spiders, feathers and sunbeams, it allows them to stake out their own impressions, to try them out for fit with how others react to the world, and thus to explore tentatively their similarities as people. It serves both to build a common world together, and to mark off and identify the ways in which one person differs from another.

The hoar frost outing

This was altogether a more dramatic occasion than the summer outing. The children came to school on this particular morning bubbling with excitement about the effects of the hoar frost on the countryside. Teacher and children sped to the park taking with them pencil and paper, thermometers and rulers. They found the lake frozen, the trees whitened and the sky an unusual pink and orange. The nature of the occasion was sufficiently specific and unusual to demand a commitment on the part of the children to follow-up work, which mostly took the form of writing and painting, on their return to the classroom. Most of what the children wrote is in the form of 'expressive'* narrative – their personal impressions and reactions. Eleven-year-old Kim was very much concerned with the effects of the frost:

> My legs went red because Mr Frost got at them. The trees looked lovely in the sun, they were pink like someone's face when it is cold. The frost is cold, oh so cold, it makes the trees stand still as if a witch had put a spell on them. Their branches stick out on end – the frost is cruel to the trees because it makes them cold and they stand still as a rock. The frost makes pretty patterns on the trees and they look as if a spider has put a web round them.

Stuart, one of the youngest of the class at eight, found his centre of interest in the lake, and its resident ducks, although he commented on other aspects of the changed world too:

> Today we went to the park and the lake was frozen. There was a duck frozen on the lake. In the distance the trees looked pink. It was very very slippery

* Language with an expressive function stays close to the speaker or writer; it verbalizes his preoccupations and interests and is most easily understood by one who knows the speaker. A fuller account of this and the other two language functions, poetic and transactional, is given in Chapter III. These function categories were developed by the Schools Council Written Language of 11–18 Year Olds Project (1966–71) and are discussed in the project's report, James Britton, *et al.*, *The Development of Writing Abilities (11–18)*, Schools Council Research Studies (Macmillan Education, 1975).

and cold. The grass was frozen, the ducks looked warm and we thought they were laughing at us coming out in the cold. The beech trees looked bright gold, their leaves like red coins lying on the ground.

These pieces paint a picture of the activities as they were relevant to individual children. The response in writing was, however, broader than this. Bryan, aged nine, stepped aside from the rushing-round activities of the other children and made a series of measurements:

> On January 5th there was a hoar frost. I looked at the maximum and minimum thermometer. During the night the temperature had been 6 C and 20 F. We went over into the park and took the temperature again. Both in the air and in the water in the lake it was 20 C. The ice was 3 cm thick at the edge but only 1 cm thick at the middle.

He did not choose to report his excitement in breaking the ice and tentatively testing it with his foot, nor is the imminent danger of falling off the supports to the platform in the middle of the lake mentioned. He chose merely to state what he found, as an objective observer.

Adam, aged nine, had a different approach from Bryan and the two other writers. He saw an opportunity to construct a fiction. It is worth noting that he remains uninvolved when a writing project is circumscribed by the wishes of others, and that in this case he found sufficient impetus to write the longest piece he had yet done.

> The fairies from Fairyland were going to conquer Britain, then to conquer Europe. When they had done that they wanted to conquer Asia and after Asia the whole of the rest of the world. Well the story starts in England when the English are fighting the fairies. One morning we woke up to find our countryside under the fairies spell. It was white as milk and shimmered like silk. It was bright as if the whole sequins and silver diaminds had fallen from the sky and carpeted the earth. When the rising sun came over the hill and caught the trees, their frost mink coats were dyed pink. The fairies catapults were made of spiders webs and wood. But the English had hundreds of fans that blew a wave of hot air that melted everything and won the war.*

The variety of writing response and the paintings reflected the open nature of this learning context. The children felt free to process the experience in different ways, confident that the teacher would receive their work appreciatively. None of the activities spread beyond the day of the visit, but what the children had felt, observed and written about became part of

* Here as elsewhere children's original spelling has been retained.

their cumulative experience of the area. On future visits there were frequent references to this occasion. In the spring Adam referred to it again, using the reference to point the changes he found:

> The fairies are gone
> The fairies are gone
> Its pretty again
> The bird sings its song.
> The water is flowing
> The flowers are blooming
> The trees are so green
> You would think the queen
> might be coming.
> The waterfall gleaming
> like diamonds and falling
> on a blue crystal floor.
> Sprays of silver leaves
> The hares are all running
> In gray woollen cloth but I don't
> Think they need it
> I may go to the folly.

Thus while the hoar frost visit was in one sense a self-contained event, it became part of the children's living experience of the world.

This work came about because the teacher and the children took advantage of chance happenings in the environment. Work previously planned was set aside. Such flexibility allows the class to take up 'spur of the moment' opportunities to capitalize on what may be transitory, but has strong enough roots in feeling to have a lasting effect. This school is fortunate to be near a country park, but it is to the credit of the teachers that they perceived that advantage.

Context 2 Exploring a new environment – a study of Craster village

The school, situated in a small town near the sea, had an intake of 250, mainly from families of skilled, semi-skilled and unskilled workers. The class was of mixed-ability ten- to eleven-year olds.

The children had been on many visits and outings before. This trip was planned as an interesting study in their last half term in the primary school. Teacher and children wanted a learning situation with a strong social element.

The children had much to say about how their time was to be spent on the two-day field trip, but the teacher organized the stay at the youth hostel and the visit to the kipper factory, and arranged for a guide to help the children in their exploration of Dunstanburgh Castle. She chose these activities knowing the children's interests and abilities. All the children visited the kipper factory and Dunstanburgh Castle. Individuals and groups chose to add to their programme, with visits to the churchyard, the anticline and the beach to talk to fishermen, and with a fact-finding expedition round the village.

The strength of this project lay in the opportunities for first-hand exploration. One pupil commented, 'You can say what you want to say seeing you've seen it', and certainly the selection and organization of what has happened processed in talk and writing is the essence of language for learning. The pupils enjoyed writing about what they had seen, done and heard rather than what they had read in books. They were aware also that some of the information was not likely to be found in books. When asked whether any unusual discoveries were made, Caroline said, 'We thought they would mostly be fishermen with Craster being a fishing village but there are only four fishermen in the village. We were surprised. But it's a quarrying town, stone quarrying.'

Much of the work centred on practical matters – how kippers are made, the purpose of the castle – but there was a thunderstorm on the visit to Dunstanburgh and this provided the perfect dramatic stimulus for imaginative reconstructions of the castle's history. The learning experiences were greatly enhanced by the atmosphere of communal excitement and social enjoyment. The children had a strong class identity and well-established friendship patterns, so that group activities progressed harmoniously.

As might be expected, many accounts of the field trip, with its wealth of different experiences, had a strong expressive flavour. There was a gap of several days before writing up from memory and notes. In the interval there was a great deal of talk and this undoubtedly helped when it came to organizing and structuring the writing.

Here are some of the children eagerly describing the kippery to a visitor:

PUPIL 1 We saw them scrubbing and putting on the salt and washing them and it takes sixteen hours altogether and . . .

PUPIL 2 And they're slit and gutted by hand and washed (the whole thing takes sixteen hours) and then there's this tube and they all get sorted out into baskets and they're put in with salt to brown and then they're tentered on sticks . . . and then put on hooks by their tails.

PUPIL 1 There's a shop just outside where they're made, where they're bought fresh, they're not even wrapped.

PUPIL 3 We all bought some kippers as well.

PUPIL 2 They're quite cheap at Craster . . .

PUPIL 1 Well they would be.

PUPIL 2 They're seven and a half pence a pair.

PUPIL 1 My Dad said they were gorgeous.

PUPIL 3 . . . cost so little.

There follows an account written by one of these girls. She has had time to order her thoughts, and has considered what the reader might need to be told. For example she explains what 'tentering' is:

When we arrived from Rennington on the Thursday morning we went to the kippering yard. There was an awful smell of fish as we went in and the first thing I saw was some ladies tentering herring on sticks. We asked the women what happens at the yard. They were very pleasant people and told us the story of the kippers. First they were split and gutted either by hand or a machine. The machine is a round wheel which feeds the fish into a covered box and inside the box the fish are split, gutted and cleaned. They are put into baskets and then taken to brine in salt for 20 minutes. Then they are tentered which is hung up on nails on sticks. These sticks are hung up in the smoke houses. Very soon the fires are lighted and the fish are smoked. At last they are dipped into whitewood chips and oak sawdust.

In contrast here is a brief and less explicit piece by a boy 'less able' in the school's terms:

The prosses that the kippers go through. fist thay are cut open and gutted and then the kippering wemmen put them on sticks with nails in and a man puts them in ther ovens to smoke. When thay came out there stacked into crates with ice.

For children not confident in writing, the struggle to get just this much down may be an achievement and a valid attempt to structure a slice of experience in writing. This child at this time found his greatest satisfaction in talk, writing being something of a chore for him.

It is the expressive element in Joanne's piece on the walk to Dunstanburgh which makes it more than just a bald account of what happened:

> From Craster we walked to Dunstanburgh Castle which was about one mile from the entrance gate to the castle itself which is shown above. It stands on a cliff overlooking the sea $1\frac{1}{4}$ miles north of Craster and two miles east south east of Embleton. Dunstanburgh seems to be a big attraction for schools. When we were there there were two older schools walking along beside us. We dumped our bags and walked around the ruins. We made our way to gull crag which was just opposite the keep which was where all the birds were nesting. Dunstanburgh is also a bird sanctuary which is why foot paths were marked out to separate the long grass from the short. What amazed me was how the gulls could nest on such narrow ledges. We stood some time watching the birds gliding and swooping as it was fascinating. Having spent about two hours at Dunstanburgh we walked back into Craster and finished off any work on the harbour and walked to the garage for transport to take us to Tock Hall.

If we compare Joanne's comment 'What amazed me was how the gulls could nest on such narrow ledges' with the sort of paraphrase we sometimes expect of children coming across other people's observations in books, we get a glimpse of the significance of first-hand experience in children's learning.

Some children tried to gather information about the village by interviewing the inhabitants. They worked with the teacher on a set of relevant questions; the list they finally used was a combination of her suggestions (she had been to the village previously with other classes) and their own.

They knocked on doors, asked their questions and noted the answers. They were fortunate to meet a group of fishermen mending their nets; with them the children had to improvise questions. On returning to school, they put their notes into order. As the children said, 'We're going to copy it all up. We're going to work on our notes we've got and then write them into neat.'

One child working from the set of prepared questions, wrote:

1. There is no doctor, nearest one Embleton.
2. The entertainment:– whist drive, over 60s, evening classes, coffee.
3. Only 1 shop which sells everything, but a mobile shop goes around.
4. There are 2 churches. Church of England and Methodist.
5. 1 school which 40 attend is called Church of England school. Nobody has passed their 11+ for 4 years.

6. Quarrying is the main work.
7. Craster has no police.
8. Craster Public House is 'The Jolly Fisherman Harry Wood'
9. Nearest senior school Alnwick.
10. Names of streets, Whin Hill, Haven Hill, Church Street, Heugh Road, Heugh Wynd and South Acres.

Another, working from notes on the interview with the fishermen, wrote:

> At Craster we talked to some of the fishermen mending the lobster pots. I didn't find them easy to talk to however I found out this much – the pots are repaired when necessary with needles like the one in my drawing above. The trawlers go 5 miles out to sea and there are 30 trawlers out in one length and there are 9 fleets. The pots are made from cane and Courene. They use any kind of bate in the fish line.

Both children see the task as one of structuring the information and presenting it to others. The first piece is quite limited. The questions themselves lead to the briefest answers, which do not give any details of the actual interviews. In the second, the pupil enters into a more complex undertaking – ordering the information for herself (she cannot take for granted a predetermined order) and making the context in which the information was gathered accessible to others. As a result she holds together both the situation of the interview and what she learnt from it.

Lying behind both these pieces of work is a richness of talk of which we have no record. However, talking to the children on their return to the classroom, we did get some glimpse of what they encountered and thought, which certainly would have been talked about in many ways.

VISITOR Did you make any important discoveries?
PUPIL We thought it would all be fishing, but there are only four fishermen in the village. We were surprised, because we thought it would be fishing, with Craster being a fishing village. But it's quarrying.

.   .   .   .

VISITOR Did you talk to anyone apart from those people in houses?
PUPIL We talked to the fishermen as well who were busy with their lobster pots.
VISITOR What did they say?
PUPIL They were too busy really. They were younger men – we couldn't really talk to them like we could the neighbours. They were asking Pauline and me in, we were asking everyone, and they would sit us down and stand and answer our questions.

VISITOR Was anyone really horrible to you?

PUPIL Well, one man, I went to the door and he had the television blaring away, and he said, 'I haven't time for youse, go on, go away.' He was bad tempered.

VISITOR But most of them were friendly?

PUPIL Yes, very helpful – there was one lady she said, 'Now I wouldn't advise you to go to this door or that one. You know, the older people who can't actually hear.'

VISITOR Did you go?

PUPIL She said it'll be all right to go to that one, so we didn't go up to the ones she didn't advise.

.   .   .   .

PUPIL We went to a pensioner's house, pensioners, and everyone asked, we tried the questions, and there was one man who looked like a fisherman, I think he might have been a fisherman in his younger days, but I think most of the fishermen in Craster are older people – middle aged. There are very few younger people there.

VISITOR I wonder why this is?

PUPIL It's so quiet. I think it's because it's quiet, there's not so much to do – most people go for busy times.

The speculation in this last observation went well beyond the narrow focus of the interviews. Perhaps in observations like these lie the seeds of more general investigation of communities. Such observations have their roots in what the children actually experienced, but call for a weighing up different from the simple recording of data or narration of what happened.

Dunstanburgh in the storm

PUPIL I liked the visit to the castle (OTHER PUPILS: Yes, yes, so did I), I liked it on the rocks when it was thundering and we were right out in the middle of it and it started to rain heavy. And there was a storm, and we were stuck there without shelter.

The children responded to this dramatic incident in different ways. They had written in the 'poetic'* mode throughout their primary-school years

* Language with a poetic function is a construct; it has a shape and pattern which complements its meaning. The stories, poems and dialogues which children write are embryonically poetic. For a further consideration of this and the other two language function categories, expressive and transactional, developed by the School Council Written Language of 11–18 Year Olds Project, see Chapter III.

and many of them chose to express their feelings about the castle in this manner without any prompting from the teacher. Pauline's poem centred directly upon this particular situation:

> *The storm*
> A thunder clap
> The sky is dark and clouded
> Craster lies as a silhouette
> The sea bestilled
> Then rain.
> Will it be a storm?
> Will it pass?
> Lightning rolls
> Then flashes.
> Everything covered.
> Wet, damp musty smells
> Rise from the old earth
> Then everything silent
> And no sound can be heard.

Other children saw the weather as a link with the legend the guide told them. (The legend of Sir Guy the Seeker, a stranger seeking shelter in Dunstanburgh Castle during a thunderstorm.) Carolyne's version of the legend was clearly based on the style of legends she had read or had read to her. In spite of efforts to rhyme, it is a powerful piece.

> *Sir Guy the Seeker*
> One dark and stormy night
> When lightening flashed and thunder roared
> A man and his horse took shelter
> Unknown to the castle and its lord.
> He stayed there for half the night or more
> Still unseen within the castle walls
> But then when midnight struck its chord
> A lady of much beauty called
> She beckoned him toward a chamber dark
> Which held a captive princess fair
> And six black knights, tall bodyguards
> A crude wooden table and a chair
> On this table a ram's horn lay
> And a jewelled sword in a gold sheath

Blow this horn, unsheath this sword
And you will free this princess to keep.
He unsheathed the sword, good and true
He gave the horn a mighty blast
In doing so he woke the guards
And was overpowered, thrown out, downcast.
In the morning he was found still searching
For the princess and the secret chamber
He will search for ever and ever
The search will never end for Sir Guy the Seeker.

Michael wrote the following sustained account, a reconstruction of events described by the guide and elaborated by the booklet. It marks an attempt by this boy to make these events meaningful to himself.

Dunstanburgh Castle
I was peering over the Dunstan plains when I saw a horseman galloping up to the portcullis. The guards let him in. He was badly wounded he said 'The Bruce has beaten Edward at Bannockburn. The Bruce's army of 8000 men are marching South, you are – are –' then he died. The commanding officer sent two men and myself up to the top of the keep. We are armed with long bows and axes. Men are boiling oil in preparation for the attack by Robert the Bruce. At dawn we could see the heads of British officers bobbing around on poles beside the Scottish banners. At 8 o'clock the Bruce's army have formed an arc around our North wall. The archers are first then the foot soldiers and behind them are the light cavalry and the armoured knights. Then at 9 o'clock the attack started the archers moved forward with the foot soilders the archers kneel down and fire hails of arrows into the castle inside the castle is in chaos. Men fall off the battlements smuthered in arrows. The comander says 'don't fire yet wait until the Scots are on our walls' 'but Captain we have already lost 80 of our 200 men.' 'Don't disobey me or . . .' but at that moment two arrows sped through the air crashing into the back of the comander killing him instantly. Now the Scots have propt up ladders against our walls and are flooding into the castle. One of the Scottish soilders has opened the portcullis. The men are waiting to pour the oil over the cavalry who are comeing into the castle. Suddenly two Scots jump on top of the soilders killing them all. The Scots have now taken everything except the upper part of the keep. Six of our men have joined at the top of the keep we are preparing to be stormed. Two Scottish soilders charge up the stairs in an attempt to take the top of the keep one of our men is run through with a slymore. I grab a pike out of the hands of one of the Scots I push it into

him and lever him through a window. One of our soilders kills the other Scot we take his rope ladder and through it over the edge after we have surcured the grappling hooks. We climb down the ladder and run to the cover of the trees. We slowly make our way back to Edward's army.

These pieces with a strong poetic function clearly gave the children much satisfaction. It seems likely that their vitality derives from a chance happening – visiting the castle in a thunderstorm. This raises the question of how far chance factors affect children's learning? Things may be saturated with meaning for children, often because of circumstances beyond our control or even our knowledge.

GROUP 2   DOING THE WORLD'S WORK

These two examples show children not merely exploring their environment but doing something positive about it. The school from which this work came takes advantage of opportunities to carry out community work which dovetails into classroom learning. In the first example the children uncovered an old coal-carrying vessel buried beneath the sand on a nearby beach; in the second, they became involved in planting and caring for trees on the local pit site which was being reclaimed.

The pupils instigated the activities in the first enterprise, while in the second the teacher saw the link between what the children had been doing in school and what was being done in the locality. The important factor is probably not who leads the way into work of this kind, but rather the quality of commitment generated once it is under way. These activities were accompanied by a particularly high level of involvement, and this seems linked both to the practical nature of the work and its close ties with the affairs of men – features which have considerable appeal for this age-group.

In each example the outdoor work either led to or followed systematic work in school. In the first the systematic element was strongly perceived to be a means of finding out something of real importance to the children. Nevertheless, this is not the only workable pattern. It seems an imaginative move on the part of the second teacher to give meaning and relevance to the tree study by extending it to a practical and highly enjoyable situation.

Context 3   Commitment to an enterprise proposed by the pupils – the wreck

The school was in a Victorian building in an industrial town near the north-east coast. Its intake was 420 – mainly children of skilled and semi-skilled workers, with some children of dockside workers and labourers. The class was mixed-ability ten- to eleven-year-olds.

The children had been engaged in a local study of Blyth and Delaval. They were returning from an outing when a group of boys discovered a wreck beneath the sand on a nearby beach known as Meggy's Burn. Teacher and children decided to undertake the painstaking task of uncovering it. It was an exciting find and the digging activity started almost immediately.

Term ended before the work was completed so the class decided to meet during their holiday to continue the activity. An invitation was extended to other children in the school, and some came along during the holidays to give a hand with the digging. A ship research committee was formed to organize investigations into the ship's origins. Thomas and Derek organized the research activities. Here is their account of the dig:

> *We uncover the wreck*
> On the Friday before we broke up for our Whit holiday, we made arrangements to dig up the remains of a ship which had been discovered beside Meggy's Burn. We met at the Mermaid Cafe armed with spades, trowels, brushes, tapes, and lunch. We walked along the beach for half a mile until we came to the wreck.
> Only two spars were showing when we arrived. First we estimated the direction in which the ship was lying and its approximate size. We marked out the area to be dug and set to work. We had to take great care not to damage anything we uncovered. It was a long tedious job removing the large quantity of sand. We moved about five tons. When the digging was finished we took the sand from between the ribs. Things then began to get really exciting because there was a lot more there than we first thought. There were 17 ribs altogether. Ribs are the framework of the ship. They were fixed to a heavy keel which ran down the centre. There were large outer planks still attached to the ribs. They were held in place by wooden pegs and in special sections heavy iron plates were attached to long bolts which passed through

the keel, the ribs and the planks. When the ship was dug out we measured its dimensions. It was 63 ft long by 29 ft wide. The piece we had was the centre section, there was no prow or stern. There were 30 peg and bolt holes. We took photographs and made diagrams. We decided to set up a 'Ship Research Committee' to see if we could find out anything further about the ship. Our research suggested the boat was a collier or hoy.

The children took photographs of the boat at various stages in its uncovering. Detailed diagrams and field sketches were made showing rust stains on the beams and bolt holes with metal and wood bolts. Returning to school after the holiday the children were eager to identify the wreck and reconstruct what her fate might have been. They contacted the local coastguard, the newspaper offices and the library, and investigated exhibits at the Nautical Museum at Tynemouth and the Industrial Museum at Newcastle. They also sought original source material from the County Records Office at Gosforth. The ship research committee co-ordinated the information. The headmaster commented that 'in the end it was a case of making an intelligent guess about what the boat was – they knew the dimensions of the ship, material, age and so on and needed something to satisfy these requirements. They settled for a collier.'

Groups of children then studied various topics related to colliers and the nineteenth-century coal trade. They made pictures and models showing what the old colliers looked like and how they were operated. One child carefully drew a map of the Northumbrian coast showing the main rock hazards that colliers had to beware of, and another drew a map showing the position of the wreck. Other children looked at mining, wagon ways, the Hartley mine disaster, the salt trade, salinity and the salt tax which involved some complicated mathematics.

They made their findings available to other children in the school by means of a large display showing how the activities progressed and the steps taken towards identifying the wreck. Photographs, writing, models and pictures figured in the display.

The practical nature of much of the enterprise generated much enthusiasm. The children seem to have been deeply involved in uncovering some of the history of their own coastline. Subsequent research on the old coal ships was meaningful to them for it threw light on the nature of what they had found by their own efforts. While the teacher guided the activities and was available to give help when needed, the children had the opportunity to show considerable initiative. This kind of learning context where children and teacher are equally eager to seek answers to questions, each contributing to the pattern and progress of the work, alters the nature of pupil–teacher and pupil–pupil relationships, and the attitudes of both to the learning undertaken. It was the children who stumbled on the wreck, who opted to undertake its uncovering during their holiday and who wanted to find out something of its past. The motivational implications of such a start to work cannot be overestimated. The task was theirs not the school's. Yet by subtle guidance the teacher made the children aware of the potential of the project, being quick to note an individual interest and to encourage and extend it.

This activity was engrossing enough to appeal to the children as a spare-time enterprise. Back in the school the work became more focused than it would otherwise have been, extended as it was by research, making pictures and writing. It was the excitement generated by the out-of-school activity which infused vitality and meaning into the systematic work in school.

At the heart of the children's search for facts about the nineteenth-century coal trade, and the coastal mining vessels was the wreck they had unearthed with their own hands. The information was essential to the effective completion of the work undertaken. A great deal of talk went on during the unearthing of the wreck, both expressive and of a kind closely related to performing what was quite a complex job. Much of the writing was 'transactional'* in function – how we did the job. One example has already been considered. Here is a well-sustained piece by Michael, describing the job of the old collier boats:

The nineteenth-century coal trade
The coal trade between the Blyth and the Thames was a big business in the 19th Century. A Hoy or Collier was a coast running vessel to carry coal, and had to operate with a minimum number of seamen. At this time nearly all the old merchants had joined the coal business and made specially designed colliers. It was 60 ft to 80 ft long and 20 ft wide. There was a forecastle and at the stern there was a small cabin for seamen. The side was so near the water that when a keel came alongside the keelman had no difficulty in

---

* An utterance, written or spoken, with a transactional function is concerned with the affairs of the world, with getting things done, imparting information, arguing a case or setting out a plan or recipe. For a further consideration of this and the other two language function categories, expressive and poetic, developed by the Schools Council Written Language of 11–18 Year Olds Project, see Chapter III.

throwing the coal inside the hold. The vessel was manned by the common seamen who didn't handle the cargo, that was the keelman's job.

The whole journey would take at least 15 days. The collier would leave port with a load of coal, weighing about 21 tons (8 Newcastle chaldrons*).

When the collier reached a port a gang of coal heavers came aboard and filled baskets with coal to make it easier to unload. The coal would be measured in Winchester Bushels (36 bushels = 1 London Chaldron) under the careful eye of a 'Sworn Meter'. After the measuring was done the coal was emptied into a waiting keel, which was about 18–20 ft long and 10 ft wide with a mast with a square sail if needed. The keel would then transport the coal to various places on the Thames. The collier would be reloaded with goods for the North and return to the River Blyth. When she docked she would unload her cargo and discharge her ballast at Ballast hill.

Michael, an able boy, read and researched widely before writing this account. He was able to become sufficiently knowledgeable to write this fairly technical account without reference to any special book. It seems quite an achievement to have internalized such difficult information to this extent. Michael commented, 'I wanted this piece to be precise for quick, easy reading.' He wanted the account to figure in the display of work to show to the other children in the school. In the following poem, Michael felt he had expressed some of his feelings about the wreck:

> The beams protruded from the clinging sand
> Forming a fence-like wall against the sun
> Like some abandoned beast in a desert waste
> Only its skeleton remains.
> Was she a busy steamer
> Belching dirt from her blackened smoke stack?
> I think not.
> More the ponderous wind-driven collier
> of an industrial age,
> Laid to rest in a watery grave
> By the treacherous sea.
> I stand on the barren shore.
> The wind blowing through my tousled hair
> And hear the ceaseless bombardment
> of the waves pounding in my ears.
> Echoing the haunting cries of those perished souls,

* Michael and some of his friends noted this word and looked up references to it to discover what it meant.

> Drowning in the sea.
> They ended their lives together
> And passed like sand
> Flowing through my fingers
> Into oblivion.

Michael and his teacher felt that in these two pieces he had made significant progress in his language development. He had managed a quite difficult form of the transactional mode and written what both he and his teacher considered his most satisfying poem so far.

Other children became deeply involved in speculating. Here is John's attempt to reconstruct imaginatively the death of the collier wreck:

Grounded
She had been driven off course by the frenzied wind and gigantic waves until she foundered on our rugged coastline. Screams of terror rang through the air as the once proud ship was driven onto the treacherous rocks. Wave after wave crashed down on the stricken boat. The storm swamped the decks. The wind screamed its curses to the billowing sails and waves pounded her leaking hull. Suddenly the wind hurled itself at the fragile sails making them scream in agony. The boat was tossed about in the angry sea. The rudder came off with a splintering crack. The boat fell out of control and the sea dragged it nearer the beach. The hatches broke and the victorious sea rushed into the hold. The weight of the coal and the pressures of the water was too much for the bottom of the boat. With an explosive crash a vent appeared. The treacherous sea rushed in. A gigantic wave leapt onto the broken ship. The sides opened and the mast fell. Men were crushed and swept away. She gave up the struggle.

An unnamed eleven-year-old wrote some rhyming couplets about the day the partly uncovered wreck was moved by the sea:

> *The shipwreck*
> There it lies all alone
> Rotting away, the beams are old.
> It moved away one spring day.
> The tide lifted it clean away.
> It lifted it from its nice warm bed
> It put it down on a cold one instead.
> On Monday we went to dig it up
> What a surprise when it was not there.
> We looked around it was not there.

We looked in despair
Someone saw it by the pipe.
Yes, that was it we shouted with delight!

This language work reflects the intense involvement which characterized the activity. It was an investigation of a phenomenon which fascinated the whole class, spreading beyond the school to spare time and demanding imagination, intuition and sustained effort. It is worth pointing out that the written language abilities of these children developed over the whole primary-school period in a particularly favourable environment. A piece like Michael's poem about the wreck represents a pinnacle of many previous efforts. The children are able, without strain, to move from writing about doing a job to writing from a more meditative, speculative stance. This particular work made demands on their language capacities and, in doing so, stretched them.

There are many different ways into learning activities and the nature of the beginning of the wreck project seems to have been a significant factor in its success. Such spontaneity in taking up an opportunity implies an educational climate where the quality of motivation and involvement are prized above faithfulness to a given context. This raises basic questions about how the curriculum is organized and to what extent we choose themes for children's work and to what extent we follow their interests and inclinations. Most schools operate in both ways, but perhaps we should be most concerned with ensuring that enough opportunity arises for child-initiated work.

Towards the end of the wreck project, June wrote the following piece:

The archaeologist
An archaeologist is a person who digs up the remains of the past and by examining them reconstructs the sort of life the people led. It is just like putting together a giant jigsaw puzzle with most of the pieces missing. The discovery of each new piece makes the picture a little clearer. We have tried to help with our archaeological dig.

The children enjoyed their archaeological dig – and when the teacher once again saw the direction in which their interests were moving, the activities were extended to a study of how archaeologists carry out their work. This led to an exploration of the local Roman remains and another project was born which, like the wreck project, was a mixture of research and imaginative writing. Projects of this kind are miniature curricula in themselves as they involve so many different activities, group, class and individual, and so many different ways of looking.

Context 4   Commitment to an enterprise proposed by the teacher – we began with trees

The school was the same as in Context 3; the class, mixed-ability nine-year-olds.

The term's work began with a look at trees in their many aspects. Each child chose a tree near his home or in a park and photographed and sketched it. It was hoped that observations throughout the year would show up seasonal changes in the shape and condition of the trees. Some of the children did bark- and leaf-rubbings.

Yvonne made these comments on her tree (the account was accompanied by leaf-rubbings and detailed pictures of twigs):

> *Trees in Bondicar Terrace*
> My tree is a copper beech tree. When I feel the leaf of the beech tree it feels nice and soft. Some of the leaves are big and some are small. The veins of the leaves are a light purple colour. On the front side of the leaf the colour is a darkish green. But when you look on the other side it is a light green. If you put the leaf to the window you can see the little yellow veins.

Neale approached his chosen tree in a rather different way:

> *Climbing a tree*
> I was in sight of the top about four feet away.
> This would be a victory
> But then I slipped
> My footholds broke loose.
> My heart was pounding.
> My hands clutched a branch to pull me up.
> I had made it!
> From the top the people looked minute.
> A winding everlasting column of smoke,
> Rose from the house below me.
> In the distance I saw a storm approaching
> So down I quickly climbed.

One group investigated how a tree grows, getting their information from books and the teacher who mediated between children and print. Here is Helen's account:

How a tree grows

A tree's roots anchor it to the ground and they pump up water containing minerals from the soil. There are special tubes in the trunk and right through the tree to the leaves. These tubes carry water. The food for the tree is made in the leaves. The food making process is called photosynthesis. The leaves need water, carbon dioxide, sunlight and chlorophyll (the green part of the leaf) then the food goes all over the tree. Photosynthesis means making with light. The branches spread the leaves, so that the light can get at them.

Teacher and class carried out various experiments to show capillary action as applied to the tree's capacity to carry water from its roots to its highest branches and leaves. The process of transpiration was explored too. Kenneth wrote an account of what was done and found:

Transpiration

On September 20th we planted some leaves in a bowl with soil and watered it well. We then put a large glass container over the top of it so it was air tight. The next day it was all steamed up. But it was not really steam, it was water that had come off the leaves. So that shows that a leaf really gives off water. We put it on a cupboard right next to a radiator. Then all the water was on the cold side of the glass, the warm part was clear. This was because warm air can hold more moisture. So it all goes to the cold part.

Stories and narratives, their own and other people's, were also enjoyed. The teacher read extracts from *Robin Hood* and *The Wind in the Willows*. In this story, Anthony wrote about a fox and an oak tree:

The hunter

One day a mother fox peeps out of the hole before she leaves her cubs. She slowly strolls through the forest where she herself was born, along the narrow rabbit path beside the river. There is a faint noise in the distance, but this does not bother her. Then what she is looking for! She sinks into the foliage like a ghost and creeps up to the unaware pheasant. Then she springs. Bah! missed. Then she freezes. Barking! That means trouble. Then a voice. There's the fox. Tallyho! Now the fox knows what the noise she heard earlier is. Hunters! She runs through the forest across the river, hoping they will lose the scent. She stops beside an old oak tree and listens for twigs snapping, but the hunters never come. She returns home. Her tricks never fail.

The school is in a mining village and it seemed valuable to take a close look at the connexion between trees and coal. Paul and Kenneth wrote what they discovered about the process of trees becoming coal, and illustrated their account with a picture of coal seams.

In the beginning – trees
Two hundred and fifty million years ago our country was covered with swamps and forests. Leaves fell off the trees. Then the trees died. These trees rotted and more trees grew. It was hot and steamy in the forests.
The surface of the earth changed, water rose and the forests were flooded. The water made mud and sand. Millions of years went by. The earth rose above the water. Trees started growing again. Water rose again. This went on for many years.
The sand and mud pressed down on each other. The dead trees changed into coal. The mud and sand changed into rock.
Layers of rock are called strata. Layers of coal are called seams.

There was much activity in the area in connexion with the plan to reclaim some of the old pit-heads, and the teacher wanted to link the children's work on trees to this development. It seemed a promising idea for the children to grow young trees and transfer them to the reclamation area. The children went on an outing to Isabella Pit-head to observe how the reclamation activities were progressing. Much discussion and writing followed the outing and it was put to the children that they might contribute to this improvement of their environment. This led to a visit to the tree nursery and hospital which Susan described:

When we went to the park we saw how Mr E—— took trees that had been destroyed by vandals and made them grow again. Mr E—— gave us some spider plants to plant. There were four greenhouses, one hot, one warm, one medium and one cold. Then we went outside and got some leaves. We got ash leaves and seeds, sycamore, beech, purple plum, black poplar. At the back of the greenhouse was a willow cutting.

Each child planted his own tree in the nursery. When the trees were sufficiently advanced to place in the reclamation area, the children returned to the nursery at Big Waters to observe the growth of their own trees. Later they were sent to be planted by the children.

Some of the photographs, leaf- and bark-rubbings, sketches and writing were displayed in a large class book, prefaced by the following comment from the teacher:

I hope that you enjoy reading this record of a term's work which you all helped to make. Most of you have a piece of work included in the book, but even if you have not, you appear on one or more of the photographs. I was beginning to think there would not be enough room for all we had prepared, but it just closes comfortably.

We are going to visit Big Waters next term. That is the nursery where our trees are, and after our visit Mr M—— will send them to us. You can write all about that for next term's book.

Keep on collecting poems and information for your own tree book.

Please read Sheila's prayer at the end of this book very carefully. You are the ones who can make it come true.

During the last term I read extracts from these books. Why not borrow them from the library and read the whole story? [List of books.]

In contrast to the previous project, in which practical activity preceded the written work, in this one the activity followed a great deal of research into the nature of trees, their growth and the processes which make them function. Its main strength was perhaps the great variety of ways of approaching the topic and the many activities which it led to – sketching, photographing, rubbing barks, planting, caring for saplings and writing. It was an exciting piece of work for the children as it kept taking unexpected turns. The satisfaction which accompanied planting trees on the reclamation area cannot be overstressed – this was certainly work with long-term results. Here is Yvonne's account of the hard work of planting:

On Friday 25th March our class went to Crofton Mile pit-heap to plant 200 trees. We left school at 10 a.m. and arrived at Crofton pit at 10.15 a.m. We took 8 spades and several trowels.

First of all we waited for Mr M who brought 2 spades and a pick. Mr C came too. There were 2 plots each 50′ by 50′. We were going to plant a 100 trees in each plot. We only had 100 plant pots because we were going to plant 100 trees without pots, 50 in each plot.

We got a good start. Mr C and Graeme dug some holes with the pick. We fillcd the plant pots with soil and put a tree in. Then we had to go for our dinner. Mr M would not come in the afternoon, so we were on our own, with Mrs R and Mr C. In the morning we had planted about 60 trees, so that left us with about 140 to plant on our own. My arms were aching. If Mr C had not come with us I don't know what we would have done. Well at the end we eventually got finished. I planted 24 trees and I was so tired.

In this work learning and living and working in the environment became intertwined. The context took account of the children's social environment and that paid dividends. The feeling that a real job was being done infused the learning with point and vitality.

This work shows that what goes on in schools need not be separated from what goes on in the world. Many children, especially at secondary level, see little relevance in what happens in school to what happens in their life outside. Clearly when work connects with what is important to a community of which the children are part such a split is far less likely. This work did not merely connect with the community – the children were actually instrumental in improving their own environment. It is generally agreed that children should be given the opportunity of exploring the environment as part of the school curriculum. Where possible it seems worth while to provide opportunities for children to participate in the affairs of the outside world.

GROUP 3   IN THE CLASSROOM: GETTING ON THE INSIDE OF UNFAMILIAR MATERIAL

In the previous four examples children were involved in activities outside the school, and a high motivational level was a welcome concomitant of the work. However, there are things we want children to have the opportunity of knowing about which are not capable of direct discovery, and teachers try to find ways of making unfamiliar ideas and concepts accessible to young pupils. Here are exemplified two different ways of helping children tackle successfully new material of a type which can seem remote and barren of meaning.

The first example shows how a wide and carefully selected range of secondary sources can help children understand material which is relatively inaccessible to them. The work centred on different kinds of sea vessels and the significance of the sea to man through the ages. As well as looking at the factual aspects, teacher and children together explored the fantasy dimensions of the sea, reading stories and poems and writing their own, looking at paintings and models and making their own.

The second class also approached their theme, a study of a Saxon community, first by researching mainly from secondary sources (although a few visits to Saxon sites were made). The teachers involved, however, were quite sure that it was through improvised drama that the new concepts became meaningful to the children. When the children were able to move beyond the secondary sources to another way of relating to the theme (in the first example through literature, in the second through improvisation), they really began to make something of the work.

Context 5   The unfamiliar being made accessible through a wide range of sources and materials – ships and their associations

This was a country school with an intake of 340; the children were of professional, skilled, semi-skilled and unskilled workers (evenly represented). The class were mixed-ability nine- to ten-year-olds.

A group of boys who had made a special study of Tudor ships gave a particularly lively presentation of their findings to the class. Enough interest was generated from this to make ships and their associations the focus of much of the children's work over the space of a term.

This topic was classroom-based in that books, films, slides, models and pictures were brought into school, rather than the children exploring phenomena on outings. Some things children want to know about are not accessible at first hand. Where no element of primary experience is present, and not many of the children have any background in the subject, the problem of helping the children to make the material their own looms large. The range of resources provided and the teacher's mediation between children and books contributed to the successful exploration of the topic. The work had a fairly firm teacher-initiated structure, although there were wide opportunities for group and individual choice. The teacher saw the project's potential in terms of developing the factual and imaginative aspects of the theme. She did not use the terms 'participant' and 'spectator' role, but seemed to have in mind something like these two stances towards experience. (See Chapter III for a consideration of the theory developed by the Schools Council Written Language of 11–18 Year Olds Project.)

First the teacher, and then the children, found out as much as possible about different kinds of ships, each child taking responsibility for discovering the design and function of at least one chosen vessel. They were encouraged to look for a relationship between the structure of the ship and the job it had to do. Group and individual work on the factual aspects ranged over modern shipbuilding, time, rate and distance studies, the history of the Thames as a vessel-bearing river, sea life, the origins of piracy, famous ships and aids to safety. Here is Kerry's piece on danger – it is rather a jumble of facts and ideas, but the expressive elements show that she is making some progress in mastering the material:

Danger
Ice is a troubel for ships – of course it will stop the ship getting through and fog is a danger for it will be very hard to see through, and also when there is a strong current it pulls you into danger, jutting rocks and coral reefs is very dangerous to the ships. Storms causes the ships disaster and many would die. But lifeboats are sent out to help the poor people. Ships must signal in fogs for disaster will be in their way if they don't. When seas are very calm it is dangerous to all ships with sails for will they go? NO! If there is no air of course the poor ships will not move. Aids can help sailors like spotter planes, lighthouses, buoys, sirents, signals of all kinds, the sea can help sailors when it is calm and the weather . . .

After looking at the very real dangers of the sea – ice, storms, strong currents and so on – the teacher showed the children Turner's painting, 'Shipwreck'. This led to imaginative reconstructions of what it might be like to be involved in a shipwreck. Drawing on the interest of a group who examined the history of piracy, the teacher read out extracts about wreckers and smugglers and as the children greatly enjoyed these, they were extended to tales and poems about mermaids, sea caves and monsters. Here is Maria's poem about the shipwreck:

> The moss on the wreck is emerald
> The crab is golden
> A fish, like a balloon, swims
> Past the sodden ship, sunk
> In watery Paradise
> The octopus' eight arms clutch
> The steering wheel as if to say
> I am the captain of this old ship
> But now on sea pasture it is

Like an old horse tired from work and
from carrying pepul from place to place.

A great variety of activities arose out of this work – painting, paper sculpting, writing of various kinds, model making, song making, movement and dramatic improvisation. While the teacher took most of the responsibility for structuring the work, there were wide possibilities for children's initiative in pursuing special points. Quick to bring the fruits of the individual and group interests to the class as a whole, the teacher also drew attention to possibilities which the children might have missed. For instance, she brought to their notice the many hazards those who go to sea must face.

The work was organized so that the children were able to approach the theme from different angles. Some of the children's work reflected the harsh realities of life at sea and the functional aspects of ships. Some focused on the fanciful side in paintings, poems and songs about mermaids and pirates. This dual focus is probably responsible for the rich variety and scope of activities engaged in: some children chose to investigate the following in depth – flags on ships, buoys, famous ships and aids to safety; teacher and children searched for and sang sea shanties, and the class listened to music evocative of the sea; one child's poem about a storm at sea was set to music by a group with the teacher's help; children wrote their own stories on the theme, 'shipwrecked'; the story of a storm was worked out in movement, and drama work was done on the theme, 'How pirates raided a ship'; some children drew, painted and made sculptures of the things they had written about

Children often respond to outings and field trips with an abundance of expressive writing, and the fact that this particular project included no element of primary experience may account for the lack of this kind of written language. There was a great deal of expressive talk, and much of the writing contains expressive elements even though its function is principally to inform. Nevertheless, it would be true to say that the children understood that expressive writing was not expected.

The writing associated with the factual elements certainly challenged the children's language abilities, for the context called not only for straightforward narrative accounts which most of them managed easily, but also for the more difficult processes of generalizing and evaluating and weighing evidence. Even the ablest children could not go far towards meeting the demands of atemporal organization as we see from Kerry's account, 'The wreckers':

> It is not right to say wreckers are in the wrong. For if you had a choice, let your children die or steal. And I don't mean hunger, I mean starving. So they have a difficult decision. So they row out to a lighthouse and signal a false alarm, so that the ship walks into danger instead of into a safe harbour. And the people who don't die and drown in the terrible waters are killed.

Although the children found much of the transactional writing difficult, the opportunity to attempt such ways of processing material may well have helped some of them to make strides in their conceptual thinking. (See Chapter IV, pages 190–6, where Kerry's written work is considered in depth.) Books were an important source of information and some children were guided by work-cards which helped them to structure their material and led them towards the most helpful books and pictures.

One of the most noteworthy outcomes of this study was the abundance of writing which had something of the poetic function. This reflected both the children's fascination with the fanciful and also the rich variety of literature which they enjoyed with the teacher. We can detect the impact that parts of the *Odyssey* and Matthew Arnold's 'The Forsaken Merman' made. Yet the children's writing was not merely derivative. Each child in this class of wide ranging abilities achieved not one, but several, embryonically poetic pieces, satisfying to himself and his teacher.

Below we have Timothy's dialogue. In the first part a coastguard orders one of his men to fix the light. The second part is a conversation between a senior and a more junior wrecker. This seems an original and highly effective way of telling the story.

> Bill
> Yes Sir. (*Saluting*)
> Hurry, fix the beam, or my kichen knife will make you wet meat.
> Yes sir. (*Saluting*)
>
> Yes Harry?
> I just had a message from the channel.
> There's a ship coming in from France with gold coins.
> Call it all off it's the coast gard.
> He's seen us
> Pack up and leave.

Surinjeet writes of a seaman's affection for his boat:

> *My ship*
> Her life is travelling from place to place.
> She travels when the
> storms and strong winds blow.
> My ship and I have fought
> Many a time with the sea.
> I feel that I don't want to go
> away from my ship.
> My ship is just like a wife or a child
> It is the dearest thing I know.

Susan's poem, 'Mermaids of the sea', captures that special vitality which young pupils bring to a theme that has caught their imagination. It is one of many.

> Frolicsome are the waves that reach the far shore
> The swift eye of a sailor scans the sea.
> A strange and wondrous voice rings like a crystal bell.
> A maiden fair singing out on the Azure sea,
> Cool breezes blowing her long golden hair
> Her blue eyes peering from under neat yellow eyebrows.
> A swift dive brings a pure shape to many a sailor's eye.
> A scaly tail slashing at the seaweed stems.
> Far down where the seahorses ride and the
> Snakes of the sea shed their scaly skins
> Where many a whale passes by and fishes dart, a cavern lies
> Decorated in shells, barnacles and sea weed
> This is the home of the maiden fair
> The Queen of the sea.

When we write poems, stories and dialogues, experience is structured in a special and rather complex way. The mermaid poems arose not only out of the literature read to the children during the project but from all the feelings and fantasies they had ever experienced in relation to mermaids and other romantic aspects of the sea. They provide another way of relating to experience, another way of learning.

Context 6 The unfamiliar made accessible through improvised drama – life in a Saxon community*

The school was situated in a small town in the north east. The children were mainly of skilled and semi-skilled workers; the class, mixed-ability ten-year-olds.

This work is rather less an example of everyday good practice, since the class teacher worked with a drama lecturer from the local university in planning and carrying out the activities. (The drama lecturer came to the school mainly for the improvisation sessions, while the class teacher helped the children with background research and provided opportunity for follow-up writing and art.) It is included because it is a powerful example of how improvisation can serve as a teaching tool, bringing alive to children the implications of incidents and predicaments which often appear to them remote and inaccessible.

At the beginning of the study teachers and children visited Saxon sites and early medieval buildings to get a feel for the period. Attention was drawn to books featuring the illuminated letters, and manuscripts were borrowed from museums so that the children could study them closely. The teacher thought it would be an interesting joint exercise for the children to make their own book. Each child chose a religious saying or biblical quotation and took responsibility for one page of writing and painting an illuminated letter. The book was authentically bound in raised bands with wooden covers. It was intended by the drama lecturer that this book should be a central prop in the drama to follow. The class teacher commented: 'The book was, in fact, to be an important symbol of learning and it was hoped that later involvement in the drama would allow for appreciation and assessment of this rather abstract notion.'

The children explored with the class teacher the kind of life the monks might have led. Some children found books which suggested what kind of daily timetable a monk of this period might have followed. Ian wrote the following poem and a prose piece in an attempt to imagine the predicament of a monk:

---

* For the account of the work in this context we are indebted to the University of Newcastle and to Dorothy Heathcote for making available to us the 'Making of History' videotapes of part of the work described.

> I walk backwards towards my cell
> My stomach empty, my knees stiff from kneeling.
> I enter my dismal store room
> And a shaft of light falls on my unfinished manuscript.
> My legs need rest so I sit on my stone seat
> There is my sheet of vellum
> And a fine quill
> And a pot of black ink
> I borrow other colours from my fellow brothers
> As I begin to sketch out my design
> I wonder,
> Is this the right life?

I went to the woods today to pick elderberries for some ink. I mixed them with some rosehips and they produced a beautiful blue. I have spent eight months on this bible cover. At last it is finished and will be joined to the other parts of the book.

These pieces draw on book research, class discussion, Ian's own feelings about making the class version of the precious book and early improvisation attempts.

Speculative talk followed about what life might have been like for ordinary people. What did they value? What mattered to them? What threatened them? What was their relationship to authority figures like the thane and the church officials?

When the drama began, the class teacher reported that this was the point when the study 'came alive' for the children. They became engaged in the issues of the period in a way that had not happened during the preliminary activities. Throughout the study the children looked up background details to make their drama work authentic, and they did a great deal of writing of their own, drawing both on their book research and on their improvisation. The drama had four main parts:

1   The people of a Saxon village have no grain and seek help from the local monastery. The monks tell them that help comes through faith in God and show the precious religious book as their authority.

2   A bad harvest comes again and the villagers, now sceptical of the power of the Christian God to alleviate their plight, pray to the old heathen god. The monks intervene, pointing again to the words of

God in the precious book. The Vikings attack and the book is hidden in the falconry.

3 In medieval times the book's safety is threatened.

4 In modern times the precious book is discovered by workmen.

Within this broad framework the drama varied greatly each time the children improvised. We studied a tape-recording of the second part in development, and later saw the children explore other possibilities arising out of the original plan for this part.

At this stage the teacher was the drama lecturer. She believed that important insights into the past could be gained by a 'living through' of the situation. By feeling their way into the predicament of the Saxon villagers, by enacting certain incidents, the children would gain some notion of the complexity of the issues involved. The history book tells them that the people of this period changed from believing in primitive gods to accepting the concept of one Christian God but, by 'living through' it themselves, the children would come to feel in their bones the gradualness and painfulness of such a change, and the doubts and setbacks which are the inevitable concomitants of such a reorganization of values.

We follow the steps by which the children came to understand something of the complexity of the issues involved. Torrential rain had ruined the corn crop and with dismay the people realized that another poor harvest was inevitable. In the following extract the conflict between old and new beliefs is evident:

(*Sound of wind and rain sets the scene. The villagers huddle together to discuss their plight.*)

VILLAGER 1 There's only one sackful of corn left, and the crops won't be ready to harvest now until at least a month's time.

VILLAGER 2 Without corn we can't eat bread.

VILLAGER 3 We'll starve.

VILLAGER 1 This corn won't last long – we'll have to do something about it. We must pray to the sun god to give us sun.

TEACHER (*as villager*) But we're not supposed to do that!

VILLAGER 1 Do it in secret then. What have the monks done? *Their* God hasn't done anything – he sent this rain.

VILLAGER 2 Yes – trust in God the monks tell us – but what happens?

VILLAGER 4 Well I don't know about anybody else but I'm going to pray to the sun god.

The villagers make their way to the mountain to pray to the stone that symbolizes their sun god. There are some dissenting voices. One villager warns: 'You will only make fools of yourselves if you pray to that stone. The sun god never brought any sun.' But most of the villagers continue their journey to pray to the god of their fathers. They face the old altar and kneel in prayer, asking the sun god to send fair weather to help the crops. The people are absorbed in their incantation and do not notice the arrival of the monks. After listening in silent anger for a few moments the monks intervene. The prayer ends with the plea: 'Rise in the sky and shine, bring life to our crops.'

MONK 1 Pagans – how dare you pray to that! (*Throwing down altar.*)
VILLAGER We can pray to who we like.
MONK 2 You have sinned! Do you know you are praising a stone? What can a stone do for you?

The monks strive to persuade the people of their error and point to the resurrection of the body and spirit as the special gift of Christianity which is referred to in the religious book. The villagers, attracted by the thought of living again after death, accompany the monks down the mountainside to the monastery and a service celebrating their return to the faith begins in the chapel. As the people pray, the Vikings come ashore and peer into the church. One of the monks sees the Vikings. The first thought is for the safety of the religious book. The falconry is decided on as the safest hiding place since it is unlikely that the Vikings would look among the birds and animals for something precious. This final part of the second stage of the improvisation was almost entirely in action and the drama lecturer commented that she wished more time could have been spent on its development. She believed that children needed at each stage in the developing drama both help from the teacher and plenty of time for exploratory dialogue before they could sufficiently understand the motivations and feelings of the people they were portraying.

Later, with the class teacher, the children varied this part of the improvisation by making the main focus a Saxon moot, where the thane hears the people's complaint against the granary keeper who, it is alleged, has been partial in handing out supplies of grain to each family. In this particular version the children experienced what it might be like to fear a famine, what it means to be under the dominance of one man, the thane, and the difficulty of deciding whether a man is guilty or innocent of a crime. Later they also met the challenge of trying to justify to hostile invaders certain values and a way of life. 'Men', they said, 'are mortal, books can live for ever. When weapons have rusted away words remain.'

We have focused on what the children made of the story and how they came to some understanding of the issues involved. It is interesting to look at another aspect – the role of the teacher in helping their understanding. She was active in two ways, firstly in pointing up the issues and secondly as a member of the community itself. Breaking in at the point at which the monks show their anger at the villagers' lapse into worship of the primitive gods we find the children all speaking at once and the teacher intervenes

> I want you to listen to what other people say – I know you have a lot to say yourself – but listen too because this is a new religion talking to an old one and this is one of the things that goes on in the world all the time . . . Men find their gods in many places and in many guises and in many ways.

We can imagine the impact of a comment like 'this is a new religion talking to an old one'. Here is the children's work after the teacher's comment set the mood, letting the children know what their feelings as these people in this situation might be:

> MONK Do you know you are praying to a stone . . . what can a stone do for you?
> CROWD (*muttering*) We've tried praying to your God . . . we can pray to who we like . . . etc.
> MONK May God in heaven help them.
> TEACHER (*now in role of a villager*) Now listen to us . . . our cornfield is ruined. We've come to every service you've asked us to and still our cornfield is wet. That stone is an old stone – a sacred stone – stone older than any man can remember.
> MONK Every stone is old.
> TEACHER That stone has stood on that mountainside since men were here . . .

The teacher now commented that the monks must somehow gather people back into the Christian fold. This stimulated the child playing the part of the monk to try to think what claims were made for the Christian god, that were not made for the sun god:

> MONK I'll tell you what God gives you, you've all been wondering what God does do. That stone can't do what God can . . . he can give you eternal life and make you live again and again.

Here the teacher seized on the point the child made, trying to show the others that the monk had chosen a very good one. The old gods did not claim to make men live again after death. In the role of a villager she said: 'if I can live twice I will worship your god.'

The child playing the part of the monk understood that the resurrection promise of Christianity is particularly attractive. The teacher wanted to show the others that this might be the one part of the Christian doctrine powerful enough to make the people consider returning to the church. It was this pointing up of the best of what the children offered which was part of this teacher's role in helping the children see the potential of drama. Clearly this teacher was more than a sympathetic bystander, for the improvisation was the means by which she judged the children's conceptual level and led them forward in understanding the situation. Timing is all important – the right moment for an intervention must be chosen, the idea must be suggested at just the optimum point.

In follow-up work with the class teacher there was evidence in the children's writing that some of the more difficult ideas were being grasped. Alison, writing in the role of the village milkmaid, showed that she had come to understand the ambivalent nature of the feelings the people had towards the monks and the church:

A problem in the village

It's been raining now for three weeks and the corn is so wet that we can't cut it. There's only a few sacks of flour left in the granary to last us until the rain stops. If it doesn't stop soon we'll have a hard time to survive. The cattle will soon die too if there isn't corn stalks for them to eat and then we'll have no milk and meat. We haven't been getting much from the forest lately either, the deer seem to be hiding from the rain.

Everyone is having trouble with the rain. It comes through the roofs and makes puddles on the floors, the clothes are damp and cold. Our children are getting cold because they're wet through. Round the village the ground is muddy and it's like a swamp, it makes it hard for us to get from place to place.

The monks are better off than the rest of us. They have stone walls and the rain can't get through their roof. It's dry and warm for them. The monks have plenty of food too because we have to give them one-tenth of everything we grow. They only pray while we are working hard getting them food. They say they pray so that the food will grow for us but it doesn't seem to be working very well.

Ian's account, as one of the monks, referred to the book in some detail. The class teacher felt that the children were at first rather slow to grasp its significance but Ian related the monk's anxiety about the book's safety to the long and tedious job of making it – something which consumed so many hours in the making must be a precious possession indeed:

The book is made and lost
I sat at my desk bent over the parchment. My quivering hand finished my part of the book. Five quills I had worn down and was now using my sixth. I sighed with relief and moved back to admire my work. There was my piece done and I was glad. Glinting gold shone from the angel round my first letter and the design was finished with a ribbon of green and silver round the edges. With excitement I went with my parchment to show the abbot. He was pleased, I could tell by the expression on his face. 'The book can now be bound' were his words.
It took a month to bind the brothers' work. Then the abbot called us all to the chapter house and we decided to bring the villagers to the chapel to pray for them and the book. When the book was opened the people rose from their knees with astonishment at the sight of such a beautiful book.
Suddenly the door was flung open and a man stood there. 'The Vikings are here' he shouted. The abbot beckoned to me. 'Quick, take the book and put it in a safe place'. I pondered, wondering where to put it. I thought first of my room but surely that would be searched? A villager shouted 'Put it in the falconry, they won't find it there'. How was I to know that it would be hidden there for many years?

Robert also takes up the role of a monk protective towards the book in this poem:

> As I paused for a moment
> While tending to the garden
> I glanced out to sea.
>
> To my horror I saw in the distance
> The square sails of Viking long boats.
>
> My senses left my body for that moment.
> Vikings! Bloodthirsty, greed-driven men
> Gold and riches their aim
> Nobody's safe from their murderous search for treasure.

Inside the church
The holy book lay unguarded
As I stood and stared my dreams were broken
By the tolling of the prayer bell.
I turned to go and my steps quickened
To warn the brothers, my friends.

In these three pieces we find children writing as a way of exploring and extending issues and ideas thrown up in the improvisation.* Such poems and stories went alongside the drama, the one activity enriching and complementing the other. Then there were the incantations and songs which the pupils perceived to be necessary in the body of the drama. At the point where the villagers returned to worshipping the old sun god, the teacher suggested that they made up their own litany, repeating each line. Here is the incantatory prayer the children made:

VILLAGER 1 Bring the sun.
ALL Bring the sun.
VILLAGER 2 Show your power.
ALL Show your power.
VILLAGER 3 Strengthen the crops.
ALL Strengthen the crops.
VILLAGER 4 Make the crops grow.
ALL Make the crops grow.
VILLAGER 5 Bring light. Show you are the true God.
ALL Bring light. Show you are the true God.
VILLAGER 6 Help us. Rise in the sky and shine.
ALL Help us. Rise in the sky and shine.
VILLAGER 7 Bring life to our crops.
ALL Bring life to our crops.

They were also aware that people needed to write and sing songs about significant events and it seemed to them likely that the Viking invasion would be a suitable theme for such songs which would be handed down through generations. Children's attempts at rhyming lines are not often notable for their success. However, Ian's rhyming couplets have a powerful ring about them and the style and form seem entirely appropriate to a minstrel's song:

* For a consideration of the interrelationship between drama and writing in learning, see Margaret Mallett, 'Improvised drama and writing', *Speech and Drama*, **25** (Autumn 1976), 15–20.

Along the shore Viking feet thunder
They come to destroy, they come to plunder
They come to kill, they come on a raid
They've gone to the monastery
Where Cuthbert is laid.

Vikings take silver and Vikings take gold
Vikings take anything priceless or old
The monastery is burned
Burned down to the ground
They've taken the jewels and good things they've found.

They've killed all the monks
They lie on the floor
Away go the Vikings
They leave by the shore.

But we're still alive
Give thanks to the Lord
Death to the spear and death to the sword.
To the sword.

These songs and incantations were written because the children felt it authentically right to include this element in their drama. There could hardly be a better reason for writing them.

Improvised drama brought home information and ideas which in our view were not accessible to such young pupils in any other way. By becoming ordinary people from a distant time they lived through particular situations and predicaments. Through speculative dialogue, and with the teacher's skilled guidance, they made the problems of a far-off period real to themselves. The associated writing reflected the vitality of the drama, the pupils frequently initiating the tasks rather than responding to the teacher's demands. Many different ways of knowing and understanding are integrated in successful improvisation – the physical 'enactive' mode, which Bruner believes has a role at every level of school learning, as well as the symbolic, particularly the verbal, modes. The insights of the heart are employed as well as those of the head. For all these reasons we believe that drama deserves a higher priority as a way of learning than it enjoys at present.

GROUP 4   TAKING UP THE ROLE OF THE EXPERT

The following two examples are concerned with children taking responsibility for the content and structure of topic work. The teacher takes the role of adviser and audience, the children make the major decisions about planning and execution.

In the first example a class explored a stately home in wooded grounds in a free, expressive and open way; they then split up into self-chosen groups and studied narrower aspects which appealed to them. In the previous two contexts teachers mediated between children and new material. Here the children had to find ways of understanding and presenting what they found for themselves.

The children in the second example worked on self-chosen, individual projects, without even the collaboration of the group. In such work children face difficulties if they have not been able to choose a topic stemming from a hobby or interest, but must deal with unfamiliar material without any ready-made framework. It is no longer a question of merely following up a teacher's suggestions or paraphrasing from a book. Despite the difficulties, such work, at its best, encourages an active approach to learning. There seems a strong case for allowing children sometimes to play the expert, especially in those areas where they already have considerable interest.

Context 7   A group focus – project on Wentworth College

The school was a middle school (nine to thirteen) with an intake of 440. It served a dying mining area which the head considered to be, in all but name, an educational priority area. Many children, in the school's terms, came into the 'slow learning' category. There was a history of previous poor educational facilities, bad housing, poverty and threatened unemployment. The children whose work is described here were the fourth-year pupils (thirteen-year-olds).

In this school fifteen members of staff are class teachers, and spend most of their time in their 'class base' or 'teaching space'. Three members of staff are 'unattached specialists' who give advice in their particular field.

For all children there are five main areas of experience: mathematics and science; English, religious education and modern languages; physical education and music; arts and crafts; social and environmental studies. In the mornings core subjects are studied, while the afternoons are given over to themes and topics in more flexible groupings. The curriculum remains fairly stable throughout the school, but there is more systematic, book-based work at the age of thirteen than at eight.

The humanities work of the school is designed to include a study of an aspect of the environment by all the children. Wentworth College was chosen as a topic with potential for development in many different ways. The children already knew something of the college as they had been taught by some of its students on teaching practice. The building, a stately home situated in spacious grounds, was within walking distance of the nearby village.

The Craster village study (Context 2) generated much expressive talk and writing, but the systematic element was not developed to any great degree. Here the children began with a personal, expressive approach, and then moved towards a more systematic consideration of particular aspects studied in smaller groups.

On their first visit the children examined the outside of Wentworth College and explored the village of Wentworth. The second visit was more planned, beginning with a visit to the Needle's Eye (a tower with a road running through it where stage coaches once passed by), continuing with an inspection of the interior of the house and ending with a visit to the woodyard and a talk by the forester. The writing which records the children's first and second impressions of Wentworth shows that they felt free to focus on whatever caught their particular interest. Both outings resulted in lively expressive accounts. David's piece is a typical example. His thoughts flow on as they would if he were talking instead of writing. Here is an extract:

> When I first went to Wentworth College I was struck with a feeling of huge coaches drawing into the yard and maids milling around. There was something about the College that I just could not lay my finger on untill my teacher told me that the building was symmetrical. I was amazed with the gigantic pillows which held part of the roof up. Then we went down the road to the old church. There I was hypnotised with the statures which laid over the tombstone with every stature there was a dog laid at the bottom of its feet. After that we went to the new church and explored around it. Inside

with all the fancy stones and the fancy decorations a different feeling was in this building, not like the one in the old church it was like a warm and satisfying feeling.

The reader gets a clear idea of the impact the experiences made, and all these children wanted to make something of what they saw for themselves. The need to make sense of what is observed is a strong feature of Denny's account. Little touches like 'it was called I think a State room' and 'they collected statues like we collect stamps' give the piece a highly individual flavour.

> On my second visit to Wentworth we visited the Needle's Eye which is a tower with a road through it. It is called the Needle's Eye and it was built for people to practice taking the stage coach through. For when the Duke wanted to go to his London home.
> But this time we concentrated on the rooms in the house we passed through the pillared hall and up some steps which had a lovely soft carpet. And at the top of the stairs is a room called Marble Hall which is a room which has statues all round the side and the room is nearly all made of marble except there is some expensive imitation marble but I could not see it. We went into a room at the side which used to be for feasts and banquets. We moved on again into another room which had a massive chandelier, hanging down from the ceiling it was called I think a State room. We moved again into a room which had lots of statues. They collected statues like we collect stamps, because in those days they had hardly anything to do.

The account of an able writer, Kay, shows evidence of development in the expressive mode. Highly personal notions and observations still occur, but she was trying to do more than record her personal preoccupations. She seems rather more aware of her reader than some of the other children, and wrote a lucid and detailed account of the structure of the house. Below are the first two paragraphs of her well sustained account:

> Wentworth is a large building which has now been turned into a college, it has a vast estate which covers 2000 acres of land, and is owned by the Earl of Fitzwilliam. The architecture of the house is magnificent, it has a fine stately appearance with a nice entrance and large wings. The wings were once used for servants but have now been converted into living and sleeping quarters for the girls. The main entrance is large with two sets of stairs up to it and six pillars in front of it, also in front of the entrance there are two mounting blocks which were for the rider to mount his horse and by just

looking at them you can picture the rider dressed in velvet breeches and braided riding coat riding off in a cloud of dust. Another thing which is noticeable is the amount of windows which overwhelm everything else. And after some discussion we found out that there was 365, an idea taken from the amount of days in a year.

From there we walked along the road until we came to another building which was once the stable block and had been turned into a series of lecture rooms. The thing that first caught my interest was the huge fountain in the middle of the stable block which although it is not workable still looks very grand and impressive and creates a very subtle air to the whole block. The stone inside the stable block makes it differ from the rest of the stone work and it gives it a more modern look. The reason of course is that the walls are more sheltered and do not get filthy with the dust and grime in the wind. From there we went back onto the road which we found later led all the way to the church which generations of Fitzwilliams have attended.

The writing in these first and second impressions reflected the openness of the investigation, and the individual's perspective on what captured his interest. The teachers intended that systematic work should follow and not precede this broad foundation of looking, and were sensitive to the fact that to move immediately into areas of focused study might well have divorced personal interest from the work which followed.

After the early outings the children were given the opportunity to choose any aspect of Wentworth as the basis of a group study. The choices made included a study of the architecture of the house itself, a look at the village of Wentworth, and an examination of decay and disease in trees. Each group based its work on what the children found out on the spot, what they were told and what they gleaned from secondary sources. Finally, large wall-folders were displayed presenting the findings of each group. Here the work of the group looking at decay and disease in trees is considered in some detail. The group, Kay, Kevin, Paul and Brent, wrote of their intention to plan and execute a systematic study:

> Our group's aspect of work is on Disease and Decay. We are going to learn about: (1) Different diseases and the trees it effects. (2) Causes of disease and decay and (3) Prevention of disease and decay and harmful animals. We are very interested in this project and we will do many other aspects of work branching off from our main titles.

It is worth noting that they saw the task as one of finding out, not one of

taking in what another deemed important – 'We are going to learn about . . .'
They also declared their interest.

The area of investigation led to close first-hand observation, but without
access to the wisdom of the forester and the accumulated knowledge in
books the children might well have been restricted to a narrow information band. The group saw the task as one of knitting together information
from these various sources. Individual children were successful to different
extents as the work quoted shows.

At the outset they planned a structure for their work. Their investigations drew first of all on what the forester told them and what they themselves noticed walking through Wentworth Forest. Here they were involved in setting down in writing what had been given to them in spoken
language, and what they themselves had seen. They wished, however, to
extend their knowledge by reading books and other secondary sources.
Here the task was different, since they were approaching information
already structured in written language. To make someone else's structure
and experience his own involves a child in a more difficult task than relating
what he has heard or seen. The temptation is often to allow the book
research to be an end in itself rather than a means of extending what is
already known. Brent in writing about fungi seemed to lean rather heavily
on secondary sources:

Puff-balls
There are several sorts of globe-like fungus of the Lycoperdon family, or as
I have called them puff-balls. The Beafsteak Fungus is good to eat if picked
when young, cut into slices and fried in butter. They are all very quick
growers and some reach an enormous size. All puff-balls dry up when old,
and when kicked, burst, releasing a yellow dust, which is composed of spores
and seeds.

The stinkhorn
This British fungus has really earned its name of the Stinkhorn, but it is
nothing like so unpleasant as some of its tropical cousins.

Brent's comment that the Lycoperdon fungi 'dry up when old, and
when kicked, burst, releasing a yellow dust, which is composed of spores
and seeds' is clearly not the kind of sentence construction that he would
normally have used. The tendency to copy chunks from books suggests
that while he was probably able to link information at first hand and

information from books in talking, he was as yet not able to do so in writing. One touch was his own, when he gave the Lycoperdon fungus another name – 'or as I have called them puff-balls'.

Another piece by Brent, 'Animals that offend trees', represents a step forward in integrating information from different sources. In this somewhat list-like piece he began with two sentences extracted straight from a book. The rest of the account, however, is an admixture of the forester's comments and personal observation.

> Rabbits are trees worst offenders. They eat the young shoots, and the tree's bark, causing retardation and often death to the tree involved.
> Deer damage the bark from young saplings, when they rub the velvet off their new antlers.
> Squirrels eat buds, berries and cones etc. and strip the tree of its bark. When this is done, even if done in small areas, the cambium layers are destroyed and the tree dies.
> If ever you see bark missing from the stem of a tree, it will be the work of the voles. Large numbers of them can cause a plague, and therefore cause severe losses.
> Moles damage nursery beds by making mole hills. When this is done, the surface of the nursery bed is damaged.

Brent could integrate what he had been told and what he had seen for himself, but these two pieces together show he was not yet able in his writing to use knowledge in books to enhance his overall way of looking at the world.

Paul's piece on the honey fungus seems to represent a step forward in using book information:

> The Honey Fungus is a harmful parasite to living trees by forcing its way into the bark and making a web-like network of fine threads. It kills the trees by penatrating them via the medullary rays, then the wood dies away. Another name for the fungus is the Forester's Curse because of its parasitic nature. It has a livid yellow top and a pale green stalk.

The odd phrase was obviously taken over from a book, but it is clear from the style that this was not a straight copy. It may be that taking over chosen phrases from books is one way of making information our own. Presumably, at best, something like Piaget's adaptation process occurs. The new information gleaned from a book is accommodated to fit the existing store of older knowledge, and the older knowledge is modified to assimilate the new. Distortions occur when either process dominates.

In the following piece Kay was able to internalize book information and so integrate it with first-hand observation and what she had been told. This capacity to use books to extend what is known already, rather than to dictate the whole structure of thought and writing, marks a significant step forward in a child's stance towards unfamiliar knowledge.

> Many diseases are caused by natural things such as deer, rabbits and insects. When deer are young their antlers grow a velvet which needs rubbing off as they get older. The deer take advantage of the rough bark and rub their velvet off on the bark, and eventually this causes the tree to die by dislodging the bark.
>
> There are many types of insects which cause disease to trees. More than often they eat away the leaves or cause like blisters at the base of the leaf, (these are shown in my illustrations). As soon as wood has been cleaned and planed for ornaments it is treated with varnish to prevent it from decaying.

Another piece written by Kay later in the study perhaps represents the best that could be expected from a child in this age-range in making information from several sources an integrated whole. The piece has a definite structure, each comment occurring in logical sequence:

> All living things whatever they are suffer from certain diseases which eventually cause them to decay and rot. There are certain kinds of disease which cause this and one of the organisms is the parasitic plant, fungi. Fungus feeds on trees usually at the base and it thrives in warm damp conditions. There are two main ways of preventing the spread of fungus diseases. One is to spray special powders over the plant or tree so that there is a thin poisonous film which prevents the spores of the fungus from developing. The other method is to breed strains of crop plants which do not get fungus diseases. A lot of the fungi which attack trees does in fact send out mushroom-like growths at certain times of the year. These fructations release several millions of seed spores which infect the other trees. This infection is very dangerous because throughout the rest of the year the fungus spreads unseen beneath the bark or into the wood. The ideal breeding ground for such fungi is the rotting tree stumps near any other unaffected trees.
>
> The forester can keep disease in check if he notices straight away the particular tree which has been affected. Another way he can check it is by felling and removing affected trees during thinning operations. If the infection is widespread he can resort to spraying the forest from the air with fungicides.

Usually the timber which is used for parts of houses is not affected because it usually stays dry and fungi needs moisture to live. One thing which does affect houses and gives the owner quite an expense is dry rot. This is one of the most destructive forms of fungus and given suitable conditions it spreads rapidly. You cannot usually tell that the fungi has invaded your wood until someone puts their foot through the floor-board. By then it is too late and you need all the timber replaced, any of the sound wood has to be treated with fungicides. Once it has been treated it prevents further infection and will not cause any more trouble.

Kay was asked how she used the various pieces of information to write this piece. The opening general statement, of a character rarely found in children under fifteen, is her own insight. She used information from books for the remainder of the paragraph, but it is no mere regurgitation, for the information is based on what the forester said and what she noticed during her walk in the woods.

In this more focused work the children did not include the expressive comments which were so strong a feature of their first- and second-impression writing, even when they were drawing on what had been seen and heard. It seems likely that they felt themselves responsible for making a public announcement about their findings (others would be reading their work-folder) and judged that personal asides were inappropriate.

Finally, here are two poems written by Paul at the very end of the study. They show his commitment to the study and his feelings about what had been learnt. They represent a different way of digesting what he had absorbed in the systematic work. Pleasing in their own right, they also show that for Paul the vulnerability of trees to certain dangers had become part of his way of seeing the world.

> *A tree's slow death*
> Pollution eats slowly into the wood,
> Rotting away the bark.
> Dealing death to the tree's equivalent of skin,
> It drops off bit by bit.
> Then parasites come to invade the bare spaces,
> Tunneling through the wood.
> And the weather,
> The rain wearing it away,
> Until death.

The stricken tree
Still, cold, and dead,
There throughout the ages of time,
Stood the stricken tree.
Hit by lightening,
In its prime,
Deformed, dismembered, and horribly bent.

Context 8   An individual focus – children working individually on self-chosen projects

a   *Individual work within a class project*

The school was a large urban school serving a council estate; the pupils, mainly children of factory workers. The class working on the project were streamed 'able' nine- to ten-year-olds.

The project was on travel – by air, sea and land. Many aspects were explored at class and group level. Later there was an opportunity to make a special study of one aspect or mode of travel. Most of the children opted, as might have been predicted, to work at the history and design of vehicles and vessels, boats, planes, hovercraft and so on, but Michael decided to work on bird flight. This, he felt, gave him an opportunity to use the wealth of information he had obtained as a keen bird-watcher and reader of ornithological magazines. He read widely for his project – books in school and from his local library. Because of his familiarity with the material he was able to use information from books without becoming slavishly dependent on them. He decided on his headings and structured his plan of work. Birds were categorized according to their manner of flying for the purpose of this study. Michael saw himself as something of an expert in this area, a view that comes out in the authoritative tone of his writing. The following piece is his description of how small birds fly.

Finches, buntings and other small birds
These birds mainly have two types of flight (a) a bounding flight, in which a burst of flight is followed by a short rest with the wings folded against the body, in which I resemble the bird to a missile. This action makes the bird bound. (b) The other flight is used in emergencies, e.g. escaping from enemies. In this flight there are no pauses, the wing-beats being fast and continuous. The families which use this flight are: pipits, tits, buntings,

sparrows, finches and larks. Pipits are small thrushes. I have illustrated a reed bunting (E). Speeds: blue tit 21 MPH, snow bunting 26 MPH, goldfinch 26 MPH, chaffinch 35 MPH, house sparrow 35 MPH, skylark 35 MPH.

This, in common with Michael's other informative writing on flight in birds, has expressive elements – 'I resemble the bird to a missile'. The way the information is structured and the successful generalizations show that Michael had a good hold on a mode of informative writing which goes beyond a simple time sequence as its system of organization. Michael also wrote two powerful poems about the movements of seabirds:

> *The seabirds – I*
> Down, down, down.
> The long winged dive bomber spiraled round,
> Down, down, down,
> The yellow billed screamer swooped like an owl,
> And dived.
>
> Chou! with a beak like a blood red scimator,
> The coal black chough swept against the sky,
> And with his ragged flapping wings we let him fly.
>
> *The seabirds – II*
> Searching, searching,
> The perky young dunlins hunt along the sand,
> With their long thin bill and dark black band.
>
> Swooping, wheeling,
> The bent snowy wings, hardly moving,
> The black headed tern swings
> Across the sky.
>
> The thick billed puffin,
> Waddling on the rocks
> Diving for fish,
> Or pulling up his socks.

There seems little doubt that these poems were the fruit of many observations of seabirds in their natural habitat. Michael himself commented that often when he saw things, especially in the natural world, something in him stirred; such memorable moments were recaptured when he later came to write. In 'Seabirds II' there is a powerful contrast between the black-headed tern swinging across the sky and the fish-loving puffin waddling on the rocks. A non-bird-watcher might suppose that the end of the poem descends to bathos because the writer is straining for a rhyme with 'rocks', but it may be an accurate image, capturing a mannerism of the bird.

Michael's expert knowledge was well known in the class, and children and teacher looked to him for help whenever the subject of birds arose.

b *Individual self-chosen projects as part of a humanities programme*

The school was an open-plan, two-year-old middle school with 700 pupils (mainly from upper working-class/lower middle-class backgrounds) and twenty-five teachers. There were five 'floating' teachers to give help to individuals at any time. The head regarded the flexibility of the organization as its strongest point – a team-teaching system operated and teachers took very small and very large groups at different times as appropriate. In the third and fourth years the children were divided into four non-streamed forms. They followed four major bands of study – humanities, maths and science, creative arts and crafts, and physical education. The class concerned was of thirty-five children in one of the four third-year bands (eleven- to twelve-year-olds).

Part of the time allotted to the humanities was devoted to individual project work. Topics were sometimes related to current and past themes explored in humanities periods, but the choice was not restricted to these. Some children chose to study ships, costumes and medicine of the Renaissance, a period already explored at class level, and others explored topics as wide ranging as the Hitchin–Cambridge railway branch, volcanoes, newspapers, and light and sight. The children took full responsibility for structuring the work. Books played an important part. Teachers were available for advice and children were able to approach specialists in appropriate areas. This openness meant that there was great variation in the extent to which children exploited the possible opportunities.

Stephen, a keen train spotter and railway enthusiast, chose to take an extensive look at the Hitchin–Cambridge railway branch. He was sufficiently familiar with his subject to map out a working structure for his study:

Foreword
The origin of the Great Northern

His work was a mixture of information already familiar from his train-spotting activities and information gleaned from books. The following piece on derailments was written quite swiftly and easily without reference to secondary sources.

> There have never been any serious accidents on the branch, and I know of only only derailment. This happened on March 21st 1970.
> Brush-type two diesel No. 5603 came off the line in Royston station at about 10.00 hrs. It was under the bridge on a crossover. The line was blocked between Royston and Shepreth.
> Another Brush type two was sent for from Hitchin. It was No. 5641. The carriages were shunted, and the engine was jacked back onto the line. Trains were running again by 12.20.
> The engine was presumably running round its train when it came off. The rear six-wheel bogie only was off. Shuttle services were being run between Shepreth and Cambridge, and through services were cut off at Royston. The rerailment was hampered rather one side by the up platform. No. 5641 with its van was on the down line.

The description of the branch was clearly a commitment to paper of a journey undertaken many times. Part of this account is reproduced here:

> Starting from platform 1 at Hitchin, the line goes along the main-line for a quarter mile, and then diverges to the right of Cambridge Branch Junction Box. On the right is a yard, and on the left a factory and then houses. The line goes along the borders of Hitchin, and then passes into the industrial area of Letchworth, the largest town between Hitchin and Cambridge. This is one of two stations where the Buffet Expresses stop. It is two and three quarters of a mile from Hitchin.
> As we pass out of the station, there is the yard, with various sidings into factories. Then the train crosses the A1 (M), and passes over Baldock on an embankment. It then runs into Baldock station, which is one of the terminuses for suburban working. From Baldock the line passes through the yard, and

past carriage sidings. Here it begins to run parallel to the AOs, separated at first by a few buildings. The line is now level, and stays about this, going through cuttings and embankments.

In giving an historical perspective, Stephen was able to supplement his own considerable knowledge about trains and railways by turning to books. Here are the opening lines of his history of the branch:

> The branch line of the Great Northern Railway to Cambridge was opened as far as Royston on 2nd October 1850. There were stations at Baldock, Ashwell and Morden. There was a small village called Norton between Hitchin and Baldock. This was part of the present day Letchworth, I do not know when Letchworth was opened.*

We have looked at the topic work of children who were successful in building on an outside hobby in their school work. These children knew their way round the chosen subject area when their project began. Pupils who do not have this advantage face the more difficult task of breaking into unfamiliar ground. The main justification for individual topic work is that it provides an opportunity to structure your own work and to select what seems appropriate. How valuable is this kind of opportunity when children are working in a new country without a map to guide them? How do children take over someone else's knowledge in an area where they have no personal foothold? At best, this can be an invitation to make your own map of an unfamiliar area – to discover for yourself what might be appropriate. However, for many children the temptation to copy or almost copy from secondary sources is too great. Can copying and paraphrasing be a way of making material your own? In the following piece Serge simply reproduced what he had read, probably from one source:

> There are many stretches of basalic lava all over the world, Deccan, Central India and the Columbia River lava plateau of the north is quite rapid and active. One of the many individual lava flows that make up different flows across Snake River basalt spread. The total volume of lava poured out has been estimated as about 12 cubic kilometres. The lake eruption was started by a considerable outburst of explosions that spattered ash not only over much of Iceland, but even over Norway and Scotland about 700 miles of the east and south-east.

This does not make a great deal of sense to the casual reader, but has any of this information become meaningful to Serge himself? Certainly it would

* Later a footnote was added pointing out that Letchworth opened at about 1900.

be sweeping to assume there was no benefit, although all the indications are that it is undigested material.

Serge included in his folder part of a translation from Pliny describing the Vesuvius eruption. Here is a short extract:

> You might hear the shrieks of women, the screams of children, the shouts of men, some calling for their children, others for parents, others for husbands or wives, and seeking to recognise each other by the voices that replied; one lamenting his own fate, another that of his family.

This is a striking piece and it may be that Serge delighted in the language and images in it. To have selected this as a writer's view of what an eruption can mean seems to have been a useful and individual way of exercising a choice. Complementing this we have another more expressive piece culled from a book:

> The liquid lava is always moving, small fountains play in a small air pocket and pieces of lava and ash fly into the air.

Perhaps this image really got through to Serge as a picture of what an erupting volcano might be like.

Later in the study, after drawing on books for accounts about volcanic activity, Serge tried to bring a personal slant to the subject by working on his own question – are volcanoes good or evil? Put this way the notion is eccentric, of course, but it is evident that he was really asking if there were any positive effects when a volcano erupted. Although the piece is not in itself successful, information from books is being used here for his own purpose:

> *Are volcanoes good or evil?*
> Some volcanos have killed a huge amount of people.
> But some support vegetation. These volcanoes usually produce plant life, when they were dormant. But Krakatoa when it was alive gave a huge vast area of fertile land, that's why people live on the island.
> Once a farmer was sewing in his field, when lava began to pour out of a hole. I think the lava had come from another volcano. Later I think plants soon grew up the side of the volcano.
> But when volcanos erupt they cause deaths and destruction.

We have looked at the attempt of a boy of average ability to make something of his study of an area which was for the most part unfamiliar to him, and accessible only through secondary sources. Did he make progress in his capacity to approach the unfamiliar? Certainly the careful illustrations and attractive presentation of the topic book suggested that he had taken some pride in his activity. Children approaching work from this standpoint are more in the role of explorer than expert.

How can a teacher help children in their individual topic work? Where a hobby is explored, little more than appreciative reading seems needed. When children are less knowing and confident in their approach to the information, the teacher tries to establish links between the children and the knowledge. This is not to say that the teacher should structure the topic – this would be to miss the point of such work – but some guidance is necessary. Would it have been unwarranted interference if the teacher had suggested that Serge consider imagining himself at the scene of an eruption? This might have been an appropriate supplement to the Pliny extract.

Even when the teacher takes a less active part in the structuring of work she must be a sympathetic audience to developing ideas and provide guidance where needed. Talking about information is an excellent way of beginning to make it your own. When children are working on individual topics they seek this chance to talk over the work with the teacher. This makes enormous demands on a teacher who sees a group of children perhaps only for forty minutes at a time. To alleviate this kind of pressure a teacher might suggest that some children work on a group topic. This would not rule out individual contributions and means that children can discuss together the structure and selection of material.

Perhaps a teacher should be actively involved even in a child's choice of topic. For while there must be opportunity for personal choice at every stage in a child's school career, the choices must be real ones. The children must be helped to see what the different possibilities are. For example, one boy wanted to undertake a historical theme but was not sure which period or character to focus on. The teacher drew his attention to the existence of some local Roman remains, and after a weekend visit the boy decided this was the topic he would like to work on. He was in a position to write about his observations at the site as well as to draw on information in books. Some mediation from the teacher between pupil and print seems to be needed by children approaching difficult areas of knowledge for the first time, and the teacher in this case gave considerable help to the boy in how to approach his reading.

In each of the situations described in this context, pupils were able to take personal responsibility for the content and structure of a section of their work. To become an expert or even, as in Serge's case, an explorer, is to become less dependent on the teacher as the authority who determines the choice and direction of the work. The pupil is encouraged to be an original thinker generating his own questions and finding his own ways of answering them. It is no longer a matter of the teacher thinking up ways of increasing motivation, for the pupil himself must take some responsibility for initiating educative and social behaviour. Pupil and teacher roles change since in this kind of work it may be the teacher who learns something about a child's hobby. The teacher's greater experience means that he can advise the pupil and point to how the full potential of the topic might be realized. We have discussed in some detail the problem of children replacing dependence on a teacher by slavery to the framework set down by a book.

It is not suggested that all the work that children do should or could be of this kind. Nevertheless, there is a strong case for allowing them to take up the role of expert, at least when they can make an authoritative contribution. Frequently, though not always, these topics are connected with hobbies and pastimes. It is true that some children in our age-range today are relative experts in electronics and space travel. We met a ten-year-old who had a strong grip on trans-lunar injection! Most children have considerable experience in the handling of pets and have observed their feeding, reproductive and parental behaviour. This period in a child's life is often characterized by collecting mania and it is not difficult to find experts on stamps. Children have wide interests outside these well-known favourite areas.

The disadvantages of inviting children to play the expert are well known. We have already suggested how a teacher might help children to make a worth-while choice. This would lessen the likelihood of children choosing again and again to explore the same theme as they move through different classes, even different schools, without any real improvement in depth of coverage – boys who choose football as a theme *ad infinitum* and girls who continually dwell on fashion and pets.

Perhaps the great contribution individual topic work brings to children's learning activities is to help them towards confidence in approaching knowledge and information. Such an attitude is not peculiar to individual topic work for it has to do with making work your own whether or not it was initially self-chosen.

Here is part of a fascinating transcript of an eleven-year-old boy, alone in a school cloakroom, rehearsing a lecture which he was to give to the rest of the class. His subject arises from a main theme which has engaged the whole year group, the early history of the earth and man. From his approach it is clear that he did not see the giving of the lecture as a testing occasion, but as an opportunity to say, 'This is how I make sense of what I have heard and read about these issues. There are not many cut-and-dried answers to problems in this area but this is how it seems to me.'

> The ice age . . . the temperature . . . as a matter of fact all the dinosaurs were dead, the temperature of our earth began to warm and all the ice, glaciers and everything that had come down from the north pole slowly went back sort of thing and melted up. Now the mammals, we had mammals as you know, that had survived, had the use of four legs at this moment. But they sort of learnt, it's funny how, I couldn't explain – they sort of walked a bit you know on their hind legs, you know, only occasionally. It was a sort of creature very like a—oh let me think, a sort of . . . sort of thing, you know bent down on four things, on four legs, like – but it went up on two legs, when it could. Now this mammal, it was . . . vigorous. It was sort of above the others if you know what I mean. It was cleverer. It could do things better than the others. Now you see this sort of apish thing began to develop in more than one way. It was developing to walk on its hind legs very stooped, so that it went down on its four legs occasionally, but it also, what else was developing, which was apart from the dinosaurs that was developed and some of the other mammals, it developed in its brain. Its brain developed very, sort of developed with its body, you know, it went with its body. It hadn't developed without its, it hadn't left its body or its body hadn't left its brain – like a dinosaur, you know, it was too big. It has such a small brain – because the brain hadn't grown with body sort of thing, if you know what I mean. Now the good thing about the dino—— the apish, sort of gorilla thing was that its brain was also developing in a small way and it was learning how to make use of the things around it, not just like the dinosaur made use of plants and ate them. It learnt how to make or how to live in something. Now say it came to a hole in the ground it would know that there he could find shelter. Now if you saw a dinosaur saw a great big cave, a cave in front of it and it knew it could live in it, it wouldn't because it's just stupid. It wouldn't even know that it could live in it.

Teacher and books play crucial roles, but in the end it is what the learner does with the information that counts.

GROUP 5   SUBJECT ENGLISH

These two examples represent typical subject English activities. The first illustrates teacher-directed reading, discussion and writing with the whole class – the most common of all text-based activities. The second shows children in small, self-chosen groups, discussing their own poems, caught momentarily in the gap between digesting what they have already composed before moving on to another writing assignment.

In important ways the two examples make powerful contrasts. In the first, the teacher does not merely chair the proceedings, he dominates them. He has chosen the text, he reads it, he asks the questions, he defines the area of the writing task, and when the writing comes in, he will pass comment on it. In the second example, the children have chosen what to read, they discuss it in their own way, and from their deliberations they move on to further writing assignments of their own choice. When they have done that, they share the results with one another in the same way.

As might be expected, the kinds of discussion generated in these two circumstances differ. In the first, the children are bound to the teacher's expertise in finding the right questions and in responding appropriately to what they say. At best, this kind of discussion can help the children to incorporate the teacher's frameworks into their own. In the second, the children are at the mercy of their own insights. At best, when they are involved and interested together, dealing with material that challenges them, they extend themselves at every point. But both have their dangers. The first kind of discussion, led by a weak teacher, can force the children into mechanical work; while the second, if what is under discussion is irrelevant to their present interests, can leave the children bored and resentful at wasting their time.

Also there are contrasting beliefs, shown in the two examples, about how children learn to write. The first reflects the view that conscious attention to language which flows from a practised pen will enhance the child's capacity to compose. The second reflects the philosophy that if the written language can be used to order experience which children have at first hand, and if in discussion they can share the experience, being responsive to both words and feeling, then conscious focusing on ways of using words will not significantly add to the child's power over language. But we must be careful not to misrepresent the teachers in either case. The teacher in the first example has a wider conception of the writing process than this accenting suggests, and the teacher in the second has often spent time with the children encouraging them to use the written language as precisely as they can.

Context 9   A class discusses a story, chosen and read by the teacher – 'The Black Hand Gang'

The school was an urban secondary school for boys, with a mixed social intake; the class, mixed-ability eleven- to twelve-year-olds.

As part of the normal English work of the school the teacher often reads stories to the whole class, then spends some time on discussion, followed by writing, and sometimes by dramatic improvisation.

On this occasion, the teacher chose the story, read it and led the discussion. The children had copies of the text. While the discussion was phased, the teacher was responsive to the pupils' contributions, following up their insights before stating his own. About half the class spoke, the teacher sometimes prompting the silent ones. Most of the writing which followed arose out of the themes of the story.

'The Black Hand Gang' is a first-person narrative about the attempts of an eight-year-old, George, to join the gang – a small group of shopkeepers' sons and two farm-hands. The gang includes George's elder brother, Joe, who is determined that George shall not be one of the group. One schoolday, George follows the gang on a fishing expedition to a pond, owned by Old Brewer, a local farmer known for his dislike of boys. After some skirmishings, including being pushed about by Joe, George is allowed to stay, and given a part of the pond into which the fish never go. It is a hot day, with the fish lying low. George is the first to get a bite after several hours waiting, and while the other boys gather round in excitement, he lands an enormous one, but nearly loses it back into the water. Joe retrieves it from the shallows in his hands, and as they, now united, glory in the catch, Old Brewer turns up in a rage and beats them all for fishing in his pond.

The discussion

There were four main elements in the discussion which lasted twenty minutes.

1 The children shared with the teacher and the class parts of their past experience recalled by the story.

> TEACHER . . . Uh huh, and are you suggesting then that you, when you read it it would be er, really as if you were fishing perhaps again, if you, do do fish?
>
> PUPIL Sometimes, but I don't really have a rod for it; if I ever go fishing it's usually um at a cottage we had, we had a cottage, and we just, if we wanted to go fishing we just messed, you know, and maybe sometimes we would, there was only once we did this, and got fish, which was very lucky, er . . . put, tie a knife on the end of a stick, and threw it in and got the fish. It got the heart. It's the only time I've ever caught a fish, ever . . . my brother and my daddy goes fishing a terrible lot but I don't really enjoy it 'cause I'd rather climb trees and do things like that.
>
> TEACHER What did it feel like that time when you caught it?
>
> PUPIL Not very, like I was only playing, you know, messing, and I thought it was fantastic, because the knife had stuck into it and the blood was pouring out of it.
>
> TEACHER Was it dead, or did you . . .?
>
> PUPIL Just as well dead, you know, it was just, its eyes were just about open under water, and it just wriggled a wee bit when we brought it up on the bank but when we brought it up on the bank we just hit its head against a stone just in case it *was* alive. It was a pretty big fish.
>
> TEACHER Have you ever seen anything at all since which reminded you of what that fish looked like when it was lying on the grass after you'd got it out of the water?
>
> PUPIL Well, there was only one thing that I've seen and it was a, not too sure whether it was a rat or some kind of a squirrel, the way it was lying in the water, just half way in the water, you know, at the side of a river, and I don't know what had happened to it, it was a horrible smell, but the fish that I caught wasn't a horrible smell cause it hadn't been lying there for a terrible while, but the fur on this animal was all silky and there was some blood over the thing which looked I thought looked like, you know, just the skin looked very scaly, the way the hair was all silky.
>
> TEACHER Fish, yes, fish scales. Yes, that was very interesting

2 The children focused upon the parts of the story they enjoyed. They responded in two ways. They either quoted part of the story:

> PUPIL . . . there's this bit here. 'The buttercups rose to my knees, there was a breath of wind just stirring the tops of the elms, and the great green clouds of leaves were sort of soft and rich like silk, and it was nine in the morning

and I was eight years old, and all around me it was early summer with great tangled hedges and the wild roses were still in bloom, and beds of soft white cloud drifting overhead, and in the distance the low hills and the dim blue masses of the woods round Upper Binfield.'

Or they summarized the narrative:

PUPIL [I like] the bit where he's hiding in the bush and Joe spotted him and come up to him and he started to run away round the pool and he ran after him and he caught him and he didn't know what he was going to do whether he was going to beat him up or just let him go and anyway he wouldn't give in with Joe he wouldn't go home and then finally all Joe's mates told him to leave him alone and let him come and he fished.

3 The children looked specifically at certain language elements in the story and, with the teacher's help, became consciously aware of the evocative phrase and telling image.

PUPIL Buttercups up to his knees, I mean, up to his knees in buttercups, it'd be pretty hard to get buttercups up to your knees because they don't grow very big, and . . . he described it well.

TEACHER Uh huh – surely this is untrue, then, why should we like something which is untrue?

PUPIL Sir, because he hasn't, he's used his imagination well.

TEACHER 'Up to his knees in buttercups.' That tells me two things. At least. What does it tell you? Yes?

PUPIL The flowers were very high.

TEACHER There were a lot, yes, they were very high.

PUPIL They were bunched so they were, you know, mostly together.

TEACHER Why does 'up to his knees in buttercups' tell us that?

PUPIL If there were just one or two scattered about, he wouldn't be able to know whether they were, what height they were, because he'd be away from most of them.

TEACHER Yes. What does it tell you about him?

PUPIL He must be very small.

TEACHER He must be small. What age is the boy? Yes, at the very back?

PUPIL Eight, sir.

TEACHER He's eight . . . his knees, he's absolutely swimming around in these buttercups.

　　　　·　　　·　　　·　　　·　　　·　　　·　　　·

TEACHER Can you think of any other phrases where we talk about 'Up to his . . .?'

PUPIL Knee high to a daisy . . .
PUPIL Up to your knees in mud . . .
PUPIL Up to your neck in trouble . . .
PUPIL You're up to here, and all that . . . full up to here . . .

    .   .   .   .

TEACHER I want you to try and find, I want you to look and see if you can find any more phrases which you like, which make you say, 'Yes, I really know what that means and that's exciting and interesting . . .'
PUPIL He walked up to me like a tom-cat that's going to start a fight.
PUPIL He suddenly cowered like partridges when there's a hawk overhead.
PUPIL There's a bit at the start like that, um, 'One of them named Ginger would even catch a rabbit in his hands occasionally. If he saw one lying in the grass he used to fling himself on it like a spread eagle . . .'
PUPIL Sir, here's a phrase: 'I wonder at the sort of fairy light that fish and fishing tackle have in kids' eyes.'
PUPIL I like the bit where it says about the man that came to hit them. 'He had a wicked old mouth, no teeth in it, and since he'd shaved his beard off his chin looked like a nut-cracker.' It gives you the impression of two big er handles of a nutcracker coming down from an ugly face.

4 The teacher speculated with the children about the nature of stories, and invited them to write. His speculations consisted of the following points
a As readers, we are interested in an *exciting* story, in *not* knowing what is going to happen.
b We also want to find out how someone else's experience is similar to, and different from, our own.
c Part of the reason for reading stories is to be reminded of our own experiences which are similar in kind to those of the author's, which can then be what we write about.
d Writing comes best when you *want to tell*, when you want to share something of yourself with other people.
e Each piece of writing builds on past experiences of writing.
f He (the teacher), as someone other than the writer, cannot tell the author what to write about, although within the school situation, he – an adult and teacher – is the primary audience to be aimed at.

This was his invitation:

TEACHER . . . [The author] told us not only of what it was like to actually catch a fish, but of what it was like to mitch [play truant] from school, to want to go along with his older brother and his gang, what it felt like to be the outsider in the gang. They didn't want him. He made too much noise, they said, whereas the boy knew he wasn't making any noise. They didn't, he was . . . stirring the water up. So they said move on down to the other place. And he was the outsider. Have you ever had an occasion when you have gone along with a crowd of bigger boys, with perhaps a bigger brother or perhaps some boys around the street, of which you felt the outsider, and I can see hands coming up to suggest times when you may have had such an experience – all right, put your hands down . . . (*inaudible*) . . . always wanted to do and finally achieved it. Which was what this boy wanted – he wanted to fish and finally he got the time when he actually caught a fish. You might want to tell me about something which you wanted – it was like magic to you it was so attractive, and you'd heard about it and dreamed about it and the day came when you actually came to do it. I'm not going to tell you what to write out, I just want you to start to write for me. Anything you like which might be, er, stirred by this story. Something that, you say, oh yes, I remember this. Or, er, that reminds me of that. And of course in this I want you to give me passages and phrases which I will like, and I will feel, ooh yes, I know what he means, in the same way as you got those from this. Yes, you?

PUPIL Sir, could it be a passage not that you really wanted to do but you wanted to go with these people? And you didn't really want to do it but you wanted to go with the people, and the people didn't want you?

TEACHER Yes, good, that story suggests a situation like that to you, does it?

PUPIL Not really, 'cos he wanted to fish, but I was going to write down a story where I didn't want to do the thing but I wanted to go with the gang whatever it was.

TEACHER Of course that's what your story has in common with that one. That there was a gang and you wanted to go with these people. So I would say, yes, that's a very good story. Something that has something in common with the story in front of you. Right. I'll give you out the pages and you'll start writing . . . Don't forget the rubbish dump that we've been talking about last week. Don't forget 'Danger – men at work' and the way in which you really thought and looked at men working in order to share something with your reader. 'The hunter and the hunted.' Don't forget those. 'Under the sea.' This is still writing, still wanting to share something with the reader. In the same way as you were doing with those.

The writing

The children started writing in the lesson, and finished the work for homework. Three pieces illustrate the range:

One Christmas day as the snow was makeing patterns on the window I heard my brother and his friends shouting outside in the snow. I was ill and could not go out, I was looking out of the window and that made me even more jealous. I pleaded with my mother, but she said no, then I asked my father he said, 'yes, but don't blame me if your of sick on Christmas day.' So I went out, we were seeing who could slide the furtherest but every time I was last. Then I gave a great big slide and I went so far nobody beat it the whole day.

> Motor bikes there lush
> My brother thought so to (at that time)
> He found a rusty one
> Determined he was to make its rusty engine roar
> It was a secret
> Him and the gang
> He was gonna mitch the lifers*
> He told me if I followed I would be sorry
> He couldn't stop me.
> I hid behind the gang
> When they had the rusty engine spluttering yet going
> I showed myself
> My brother made some fus and truble
> But the others said they wanted a laugh
> So I got a ride
> Well I came for it and got it.
>
> * Lifeboys Brigade.

The outsider

The boy had been sent to the other end of the pool because he was new, an outsider. This I read in a story called, the Gang, though it was not exactly the same words. I pondered this passage again and again and then suddenly remembered a passage out of my life.

It happened when I was about seven, a young lad in a big world. My daddy had arranged for me to join the lifeboys and I had never heard of them before. So there I was sitting in the house one hour before it started all neat and tidy. I can still remember what I wore, a tight fitted navy wooleled jumper and a pair of slack shorts navy again. I wore navy knee socks which kept dropping down on me and on my feet I had a pair of leather black-polished shoes. The minutes had went very slowly since I had eyed the clock several times. But finally to my uncontrolled curiosity we were on our way. This we that I refer to was my mum and me.

The lifeboy building was twice the width of a house and had six gigantic plain glassed windows surrounding it. It was rather unfortunate for me that

I was the only new joining member, and imedially Mum left I knew how lonely it would be for me. Everybody seemed to pass me by and I could not help but notice a hint of distaste. I was slowly being stabbed to death because I had no friends. Suddenly I tripped and fell on the polished floor, and the boys around me started laughing. Suddenly we were the closest of friends. Suddenly I was able to join in all the games. Suddenly I was no longer the outsider.

Opportunities offered by the lesson

This kind of lesson represents one of the most familiar forms of English in the secondary school. It offers many opportunities.

Hearing a story for its own sake. The story was well chosen, touching a common preoccupation of many boys in the pre-adolescent phase – a concern to belong to a group, especially one which indulges in quasi-illegal expeditions. The story was brilliantly read by the teacher, who was able to present the dialogue in different voices, and to maintain the on-going narrative with a keen excitement. If the lesson had stopped at this point, something significant would already have happened.

Relating one's own experience to that presented in a story. Telling a personal anecdote recalled by the story is an appropriate beginning to the class's discussion. The pupil who, under the promptings of the teacher, told of his experience of fishing, followed by his memories of a dead rat (part **1** of the discussion), was opening up for himself aspects of his experience against which the story had to be understood, and in terms of which he would judge its significance for himself. In doing this, he also shared with others his own insights into, and feelings about, those incidents. It is against such a background that the story has first to work. Furthermore, such incidents provide touchstones for the individual to judge the ways in which the story is appropriate to life.

Exploring ways in which the author presents experience. Parts **2** and **3** of the discussion present three different ways of considering the story. In part **2** the first response – quoting part of the story – enabled the pupil to get his own voice around some of the language, and by doing that he was getting the feel of the flow of the language from a practised pen. In the second response, the pupil condensed the narrative to the bare bones of the plot.

The significance of this response may well be that children need to have the skeleton of events clear for the more subtle patterning in the story to become available to them. Part **3** represents a very different approach, best characterized as an explicit focus upon language. Tentative discussion of the meaning of the metaphor 'up to his knees in buttercups' was seen by the teacher as a search for meaning, not as an exercise in labelling language devices. It directed the pupils' attention to one way in which writers present their meaning indirectly. The pupils had some difficulty in unpicking the meaning. The discussion then spread out to incorporate expressions of the same kind available in the idiomatic speech of the pupils, and telling images in the story. It is difficult to judge what this achieved for the pupils. There was no evidence that the kinds of idiomatic expressions marshalled in the discussion were used by the pupils in their writing. We argue in Chapter IV (p. 209) that focus upon language may well divert attention from the search for meaning and significance.

Picking up from the teacher, and then applying, an overall view of the nature and purpose of story-telling. The teacher provided a context in which the children could begin to consider themselves as writers. An essential part of this is contained in the way in which he invited them to write. The tone of the invitation was almost incantatory – his own total commitment to the centrality in the curriculum of reading and writing stories was so infectious that the pupils entered into the writing task with a rare will. His words in the transcript cannot do any justice to the way in which he carried the pupils along with him.

Writing about themselves in an area to which they have been alerted by the story and the discussion. It is clear from the writing that the theme of the story touched their lives at many points; all but one pupil retold a personal incident, the exception being one boy who retold the original story. We discuss in Chapter IV (p. 171) the nature of stimuli which give rise to writing, and suggest that the personal experience of a particular child is the most fruitful quarrying ground to explore in writing. This particular set of work bears that out.

Hearing others read their stories and poems, coupled with the opportunity to read theirs. The completed writing was mounted in the classroom and accompanied by pictures, and some pupils read their work to the rest of the class. This writing then became the background to further work, in the sense that the teacher and the pupils referred back when setting out on a new assignment. By doing this, the teacher encouraged them to see their writing not as final end-products, but as part of a continuing process of mastering the written language.

When the teacher takes such a major responsibility as here, the presumption is that his greater experience of life and literature, his adult and specialist insights into the processes of reading and writing, take the children further than they would be able to go on their own. There is no role conflict between being a teacher and being in charge of the proceedings.

Certainly, the reading of stories has a central place in the curriculum. Younger children in the age-range, though, cannot so easily maintain such a clear focus as was demanded in this lesson, nor conceive of the story, the discussion, then the writing, as a continuous sequence, each part building on the other. For these older pupils this lesson represents a good example of one end of the scale, but we would also want them to have lessons where their insights could be explored less in the teacher's terms and more in their own.

Context 10   Children discussing their own work in a small self-chosen group

The school was a comprehensive coeducational school with a wide social range. (It was the second year of establishment.) The year-group was of mixed-ability twelve- to thirteen-year-olds, and the self-chosen group comprised four boys and two girls.

The group

Here is a thumbnail sketch of members of the group:

A (girl): sparkly, attractive; fluent reader and writer; not noticeably a thinker – no evidence in her work of real thrust; hardly ever initiated within the group; a fairly recent member.

S (girl): the oldest for her age in the group; clever; competent worker, but did not easily relate to her school work; related much more to people; a close friend of D.

C (boy): very shy and often withdrawn; felt that he could not cope with much of the curriculum; beautiful handicraft work, from which he gained some status; very poor at writing, inhibited by very poor spelling.

R (*boy*): sensitive; conscious of his appearance; quite keen on work demanding the collection of information; poor as a writer; without the support of the group, his work might well have deteriorated.

G (*boy*): slightly anxious; very interested in mathematical puzzles; read wildly improbable science fiction, but hesitated either to read or to write on themes about social relations; could see no use for writing to sort out the social world.

D (*boy*): more able than many thought; kind and considerate to other people; avoided confrontation; supposedly could not read when he left primary school, but was one of the best in the year group by the end of his first secondary-school year; often in a dream world of his own; liked to do things in his own time.

The discussion

On this occasion, the group was discussing some poems and stories they had written about their families. We joined them one hour into the discussion, at the point when they moved from one poem to another. (For the purpose of analysis the discussion has been divided into eight parts marked on the transcript.)

1

C My grandfather, he's always watching telly, cowboys and Indians.
D Oh my . . .
R Does he . . .
D He's still going strong then?
C Yeh.
R Are you *sure* he doesn't do anything else?
C My grandfather used to play golf.
D Mine never watched telly, never watched it at all.
A I watch about one-and-a-half hours a night.
S I watch about that much.
A I suppose it's quite a lot.
D I watch Morecambe and Wise.
C Yeh, that's a laugh.
D Most programmes are useless.
R Terrible.
C My nanas are both going strong.
S Mine died. One of mine died in '63 or '64, I can't remember.
R My dad's grandad, I can remember him, you know.

D Your dad's *grandad*!

R Yes, he was nice, I can remember quite a lot really.

2

A Shall we read another one?

S Yes, let's read D——'s.

D You read it.

R I'll read it. (*Reads.*)

> *My grandfather*
> He stood deep in thought
> While the milk on the stove
> Boiled over
> > His eyes with no sentiment
> Flickered
> > Stared on and on and gone
> An old chair creaked as he sank down
> > And his mind ticked on.
> In the endless fields of thought
> > of great rivers so long
> Of wrought-iron bridges
> > To cover the rolling mind
> > Of my grandfather.

S That's good.

A Very good.

S Can I see it? I'll have to read it again.

C Yer, let's see.

(*Murmur of voices.*)

S It's very good. It's very true to life, true to his grandfather.

A Do you know his grandfather then?

S No, but all he's told me, he talks about him a lot.

G I don't understand the last part, the bit, that line about 'wrought-iron bridges'.

R I think it's there because it sounds good. I read it and thought 'that's good' but then I thought 'well, what have wrought-iron bridges to do with it?'

D Well I suppose, I suppose I did kind of well write it or it kind of came; but I think it is right.

S Why?

D Well the main thing about him is he is like a bridge. I remember, well he's always coped with things, climbed over obstacles, made kind of, well bridges you see across, between things, between us, too. Do you see?

G I suppose so.

3

S I think I see. Grandparents are often easier to get on with than parents. They patch up quarrels, don't they?

D Yes, it seems to be, well easier with them, they don't make such a big problem out of things.

A My parents say my grandparents spoil me.

C It's because they haven't got, well, the same responsibilities the parents have got.

D In some ways they're like children again.

A Yes.

(*Laughter.*)

4

D 'Wrought iron' was because he does everything well and because in his day bridges were made of, well were made of wrought iron not cement.

R Yes.

(*Confusion of voices.*)

G He's thinking of the past, isn't he, things like, that have gone before. He doesn't notice what's happening now.

5

G Old people are like that, my gran, she remembers everything when she was a girl, but not what happened yesterday.

S Yes.

A That's right.

R Yes.

S I wonder if it's true.

G I think . . .

R If what's true?

S Well, sort of what they remember, like it was always better then, in their day – even the weather.

(*Laughter.*)

A Or else, 'I didn't have all these things when I was a girl', and 'I wasn't allowed to do that', and 'Think yourself lucky'.

(*Laughter.*)

R Well, they can't just make it all up, though. It can't be, well, very nice to be old.

S No, and not be able to do things any more.

6

D Well, we all change things that happen.

A What do you mean?

D Well, if I do something wrong, or get, well, you, embarrassed, well I think about it, and do it again and again in my mind. I sort of act it out.

G Yes I know.

D I make it, well, better, till it stops worrying me.

(*General murmur.*)

7

G His grandfather doesn't sound as if he's changing things, or making things up. He's just thinking and remembering. It's sad, it's a sad poem.

D *I* don't think it's sad. You see, he does that. He's thinking and the milk boils over. He always has his eggs boiled hard. I don't think he ever had a soft-boiled egg in his life.

8

S Do you remember that poem about the grandfather 'A Moment' . . . 'A Moment of Respect.'

D That was good. That was a sad poem. It more describes . . . that bit where they all move their watches on.

S Yes they all, all the family depended on him.

D Our family is like that.

In part **1** the children, in moving from the consideration of one poem to another, are in a free-wheeling stage, collecting together information on their grandparents, and quite loosely recording details of their own behaviour. They do not penetrate far below the surface – there are no grand new insights – for it is in the nature of this kind of talk to build up and maintain a common platform of sharing and trust within the group. It may well be that periods of quiet gathering are a necessary condition for the period of thrust which is to follow.

In part **2** the group considers a new poem, one which fits into the context established in **1**. The poem immediately catches them up, so much so that they wish to read it again. They then make a predictable move – they set out to understand what they cannot construe; G poses his puzzlement: 'I don't understand the last part . . . that line about wrought-iron bridges.' R tentatively suggests the expression is there because it sounds good. Many a discussion has foundered at such a point, because if poems are merely left at this level of understanding, the critical relationship between language and experience cannot be explored. The fact that the author is present, able and willing to give relevant answers, provides the possibility of moving on. His first answer is to R's point: 'I suppose I did . . . write it or it kind of came' – that is to say, it had the right feel, it sounded good. But he then provides a critical key: '*I think it is right.*' He then expands this point, which is partly to answer G's puzzlement: '*Well, the main thing about him is he is like a bridge . . .*'

In part **3** D's explanation of the meaning itself needs to be explored, which the group do by assembling a set of relevant generalizations about what grandparents are like.

In part **4** D then returns to the original image, adding to his previous explanation a detail on the significance of 'wrought-iron'. His answers make a great deal of sense about the image, although one wonders whether any of it was consciously in his mind as he wrote. His first answer, '. . . *it kind of came*' is probably nearer to the actual process of writing, in that such an expression collects together a complex set of half-felt associations, many of which can only be retrieved after the event. It may well be that D discovered a good deal in the process of having to explain what he meant. G now puts a general gloss on the poem: 'He's thinking of the past . . .'

In part **5** they then gather together examples of how grandparents live in the past, and how they rebuke the younger generation. For all the humour, they still maintain a serious consideration, determined to enter into what it is like to be old.

In part **6** D, following up the suggestion that grandparents may well misrepresent the past (S's speculation about the truth of '*like it was always better then, in their day – even the weather*'), observes that 'we all change things that happen'. This is a somewhat astonishing observation in its accuracy and potency – we falsify what is uncomfortable in experience in order to come to terms with it, to digest it. It may well be the first time that such an essential fact of humanity has become part of their awareness.

In part **7** G tests the relevance of the observation to the poem, rejects its application, then makes a total judgement: '*It's sad, it's a sad poem.*' The author, somewhat fiercely, denies that judgement. His grandfather was a ruminating character, more given to thought than to action, and certainly he was happy in being like that.

In part **8** they bring in another poem which they had explored in previous discussion to add to what they are discussing now.

These eight sections are part of a continuous whole. Part **1** is a run up to the new poem and **2** introduces the poem, but all the other parts have their roots in preceding parts: for example, **3** depends upon D's explanation of bridges in **2**, **4** depends upon S's speculation in **3**. The continuity depends upon what occurs in the discussion itself, hence its development is not one which could be predicted in advance, or deliberately planned to occur. The children follow their noses. Such a pattern contrasts with that of most teacher-led discussions, which tend to be predictable along pedagogical lines and to proceed like Socratic dialogue, with the teacher asking the questions and the pupils responding. Only two parts of this discussion begin with a question – **2** by a bare procedural request, **3** by a mere substantive one – and there are few questions throughout. The dynamics of the process are much more an accumulation of supporting statements and relatively open speculations which allow the children to progress without disputation.

How far does the group achieve school objectives?

The discussion fulfils almost all the conditions that an English teacher might lay down about the discussion of poems:

a   Children should respond to the whole of the poem, as well as its parts (parts **2, 4, 7**).
b   Children should relate the poem to their own knowledge and experience, with the two-fold purpose of penetrating further into the poem (parts **3, 5**) and understanding themselves better (part **6**).
c   Children should relate what they presently read and say to what they have read and said in the past, principally in order to build up a cumulative insight (part **8**).
d   As an added bonus, children should expand their abilities to respond sensitively to the properties of language (parts **2, 4, 6** and **7**).

In these respects, it is difficult to see how the presence of the teacher could have greatly enhanced the propriety and penetration of the discussion.

How far is this discussion a worth-while social experience?

The children deal sympathetically with one another, so that even a relative newcomer to the group, A, can make a contribution and be listened to. They also all play a part – D, in his capacity as authority on the poem, plays the major role, S maintains the speculative tone, G continually directs the group's attention to the poem, C makes one significant remark, R reads the poem and contributes supportive agreement. The quality of their listening and attention is high, in that hardly any statement of weight is ignored. Very significantly, they can celebrate their solidarity with the occasional group laugh.

The main opportunities

Small-group discussion allows greater freedom to the pupils than can occur in the one to thirty (or more) ratio of the average class – greater freedom to find their own way, to make what they know relevant to what is presently under discussion.

To offer this freedom is, of course, to run the risk that pupils will become distracted, and spend their time on matters which the school does not deem important. To forestall that possibility, many teachers provide the group with a set of objectives. Such a guideline was not necessary in our example. Here the group was well motivated, interested in what was before them. That was not accidental – the fact that they were discussing their own work was a built-in incentive, which dovetailed neatly into the area of discussion, an area in which they had a rich and relevant personal knowledge. Even so, it is doubtful if they could have brought that to bear in such an open and speculative way in a whole class. It is in the nature of the self-chosen group, with its history of shared assumptions and mutual trust, to create the security for individuals to venture their tentative speculations without fear of contradiction or ridicule. Many teachers strive to achieve this atmosphere in the classroom, but differences in personality, and the often present sense of rivalry in the group of thirty or so, militate against it happening frequently.

The small group also offers a better training ground for listening than is available in the larger class group, and a more congenial arena for the withdrawn and reticent to speak up. In any class lesson, an individual may be called upon to respond perhaps ten times. In the present example, which is about three minutes long, the smallest number of contributions is seven, the greatest eighteen, and almost all the utterances reflect a high level of attention to what others have said. Further, C, who according to the teacher needs to be drawn out, makes a contribution without strain.

The role of the teacher in group activity cannot be easily determined. The more he imposes a pattern, the more likely it is that pupils feel they have to keep to it. On the other hand, many groups can flounder. One form of control exercised by the teacher in the example was the frequent tape-recording of the group's talk, which could then be monitored, so that further points could be taken up if necessary. Much more important is the total context in which such discussions occur. These children had been working in groups with the same teacher for upwards of twelve months. Further, the integration of English with other humanities subjects had freed big blocks of time – all through mornings and afternoons – time for the small group to settle down and for the discussion to develop. Good teaching, too, lay in the background. Previous talk with the teacher, talk which had led them in and out of poems, but remained in general sympathetic to their point of view, contributed in no small way to the group's confidence in tackling the work on their own.

Finally, while this teacher would endorse the view that children need to talk in order to learn, and would support a radical claim that 'talk for talk's sake' is an important commitment of the English teacher to the language development of pupils, she also sees this talk as an intrinsic part of the conventional English programme, the network of activities of reading, writing, talking and listening.

GROUP 6   ENGLISH IN INTEGRATED STUDIES

Some secondary and many middle schools have seen advantage in 'integrating' the curriculum. The various schemes under this heading seem to have one thing in common – an allocation of time, often as extended blocks covering whole mornings and/or afternoons, equal to the amount which would have been spent on the separate subjects. The two examples here illustrate some of the problems involved, and give some idea of what happens to English when it is integrated with other subjects.

In the content-centred approach, in which materials once dealt with under separate subject headings are brought together in a co-ordinated framework, the organization is usually in terms of topics, and the specifically English content is often literature of the relevant period. This kind of integration seems to occur when English, history and geography are merged together. An activity-centred approach brings together specialisms thought to have a common purpose. Planning tends to be ad hoc and provisional, the teachers and children consulting as they go. The English activities are reading, writing and discussion, in many respects as in a separate programme, except that they may arise from, or be developed by, the other specialisms. This kind of integration occurs when English merges with art, drama and music under such headings as 'the creative arts' or 'the expressive arts'.

The contribution English makes in the first kind of course lies as much in the language activities as in the content. The accent is on talk and discussion, which plays a positive role in helping the child cope with unfamiliar material; and making the impersonal context personal, by writing in a fictional guise, helps the children come to grips with foreign places and historic times. In the second kind of course English appears to receive more than it gives, for it seems that the expression of feeling involved in art, drama and music is put to good effect by the children when they read and write.

Context 11   Humanities course and expressive arts

The school was a comprehensive school (reaching the end of its second year), in a suburban/rural setting. It had new buildings with good facilities, suitable for setting up a humanities area with resource centre and adjoining classrooms. The intake was mixed both socially and in ability. The work described is from first- and second-year units.

In this school English was integrated with history and geography to form a humanities course, and also played a central part in the expressive arts, with drama and music. In the former, it was fully integrated, the relevant specialists planning a coherent two-year course. In the latter, there was a much looser partnership, the specialists free to call upon each other's expertise, and from time to time joining forces to produce a year-group spectacular, or in smaller ways co-operating to reinforce certain studies.

The humanities course

In general, this was a topic-centred course organized under the following termly headings:

1 The structure of the earth/prehistory.
2 Prehistoric Britain; how man survives; language and communication.
3 The medieval world.
4 Ancient civilizations; Greece and Rome.
5 The Renaissance and exploration.
6 Agriculture and village life.

The second unit was something of an exception. The children had the choice of concentrating on one of these topics, although they were expected to spend some time during the term on the others. With the other five units, the children all covered much the same ground, although it was part of the team's thinking that depth of study was at least as important as a wide coverage, so that individual children and groups to some extent followed their own interests.

The topics in each term's unit, drawn together from each subject area, had been chosen to reinforce one another. A good example is the outline for the first unit, 'The structure of the earth/prehistory':

> *The structure of the earth.* An introduction to the physical world; modes of formation of rocks and associated scenery. Concept of geological time-span, and evolution of life; and use of fossils. Concept of climatic variation and its effects, landform changes and the concept of gradual modification by agents of weathering and erosion. Study of earthquakes and volcanoes, and their effects on man. Some field study.
>
> *Prehistory.* An introduction to the idea of change and adaptation to different environments; to the work of palaeontologists and archaeologists; to the concept of time. A consideration of life-forms from Pre-Cambrian to Post-Pleistocene eras: the ages of invertebrates, of fishes, of amphibians, of reptiles, of mammals and finally the emergence of man as the predominant primate.
>
> *Creation myths.* Work on creation myths offered by English specialist. Discussion of ideas of what existed before the creation of the world, e.g. Genesis, the Greek idea of chaos, Egyptian ideas of water, 'the deep', dark-

ness, the idea of 'nothing'. Out of these states the emergence of order, time and light. Concentration on Northern myths. Movement, drama, art, music, reading, writing. Similarly the creation of man: the Prometheus story. Survival without fire, Prometheus stealing fire for man, the first fire, fire as life protector and life destroyer. Literature available. Roger Lancelyn Green, *A Book of Myths* [Dent]; Roger Lancelyn Green, *The Saga of Asgard* [Penguin Books]; Barbara Leonie Picard, *Tales of Norse Gods and Heroes* [Oxford University Press]. Also a collection of poems, extracts, pictures about fire.

The planning/teaching team were also aware that the nature of their specialisms might require the development of particular skills, and the acceptance of special approaches to the material under study. The introduction to the fourth unit makes these beliefs explicit:

> *History.* The nature of historical evidence. Group work on a wide range of historical documents, not limited to any particular period.
> *Geography.* Historical evidence on maps. Use of simple sampling techniques to record data and try to analyse distribution patterns, e.g. of prehistoric sites, Roman villas, etc., on OS maps. Location of villages – discussion of factors.
> *English.* Nature of reminiscence; children visiting a local historian, taping him talking and discussing. Memories of grandparents, parents; comparative accounts of the same event. Personal writing about their own memories, selection and emphasis. Nature of fiction, truth, legend. Oral transmission, broadsheet ballads, newspapers and other media.

The teaching team – one specialist in each of English, history and geography to a hundred pupils in a year group, supported full time by a craft teacher and part time by a remedial specialist – planned the course together, and took individual responsibility for preparing materials and guidelines from their particular subject areas. In working with the children they acted as specialists, available for consultation as the need arose. Five one-hour-ten-minute sessions were spent on the work, timetabled so that each child spent at least one whole morning or afternoon on his chosen field of study. Each teacher was responsible for a group of twenty-five children, a class-size group that met together at the beginning of each session to choose working groups and topics for study, and at the end of the session to report progress, and to receive comments and further direction. Within this class set-up the breadth and depth of coverage was monitored across the whole humanities field for each child. The conscientious teacher-tutor could ensure that all the children covered most of the field in some detail and could support individual children in depth study. This system, too, allowed for the fact that individuals might wish to spend a month on one topic or predominantly on one activity. Sensitivity to developing strengths and coping with weaknesses was something prized by the team – to know a child's work in detail across a quarter of the secondary-school curriculum is something not often achieved with a subject-oriented time-table.

The basic working unit was the small, self-chosen group which remained intact until the group endeavour was brought to some stage of completion. Apart from that proviso, no important restrictions were placed upon how many different groups a child might be a member of. The formation of the groups tended to rely upon friendship patterns, rather than ability group-ings. Within the groups, the working mode was discussion. The children were expected to share their wisdom and knowledge; they were encouraged to formulate questions to which the group would then find answers; they were expected to report back and to justify their activities to other class members. When they produced writing or maps, wallcharts, painting, etc., it was expected that a wider group would enter into informed discus-sion of the products. For most purposes, the teaching team valued the function and efficacy of the spoken language above writing.

The English contribution

The responsibility for the reading, writing and spoken language develop-ment of the children was held jointly by the team. Nevertheless, the English teacher's access to relevant literature played a major part in such development. For every unit there was a rich and varied reading list, in some cases material which easily integrated with work from the other sub-ject areas. In the unit on the medieval world, in which the central history components were a study of kingship, religion, land tenure, town and country life and the origins of the town, contemporary writing such as the *Canterbury Tales, Sir Gawain and the Green Knight*, and modern versions of the Arthurian legends such as Alan Garner's *The Weirdstone of Brising-amen* (Collins, and Penguin Books), were more than supportive material. In other units, reading material branched out from the main study. In the unit on the Renaissance and exploration, the English component started with some work on the historical period, but quickly moved towards science fiction and space exploration, in which conceptual links exist with Renaissance exploration and the men who carried it out. While the history component was concerned with the revival of ancient cultures, the Copernican Revolution, the exploration of new lands and the 'conquering' spirit of man, and the geography component with the physical geography of the Mediterranean, the English work took a line through space exploration and science fiction as a present human endeavour to push forward the frontiers of knowledge and come to grips with the unknown.

A more complex aspect of the English teacher's role lies in the dynamics of what is done with the material across the humanities field. The English teacher in this scheme put the problem as follows:

> I suppose the greatest revelation to me was to see the difference between a child working in a field and producing a piece of writing – about himself or something he is interested in, or a story – and the kind of writing he did in history or geography. Even when history and geography materials have been presented with a lot of discussion and through interesting activities, the writing seemed to cause tremendous difficulties for them. Also, I found myself looking at textbooks because the children were having difficulty with them. For example, when we were doing something on the medieval period, we worked with a splendidly illustrated book about knights – illustrations of clothes and armour – which contained passages about chivalry . . . Chivalry is a concept which needs illuminating but what the children were doing *was copying out of the book and drawing the pictures* . . . We were constantly finding concepts like this which were just dead on the page, and trying to do something about them either in drama or talk or writing . . . This is part of the problem in the secondary school. Children suddenly come into contact with an enormous range of secondary experience, different kinds of talk and writing, different expectations of different subject teachers, and there seems to be a very big gap between where they presently are – children of 11 and 12 are still very subjective – and what these materials and expectations demand of them . . . What we found ourselves doing was trying to mediate between the children and the information they were being asked to handle . . . We therefore began to insist on discussion before writing, to encourage the children to share any personal experience relevant to the topic in hand, to engage in dramatic activities built around aspects of the topic, and to plan and execute as many field trips as possible.

These comments go right to the heart of a central problem in all teaching – how to help the pupil make coherent meaning out of his educational experience, whatever that may be.

Some of the problems connected with English in integrated studies are illustrated in the following examples from the work of two pupils: Kim, a first-year pupil working on the first unit; and Karen, a second-year pupil working on the fourth unit.

Kim's work, like that of most eleven- to twelve-year-old pupils, illustrates clearly the difficulty of reproducing fairly remote material with no attempt to process it in any way. This extract (together with many other pages) comes straight from the original source:

> *Neanderthal man*
> The skeleton of Neanderthal man shows a rather short man but a powerfully built one. He stood just over 5 feet tall. His hands and fingers were short and stubby, so were his feet. This is shown not only in his bones, but also in some actual fossiled footprints of a Neanderthal man. Altogether he was heavily muscled and imensly strong. His face has three Neanderthal distinctions, a receding chin, larger cheeks, Man's footprint and prominent brow ridges. These curve over each eye, they continue and connect over the nose. This is what gives Neanderthal man his classic stone-age beetle-browed look.
> Compared to Australopithecus, Neanderthal man seems almost civilized. But he was well able to look after himself. Also he could probably speak a crude language. They had pondered on the nature of death and probably had felt the first primitive stirrings of religion.

This slavish copying serves no good educational purpose. It is very common in all schemes of work which use workcards to organize the pupil's day. Such activities not only occupy time; more damaging, they may convince the child that he is actively thinking and learning, because he labours hard to fill up the pages.

Kim and her group had been contentedly engaged in similar work for several days, when they were directed towards an Escher print of prehistoric monsters. The print powerfully affected them, and a lively discussion followed:*

> S I need to be, well frightened, of of things kind of changing in my room.
> M Yes, I know . . .
> (*Confusion of voices.*)
> S My coat hangs on the back of the door, my bedroom door, that is, it looks, well in the dark, it kind of looks like a person.

* Kim's comments are italicized.

M Yes, I know.

J It's like that with everything, there's just the, um, the shape.

M Yes, it stays the same shape, but it um, it . . .

J Becomes something else.

M That's right . . .

(*Confusion of voices.*)

TEACHER Yes, all the familiar things become quite changed and frightening, don't they?

('*Yes.' Laughter, several voices.*)

K *Especially if you've seen a film, something scary on the telly, or read a, well, a ghost book, or a mystery, or something.*

S Yes, I remember this film . . .

K *Yes, I sometimes do that on purpose* . . .

(*Confusion of voices.*)

TEACHER How on purpose, Kim?

K *Well, I suppose I, um, like to frighten myself sometimes, when I'm warm and I know it's all right, really.*

M Mm. I do that too.

TEACHER What was the film you started to say?

S Well, it was this, um, this film late on telly one Monday night. It was, er, about um, Dracula and things like that.

F I saw that, it were good, it were ever so frightening. I kept my light on after that.

M I used to make my parents leave the light on all night.

(*Several voices in agreement.*)

F I used to look under my bed, behind the curtains, in my cupboard, every-where to see if anyone was there.

(*Laughter, agreement, 'I still do'.*)

TEACHER I used to do that too; I used to run down the stairs too to get back into the sitting room, as I thought there was someone behind me with a knife.

S Did you? Did you really?

TEACHER Yes, I did.

F How old were you?

TEACHER Oh, about eleven, I think.

K *This picture here reminds me of a dream I used to have.*

M What was that?

K *Well, we always had this, um, this big book, a kind of encyc . . . encyclopedia, I think it was. I used to look at this picture of a dinosaur and I used to look at it and I didn't really know what it was, I used to dream about it coming alive and well, I suppose it's silly.*

J   No, go on.
K   *Well, it used to come alive and crawl out of the book and do things and then go*
     back before morning. I remembered it when you showed us that picture.

Taking her cue from this, the teacher introduced the group to a poem on
monsters, which kindled similar discussion. Kim was a major contributor.
From this point on Kim was involved, excited and interested, and she
launched herself into some creative work. First, she wrote a vigorous
poem:

> *The pteranodon hunt*
> 'Hui anu!' Cries the witch doctor,
> 'Hui anu!' Cries the chief.
> 'Hui anu!' Cry the men,
> 'Hui anu!' Whisper the women.
> The children are silent,
> The witch doctor dances a spell,
> 'Hui Anu, Mano Huai, Abu Liamy',
> His voice contorts and contracts,
> With his excitement of the hunt,
> The hunt for the dreaded Pteranodon,
> The 'Soul of the Evil Dead'.
> The witch-doctor finishes – he sits down.
> The children are silent.
> Silent and afraid.
> Weapons are picked up.
> The men stride out of the village
> Out into the bush.
> And then . . . A warrior screams . . .
> . . . High, high above on the cliffs,
> Sits the monster, flexing his wings.
> 'Aaaaruagh', he screams and flies,
> The sky goes dark, the sun blocked out by the monster's wings.
> It swoops, the men let loose their weapons,
> It screams, in agony and falls.
> The men return home – triumphant.
> The children chatter.

In this, the primitive tribe – ancient man – and the Jurassic beast were
brought into a meaningful juxtaposition, and this suggested to her a
richer, more personal, more informed context for at least some of the dead

facts she had slavishly reported before. She constructed a narrative, 'The quest for the death lizard expedition,' which enabled her, in a fictional twentieth-century guise, to make something for herself of the ancient world. What was it like?

Kru Miauon – old world

It is still and silent in the forest, quiet and dim no one is awake. The first rays of sunlight creep over the path alighting on plants and hollows where animals are asleep, creepers hang from branches, swaying gently in the slight wind. Insect-trap plants stand upright, the traps set. They seem to be lifeless, in the stiffness that comes after death. But they are not.

The first awakening occours – a large dragonfly zooms from the trees whirling, circling about creepers and plants as if he was an awakener for all the other creatures. A tiny shrew-like creature scampered up a tree, he scratched a piece of bark off, it fell and woke a squirrel. The squirrel chittered angrily and turned to a half-eaten nut. Bees came streaming out of a hole in the side of a thick trunked tree, buzzing excitedly, as the sun rays flitted across their yellow and black bodies. Animal after animal awoke until the forest was alive with activity, but all the while they seemed to be nervous and cautious, constantly looking over their shoulders at something – but what!

And then it awoke! A great mound of dry earth arose and shook. The earth tumbled off and an ugly snouted head emerged. Leathery feet thudded down and crushed plants and saplings. Birds screeched and animals scampered to the safety of rocks and trees as the snuffling spiked monster groped ungainly towards the edge of the forest. Its long tail thrashed out at tree trunks grooving them deeply. He crashed away and was gone. All that was left were his footprints. The forest relaxed.

What would it be like to be there oneself, even if in a persona of a twentieth-century hunter, rather than as herself?

Hunted

(As related by Gary Trent, a writer, to the rest of the 'Quest for the death lizard expedition')

I was plodding moodily across by the great fish lake under the overhang cliff. Then my skin began to prickle and my spine contracted tightly. Looking behind I could see nothing, I relaxed but quickened my pace. On the far side of the lake I heard a cross between a snuffle and a grunt muffled in the thick foliage. I began to sweat, a cold clammy sweat. I knew something was tailing me and I had to get away – Fast!

A large prehistoric Triceratops stuck its ugly, three horned head out from the trees. A sound, I suppose it was a growl, was emitted from the brute's flabby throat. It advanced covering ten yards at each stride. I froze. It splashed through the ten feet deep water in the great fish lake, I stared disbelievingly at the ground spread out before me.

Then my legs came to life, I just turned tail and ran, hoping the brute was a cumbersome creature and could not move fast. Unfortunately for me, the Triceratops could manage a gallop of about ten m.p.h. As often as I could will myself to, I stopped and flung rocks at the creature, he flung them contemptuously away with a baseball glove front foot.

Up till now I had kept a clear head but then I paniced, I ran blindly on into the forest, brushing hairy stemed plants from my face as I ran into them. A fallen tree trunk across the path halted me I had to climb over, my weak legs gave way and I fell banging my head as I did so, and rolling under the thick bark, the monster went crashing away and I was forgotten.

With these, which she read to her working group, under her belt, she then extended and amplified this narrative into a full-scale story.

Kim's basic strategy to envisage the ancient and savage world was to people it with creatures and people she could realistically imagine. This strategy, if not suggested by the English teacher, was certainly supported by her. The sacrifice of actual accuracy was, in her view, compensated for by active intelligence at work. At the very least, there was personal investment in the study. However, the challenge could be made that such work does not help Kim to become an historian, or a geographer, for to do this she must learn different frameworks for ordering material. That challenge may not be met by claiming that the writer has created a world with some personal significance. But then nor is it supported by what Kim had been doing with the textbooks.

The children working on the second unit were expected to produce a folder on a topic of their own choice, presenting varied materials showing different approaches to the subject. A number of teacher-led sessions were timetabled, sessions which drew attention to different modes of treatment. Karen attended four such sessions as follows:

1   A scene, planned and acted by a small group to the rest, of an incident in a shop. Comparison of interviews and accounts of what each onlooker thought he saw.
2   Listening to tapes of snatches of conversation and trying to establish settings. Making tapes of people talking, transcribing them and comparing dialogue in fiction and plays.

3 Interviews – practising interviewing people in a variety of situations for a variety of purposes.

4 Newspapers – looking at different treatments of the same story.

Karen chose to work on the 'Loch Ness monster', a topic which was then revived in current speculation, and which she felt offered her a wide range of varied materials. Like a good researcher, she wrote away to relevant bodies for information, but, as so often happens, she had to rely on her own wit and invention, because the information was so long in coming. The resulting folder was all her own work.

In sixteen sections, she tried her hand at various modes of presentation and kinds of investigation. Chief among these was what we could call eyewitness description, which appeared in two forms, the first a collection of various statements, under the title, 'If the description fits'. Here are two examples:

> *Gillian Downs 1964*
> I saw the monster while I was playing hide and seek with my freind Carol I hid behind a bush just beside the loch Och and I turned round and . . . and there it was the monster of the loch just there floating in the water about half way across the loch it was ever so big it was. It was black and grey and it had a triangle head and a sort of long gooses neck. I was frightened so I ran away home, oh it had four humps on its back.

> *Mr Macnair 1968*
> I saw the monster at a front view while I was fishing in my dingi. When before me there was a termoil in the water then a head and neck emerged about fifty yards in front of me it had a dark grey skin two small nostrals and slanted eyes with a very long thin neck suporting an oval shaped head it towered up from the water at about twelve feet. I must have seen it at about six o'clock in the morning.

The second kind was the on-the-spot interview, which drew directly on the class lessons surrounding the project. In most of the interviews there was a dual focus, partly on the information, partly on the people being interviewed:

> REPORTER Gooday I'm interveiwing people that have recently seen the Loch Ness monster.
> MRS SHAW Och I, me and my Burt saw it yesterday out in the loch swimming about it was. Och the nou its not a monster my Burt says its some kind of prehistoric animal it had ten humps and an enormous head ever so long it

was, at least a hundred feet long ask my husband. I'll go and get him. Burt, Burt come here a minute will you I've got to go now.

REPORTER Your wife tells me it was a hundred feet long with ten humps, is this so?

MR SHAW Well I, my wife has always exaggerated a little really it was about thirty-five feet long and it had a tiny head and I'm not sure how many humps it wasn't very clear with the mist decending on the water but I took some snapshots of it if you'd like to see them their not very clear I'm afraid. You see in the first picture it was very dull and bleak in the second its a little clearer because there was a crack in the clouds just then. Och I'm still not sure I beleive in it it might have been some kind of optical alusian or something floating on the surface of the water with all that mist around I couldn't be sure of anything. Although some in the nearby villages and towns swear theres a monster or some kind of prehistoric creature although what it could live on I don't know.

These pieces are typical attempts to come to grips with impersonal material, personalizing the information by building up a character who becomes a mouthpiece. Here Karen is trying to produce eye-witness accounts by actual people speaking in their own voices about what they saw and believe.

The people envisaged by her are ordinary citizens, with no special claims to make, no professional stance to take up. The scientist, though, does have a special role. He classifies instances under categories:

Scientist Mr Zorronbull said, 'If there really is a monster it would be a desendent of the prehistoric animal the Brontasaurus or the Centiosaurus which lived by swamps and marshes during the Jurrasic period. This animal had a long neck a small head a large round body and a very long tail measuring from head to tail at about sixty feet and all of these descriptions tallie with the descriptions of those that have seen this animal. The only difference though is that the monster has humps, seven I am told.'

He develops theories to account for exceptions:

Miss Arkinsaw, Mr Zorronbull's assistant, comments, 'Yes well I, I've been working on the idea that when this animal was living it lived down in England but then there came a, ah some sort of drought and because these animals had very small brains therefore very stupid animals so most of them just stood there and died but the longer the drought lasted the more of them were born so gradjully the animal evolved and grew humps on its back like cameles to store water and food and this particular animal got more than its fair shaire of brains and it must have walked at least three hundred miles to Inverness where Loch Ness is now and as it was such a big loch it survived up till now which is some kind of miracle. If it actualy is there?'

He also writes objective reports on investigations, drawing conclusions from the data available:

Over the years we have collected and recieved small finds from the monster itself or beleived to belong to the monster. Among asorted items there are a few teeth and aparently toe nails which must have some how fallen of in some way we have managed to collect enough nailes to asemble a foot or a paw what ever you like to call it and have drawn in the actual foot so far we have found four nails of varying sizes. There for it must have four toes from the pictures we, and others have taken it lookes very much as if it must have webbed feet which were evolved over the years to help it swim.

(It is interesting that the impersonal tone is interrupted by the voice of 'common man' or, to put it differently, that an expressive element intrudes into what is basically a transactional piece.)

Finally, there is the geographer, who is represented by a scale map of Inverness, and this piece of writing:

Putting the monster in its place
The villages surrounding the loch would obtain a very low income if it was not for tourists buying expensive souveneirs and taking boat trips on the loch and variose other things. I dought that any of them would make much of a living without these buissnesses on the side. The land is only really good enough for grazing land for sheep and has a lot of trees and bushes. Working on these lines if the ledgen wasn't there then most of the villagers would have to mouve away to Nairn Moray Banff Aberdeen which are the nearest big towns. They would have to work in Hydro power Alliminium stations and cole mines or any other industry and use these resourses therefore we call it the rurual depopulation of Inverness. Around the loch there are variose industries chimneys and cooling towers needing the loch a few years ago for power. The land around the loch is very bare except for a few bushes and trees dotted here and there.

This piece is of particular interest. Is the writer using her own voice, or is she pretending to be a geographer? Add the superscript 'Miss Wilkins, geographer, said' prior to the piece or 'This is what I, Karen, want to say' and the text would be equally suitable. This suggests that if the writer assumes the role of a specialist, the gap between speaking with another's voice and speaking with one's own may not be as wide as it sometimes appears to be.

The expressive arts

This aspect of the curriculum was not topic-centred or planned as a common course, in which the staff acted as general teachers to the whole group. Each teacher (music, drama, English) acted as a specialist, promoting ideas and activities which arose within the subject, and working with a third of the age-group as a class unit. The stable group resulted more from an organizational need than from subject divisions. Experience had shown that once the groups in the class, or the class as a whole, had set out to develop some activity, the unplanned arrival or departure of children disrupted the work.

Through their subjects the team pursued a common purpose. Music and movement, song and poetry, dramatic improvisation and fictional narrative formed natural pairs, and together provided children with their best school opportunity to structure and express a wide range of feeling. This commonality of purpose led to two kinds of co-operation. Activities initiated in one area could be further explored in another. A story read could become the basis for dramatic improvisation, and music could be created to accompany a dramatic scene. Also, activities for the whole group were organized, which by their nature required joint work – for example, film making and plays.

The first-year group presented a drama and music production, called 'The creatures', a programme of improvised movement and created music to represent the animal world. Integral to the programme was a reading of their own writings composed for the occasion. Many eleven-year-olds write about animals, perhaps because of their consuming interest at this age in living creatures other than themselves. In this particular collection of work the children had clearly thought very carefully about the kind and quality of movement in the animals they wrote about. This aspect of animal behaviour was discussed during the writing activities, but more importantly was the basis of the dramatic movement, which clearly succeeded in imprinting the movements 'in their bones'. When they came to write they had more to draw on than an arbitrary use of descriptive words.

There were no pets, if one excludes this solitary tortoise:

The tortoise
In the corner near the tomatoes
There is an old old stone.
Suddenly it comes to life
From one end a brown wrinkly head appears
Then a leg and another, then two more.
Scaly and shiny they appear each with four sharp claws
Now the tail has appeared
Short, fat and stubby with dark smooth scales
With a mighty heave it lifts up its old shell
And slowly lumbers off.
With its head wobbling and its claws digging into the ground
It gradually approaches the lettuce on the grass
Then it opens its wide mouth and bites at the leaves
Tugging and pulling at them until it gets a nice big piece
It chews it over and over again then swallows it
Afterwards it moves off to a sunny spot and rests there
Gazing at the stone wall
Soon it falls asleep until the sun comes out again.

There were the gentle and timid creatures:

The dik-dik
The dik-dik, tiny, graceful and full of life,
He darts, squirms and weaves between bushes and trees.
The dik-dik is as graceful as air itself
Moving swiftly over the hills.

Eyes bright like tiny stars but cautious and quick to
  realise danger,
The larger animals seem slow and dumb against the tiny
  dik-dik.

The jungle bush is good for camouflage
But not for the tiny dik-dik, he has to keep on the move,
Eager to keep away from the lions and leopards.

The tiny dik-dik cries like a bird, so sweet.
He is very shy like a boy when he meets a girl.
The dik-dik, sixteen inches high, small but oh!
  so beautiful.

There were the insects:

I watched an ant
One solitary ant marched across my book.
How large I must seem to him,
I held him up to my eyes and watched him,
His legs marching – One . . .two . . . one . . . two . . .
Across the roads of the words,
One . . . two . . . one . . . two.
Three legs moving, then three legs more,
Brown head waving, roving around,
Mouthing the smells, the air, the smog.
Eyes swivelling around,
Our gaze meets.
Brown, metallic body,
All segments stiffen.
But he marches on,
One . . . two . . . one . . . two.

Finally, a bird, which (by courtesy of Carl Sandburg's poem, 'Wilderness') has taken up a different habitat:

The albatross
I've got an albatross in me,
A lonely albatross, a wandering albatross.
A swooping cavorting albatross,
An albatross so wild he tears me in half.
An albatross that dives and banks in his endless search for food.
I've got an albatross in me,
An albatross so sleek and graceful.
An albatross so fast and swift,
An albatross that curves and banks in the wave-swept wind.
I've got an albatross in me,
An albatross that plummets in ever decreasing circles.
An albatross that skims for years through curling waves and hydrophonic winds.
An albatross streaked black and grey by harmonic winds and waves.
An albatross that nears its end in screeching winds and echoing waves.
An albatross that will face its death on splintering rocks and whirlpool waves.

Context 12 World studies course

The school was an inner-urban, working-class comprehensive school (eleven to eighteen), divided into junior and senior schools on two sites. There was some exchange of teachers between sites, but those working on the world studies programme for the eleven- to thirteen-year-olds formed a stable group. The work described is from second-year units.

The world studies course was organized round physical and economic geography, and the history of man. Early in the course the children studied such topics as:

1 The earth
2 Mountain areas
3 Equatorial areas
4 Arctic-tundra areas
5 Early man

These provided background to a more specific study of the civilization of such countries as India, China and South America. Exactly what constituted the course depended upon the teaching team, which was continually revising sections and preparing new areas of study.

The specific teaching/learning sequence had a common pattern. Each week began with a lecture given by a member of the team to a whole year-group (sometimes a film was shown), and the lecture was usually followed up in the succeeding lesson to crystallize difficulties and misunderstandings. For much of the time, the children did individual and group research (using reference books and filmstrips), organizing both with the help of work-cards prepared by the teaching team.

Nine periods a week were allocated to the course, generally blocked into year-groups operating for a whole morning and a whole afternoon, with two additional sessions. Individual teachers, while being responsible for a normal class unit, were available to other pupils for consultation and help.

The teaching team was a mixture of subject specialists but they acted in the programme as general teachers, each responsible for the total work of the class. Where they felt deficient in the curriculum, they made it a special task to learn from their colleagues, so that they had a growing competence across the total area.

The English contribution

Two aspects of subject English work played an important part. Children can often feel empathy with the predicament of people in other places and at other times, and when this was apparent, the children were invited to enter into a role and write from another's point of view. There was also an emphasis on small discussion groups, with pupils often using a tape-recorder to monitor their work.

Side by side with these were other familiar English activities, but these were not often thematically connected with the world studies programme. The integration was as much in providing joint time for the humanities work as in subject content. However, many of the children themselves saw the normal English activities as part of the world studies course, and not as something on a timetable called English.

The second-year children studied China, both ancient and modern, in some depth. Two sections of that study illustrate well the opportunities open to explore individual imaginings. First, they studied the building of the Great Wall, and considered its significance. The work-card reproduced below gives some idea of the historical/geographical study.

The Great Wall of China

1 When was the Great Wall built and how old does that make it?
2 How long and how high is it?
3 Why was it built?
4 What does this suggest about the relationship between China and her neighbours at this time?
5 What difficulties would there be in building the Great Wall? (Think of the size and relief of China.)
6 Would a wall by itself be an effective defence or would other measures have to be taken as well?

Then, as part of the work, the children wrote fictions on whatever caught their imaginations.

Battle of the wall
The war was bloody
A garason wrecked

Men with slit throats
Lieing down dead
Surrounded by blood
throats hanging out
The fire put out
By one man's blood
Up above fling round
Is the crow so large and so black.

One man's horrors
The life of a man out of a million people building and defending a wall, for their country. The wall is a Great Wall, it is also a great battle. Hundreds died some sick too sick to tell the tales of those who were dying were thrown in the foundation. I have been here many a long year. Twenty? Time flies to quick to count I cam a young lad of twenty six. Some came younger at fifteen some left as old men some never left at all. Fight what for? nothing my wife my son I left behind me to fight I'll fight till I am dead or sick of hunger I am a slave to my country. The letters I right to my wife I doubt if she has got them No letters I recive A man lies down beside me dying near to death, He lied quite still for a moment no speaking as if he was praying. He got up and walked over to another man not seeing the Barbairan climbing the wall not seeing him come behind not seeing the end.
One man's horrors
One man's dreams.
One man's wife might dread in strife
One man's wife thrown away for war
One man's heart shall not beat
One man's soul is now free
One man's life is now forgotten
But some shall live to tell the tale.

Neither writer pretended to be either historian or geographer. They were fiction writers, and historical/geographical accuracy was not their concern. Neither of the pupils was very able in written language, and assignments which required formal and coherent presentation of facts were a struggle. Here, although some would quarrel with the mechanics of their presentation, they both painted stark, realistic pictures.

The class also studied the political history of China in the post-war period. One pupil covered an aspect of this history, the dispossession of the landlords, by constructing a narrative, an encounter between peasants, landlord and a communist party member:

The trial

Late one night whilst all the peasants were in a kind of Chineas cafe smoking a communist party member ran in shouting 'The communists have taken over in Peaking.' Not many people new what this meant only the young people new. There was a fuss about what it had to do with them, but in the end he perswayded three of the youngers to go and fetch the landlord to put him on trial. Whilst they were gone of the people began to doubt their disision but the communists and some youngsters began to win the older people to their side and the nealy old sticked to their side and never theought the younger generation may want a change. When they arived back at the cafe everything went quiet even the brave young sat down not nowing whether to grovel or not. In he strolled the Landlord himself it was quiet for about 5 minutes then the communist went round and reminded the people, what he had done for them. Then the people started to accuse him of things like you killed my son or took wives or daughters for slaves. He just laghed then one of the gards hit him across the back of his knees he fell on his face he tried to get up but they made him stay on his knees one woman threw a bowl at him it hit him on the sholder he fell back then everybody rushed forward they stamped on his face and they kicked him in the stomack this on for quite a while till they realised he was dead.

Another took up the role of a communist party member, and gave an account of a similar incident in the form of an official report:

Dear Governor

This is my report about Ho-run village where I have been sent to. In this village there was two main landlords one was no trouble and he ran after he found the people were riseing he left the deeds of the land behind. The other was more trouble. There was a big meeting in the village with the peasants and the landlord the landlord said he would not give up his land I said he would have to if he did not it would be taken from him and he would be shot. All the peasants cheered and all the way through the meeting he did not say another word, and it did not take long to find him guiltie he would be shot at dawn there wer no trouble volunteers and the sentence was carried out. Life is better in Ho-run now and some people have all ready started farming.

Yours faithfully
Miss J. Smith

These pieces reflected more of the historical content of the course than the previous examples, but neither teacher nor pupils would judge these pieces by their historical accuracy. Both would apply criteria similar to those they would use with fiction writing. But both would also believe that approaches like these to historical material help to bring the past alive, and contribute to an interest in the period under study.

It was a feature of this course that the children discussed their work at great length, usually in small, self-chosen groups. The end-point of their work on a particular study was often a review of the display they had made, of what they had written, read and learnt. The writing would not be regarded as an end-point, as it is in many schools where they close the exercise book on the subject once the child has committed his understanding to paper. Rather, writing was seen as just one language activity which contributed to structuring information, and for many children not the most important one.

Here is a discussion between three boys, working by themselves to review their work on the Spanish conquest of Mexico:

R Cortes went from Spain to Cuba.

J Even though the Governor didn't want him to, did he?

R He did.

J No, the Emperor of Spain didn't want him to go.

R He did.

J He didn't, he sent a messenger after him to stop him from going.

R He didn't. Cortes went to Cuba to seek his fortune.

J Yes.

R But, when he left Cuba.

J Yes, well, when he got to Cuba, the Emperor wanted him to go to the west because he heard of great riches over there, didn't he?

R Yes.

J But then he found out he shouldn't have gone.

R And the Governor of Cuba tried to stop him, but he didn't. Then they sailed over to the River Tabasco —

J Tabasco where there was . . . well, a bit of a war, wasn't there, but they won it easily because of the horses they had. They thought it was one person, didn't they, a horse and man?

R Plus the cannons.

J Yes, the cannons. And they frightened them because they'd never seen them before. Oh yes, er, from Cuba, though, he sailed with 353 soldiers wasn't it?

R No, 553.

J That's what I said.

L . . . 180.

J 180, yes, and 16 horses, no 14 horses, 16 cannons and a few firearms. Oh yes, from the River Tabasco they sailed to Vera Cruz which he named himself, didn't he?

R Yes.

J And he made a settlement there, didn't he, with a few men?

R Yes.

J And then from Vera Cruz he marched his men across the land to —

R Mexico.

J Mexico. Oh yes, at Vera Cruz to stop the men mutinying he burnt all his boats.

R Yes.

J And then er oh yes, when he got to Mexico he didn't believe it because it was too grand, wasn't it? All gold . . .

R And when he got in there he was greedy . . .

J He took —

R He tried to take over Mexico.

J No he never. No he never. He went . . . Montezuma . . . Let him . . . greedy.

L So he took him home as a hostage.

J And then he began to feel uneasy because all the natives . . . (*inaudible*) . . . speaking his language.

R Yes and when they went to call them down they told Montezuma to say something.

J No, but then they captured Montezuma, didn't they, and then when Cortes left to fight Nazu, wasn't it, or something like that.

R No, Narvez.

J Narvez, yes. Yes, the man he left in charge massacred all the priests, didn't he?

R Yes.

J Chopped their hearts out.

R Yes, when they uprised, em . . .

J When Cortes came back there was a big uprising, wasn't there?

R Yes, and Montezuma was taken.

J No. He asked Montezuma to talk to them because he was friends with Montezuma.

R Yes but they stoned him and he died.

J Yes, a few weeks later.

R And they were drove out of Tenochtitlán —

J Or Mexico, yes —

R And then —

J And then he —

R Come back with more natives and that and he were there by ship —

J Yes and he cut off all the ways to it, didn't he?

R Yes.

J And so they died of smallpox and disease and lack of food and water.

L Some were still survived.

J Oh yes, only a few. There's still a few people nowadays that speak the Aztec language.

R Yes.

L Yes, but if you go to where the new cities have been built and you dig up they find lots of —

J Yes.

L Remains of them, yes.

J Or something like that. Well, what do you think of that topic? Do you think it was any good?

R Yes, I reckon it's all right.

J Do you think we learnt a lot from it?

R Yes.

.   .   .   .

J Well, can't think of anything much more to say, can you? Yes, what was that lady's name who could speak Spanish and —

R Donna Maria.

J Oh, Donna Maria.

R Who translated for him.

J That's right, translated it when Cortes talked to Montezuma.

R Yes.

J That was right. It didn't last very long, did it, the Aztec civilization.

R No.

J A few men though could destroy a huge population like that.

R If they had the things.

J Yes, 'cause the advanced weapons and everything, didn't they?

L Yes, but I thought if all the Aztecs got together they could have swarmed them all.

J Yes, well that might have been it because no organization.

R The end.

J But the Spanish had organization and plans.

R Yes.

The primary objective is the pooling of information to make up the historical narrative, which more or less answers the unspoken question, 'what happened?' (The detailed work which the children have done in their work-books is reduced to skeleton form.) There is nothing remarkable about this episode. The children have a common objective, so they do not make anything of their disagreements, but move ahead at a steady pace, one person supplying deficiencies in the account of the others. They have a clear strategy for doing this. One of them tells the story (J), while the others occasionally challenge, but more often supplement, his account. R plays the major part in this. He knows more about the details than either J or L, so he is in the position continually to agree, or put in a critical detail. He is the sustaining audience. L does not get much of a voice in, either because he knows less or because he is dominated socially by the other two. The flavour of the whole is co-operative rather than competitive. It does not release any special insights. It represents the humdrum aspect of normal work. But the children are learning – learning to take a serious attitude about what they are asked to study, to co-operate with one another in the learning task, and to get satisfaction from what they have reaped during the study. If they see historical events as adventure, rather than as an invitation to critical analysis, at this age we should not be unduly concerned.

The teachers were keen to let the children work by themselves. But they also joined them for discussions, nearly always in small groups, when they tried to get the children to consider aspects of the work which, if left to themselves, they might not have attempted. In the following example, four boys talked with their teacher about the Indian caste system. The teacher knew well enough that one of the major difficulties in learning about other cultures is that of relating factors in other societies to your own. This is influenced by the degree of conscious understanding people have of the cultural patterns of their subculture, and those of society at large. This can only be acquired gradually, and here the teacher is helping the children to articulate such understanding as they have. There are many difficulties. They begin on the caste system:

> TEACHER Now, what I want you to do is to talk about the Indian caste system. Start off by saying what it is. Anybody want to start? (*Extended silence.*) What's caste?
> (*Inaudible whisperings.*)
> PUPIL I I've got . . . it's the one about the Indian er classes are split up.
> TEACHER Yeah, go on. (*Pause.*) How are they split up?
> PUPIL I Well, the police are all big and powerful and the little peasants, you know, the er, the er road sweepers and that like, er, are the lowest lot like.

TEACHER Yes, how many castes are there?

PUPIL 1 Four.

TEACHER Four main ones. How would it affect your life, what caste you were in?

PUPIL 2 You couldn't change from one caste to another.

PUPIL 1 No.

PUPIL 2 If you were a road sweeper, you couldn't if you'd got a lot of money you couldn't be, er, called one of the rich people, you'd still be in the lowest class.

TEACHER Yeah . . . Um . . . How would it affect you? Could you be low caste and rich?

PUPIL 1 Yeah, but you'd still be . . . (*inaudible*) . . . low class.

PUPIL 2 You couldn't change from one class to another.

TEACHER Would that matter if you were rich?

PUPIL 2 No. No but it would be a better life for you but you won't be able to go up in class.

PUPIL 1 No, you won't be able to say, well I'm one of you now.

TEACHER Well what about your children?

PUPIL 2 They have to follow you.

PUPIL 1 They follow you.

TEACHER Why can't they go up?

PUPIL 2 Because you're still alive and you've got to follow them . . . they're in.

With the teacher's help they pinpointed the ways in which the different castes keep separate. They then proceeded to link caste divisions with racial and religious divisions within English society. The teacher tried to pin them down to make explicit statements about English society. This did not work. The teacher wished to exclude colour discrimination, presumably to concentrate on rich/poor, working-class/middle-class divisions, whereas the children did not wish to shift beyond colour discrimination at this point. The discussion quickly moved to an anecdotal level.

TEACHER Well, nobody talks about the caste system in Britain.

PUPIL 3 Oh no. You can see it though, can't you?

TEACHER What would you call it? Would you call it a caste system?

PUPIL 3 Not really, racial relations, really.

TEACHER Racial relations apart? Leaving . . .

PUPIL 3 We're just not friends.

TEACHER Leaving coloured people out of it. Just among English people.

PUPIL 3 Just don't want to know.

PUPIL 1 Well (*pupil's name*) is English and he's coloured . . . Quite a lot of people.

PUPIL 3 Umm.

PUPIL 2 Yeah, it's like after the war, if a West German comes over here or something and they go 'Oh he's German, don't want to know about him'. Like that film where that woman was a Jew, and they shoot her son, a Chinese.

PUPIL 1 Oh yes.

PUPIL 3 Some people would think a bloke, he's coloured and he's got a coloured father, and he's born in England, goes for these walks round and people just stare at him . . .

PUPIL 2 Yeah . . . (*pupil's name*) comes from Jamaica.

PUPIL 3 He's worried cause they're more English than he is. Been here longer than him.

PUPIL 2 Yeah what about . . . There's a bloke, he was white, right, and then he was ill.

PUPIL 3 Oh yeah and he turned black.

PUPIL 2 Turned black, yeah.

PUPIL 3 No, that was the one who was black and turned white. The doctor gave him some medicine.

PUPIL 2 Don't know . . .

PUPIL 3 It was, and he tried to sue the doctor. That's right, cause he wanted to stay black.

After a pregnant pause, the teacher returned to a major distinction in the caste system, which was soon lost in comparison of religious differences, and which went on to the religion of the children themselves The teacher then asked another question, looking for a definition of class differences, to which one of the children offered an 'astonishing' personal example. (Shortly afterwards, when this child was asked whether his example meant that you could or could not tell class membership from spoken characteristics, he said he didn't know.)

TEACHER In India . . . are all high caste people rich?

PUPILS No, no, not all.

PUPIL 3 Just all in that caste, you don't have to be rich or not.

TEACHER Well if you're high caste and fairly poor.

PUPIL 3 You have to work harder to get the money to make up.

TEACHER Do you get any advantages from being high caste then?

PUPIL 3 Not really, just (*inaudible*)

PUPIL 2 . . . Stay common, stay with your own caste.

PUPIL 1 It's the same as religion, isn't it – they've got all different castes, we've got all different religions . . .

PUPIL 2 Yeah, but they've only got two religions in the country.

PUPIL 1 . . . Catholic, and all that . . . Protestant . . .

TEACHER But d'you think that one is sort of higher than another? One is regarded as more . . .

PUPIL 2 What, in the highest class?

TEACHER Yes.

PUPILS Oh yes, yes.

PUPIL 2 The one that has the most money . . .

TEACHER No, before we were saying there were all different religions in England, well is one religion regarded as higher class than another religion? Are Catholics regarded as higher class than Protestants, or the other way round or what?

PUPIL 3 Well they're always fighting so you can't tell, can you?

PUPIL 2 They vary . . . in Ulster —

PUPIL 1 Well each religion considers their religion as the proper one and er . . . all the rest are a bunch of savage pagans.

PUPIL 3 And you usually find, you usually find that when they're poor people they're mostly Catholics. Cause they believe in . . .

PUPIL 2 No . . . How d'you know?

PUPIL 3 Cause most people are Catholics who —

PUPIL 1 You might be Catholic.

PUPIL 3 I'm not Catholic.

PUPIL 1 Aren't you? What are you?

PUPIL 2 I've only been to church once.

PUPIL 1 So've I only been to church once.

PUPIL 2 . . . Watching a girl get married, that's all.

PUPIL 1 What was that for?

PUPIL 2 School.

PUPIL 1 Oh, yes.

PUPIL 2 I had to be away that day.

TEACHER In England, do you reckon you can tell someone who's higher class?

PUPIL 1 Yeah, by the way they talk . . . on the bus yesterday, me and my sister, got on this bus, and when this bus conductor came up to us 'Oooh yees, fares please' came out all posh. And it's a bus conductor! (*With astonishment.*)

The children then went on to enumerate their candidates fo upper class membership (the Queen and Ted Heath), for middle-class (Harold Wilson), and those who are the rich (business tycoons). At this point, the teacher left the group, suggesting they continue their talk. In it, we had some glimpse of what these thirteen-year-olds perceived as discrimination, but their ability to control an orderly pattern in the conversation was not sufficient to allow them to remain cool. After the quoted excerpt, there was violent argument, mostly inaudible, covering racism and world conflict, mostly in the 'yeah but' vein.

TEACHER Look I'm going to leave you for a few minutes, 'cause I've got to go out, but I'm going to leave the tape on – you carry on talking. Don't stop.

PUPIL 1 What about?

TEACHER Same subject, caste, and what is, and the, whether England is like that, has got the same sort of system in any way. OK?

PUPIL 2 Right.

PUPILS (*Hesitation.*) Well er (*coughing*) um . . .

PUPIL 1 Most people go to America, yeah.

PUPIL 2 Australia.

PUPIL 3 Not America, Australia. That's where we might be going.

PUPIL 2 If we emigrate, not Australia, no.

PUPIL 3 We will

PUPIL 2 No we'll go to New Zealand.

PUPIL 1 Pakistan! (*Laughter.*)

PUPIL 3 Yeah, they'd love you in Pakistan and all.

PUPIL 1 They'd probably rob you, take all your money.

PUPIL 2 Yeah, leave yer . . . (*inaudible*)

PUPIL 4 You wanna watch (*name*), I'll get a skinhead over here.

PUPIL 1 Oh yeah! Let me put a skinhead in the middle of East Pakistan.

PUPIL 3 He'd run . . . (*inaudible*) wouldn't he?

PUPIL 2 He wouldn't know what to do.

PUPIL 1 They'd try and get their own back

PUPIL 2 If I took a kid of about eighteen into Pakistan . . . say he's got, you know, Pakistan, he go in the barber, barber go, 'Trim please'. Barber cut all his hair off, you know, then he's a skinhead, then they can beat him up.

PUPIL 1 Yeah then they could still beat him up. And it's really race, racial, isn't it?

PUPIL 3 Relations . . .

PUPIL 1 Racial, you mean, not relation discrimination, is it?

PUPIL 3 Racial discrimination.

PUPIL 1 You know there's a lot of that in this country now.

This example seemed to expose the gap that exists between intuitive understanding of your own predicament sufficient to live your own life, and the knowledge and wisdom to be gained about your own situation by entering through imagination into other social structures with an equal sympathy and understanding. The writing 'in a role' of the earlier examples was one attempt to bridge the gap, but there intuitive understanding of man was uppermost. In this example the attempt was made consciously and rationally to rehearse the contrasts between the foreign and local society, an attempt which only partly came off. Nevertheless, the role played by the teacher in discussions of this kind – the encouragement of the children to make explicit comparisons without losing touch with the reality of either society – cannot easily come from a pupil, unless he has mastered his own egocentricity sufficiently to be able to take over that role. The teacher was here attempting small moves towards enabling all the pupils to do this.

II. Systematic learning: what is involved?

Many younger pupils flounder in areas of the curriculum where personal experience and response seem less relevant, and the focus is on acquiring a new technical vocabulary. This was evident in much that we saw; the pupils exploring Wentworth College (Context 7), for example, seemed under most strain when systematic work began. The studies of L. S. Vygotsky on the formation of 'scientific' concepts are a helpful framework in which to consider the problems pupils meet with formal knowledge.

When a child learns a language, he takes over something which is the common property of the community. He takes over the range of categories of experience and understanding his community has found useful. Thus words often come as part of a system – for example, 'father', 'mother', 'daughter', 'son'. (This is not to say that a system is acquired all at once or that a word has a place in only one system.) When he goes to school he meets new concepts and thus new words and new ways of categorizing experience. Taking over Piaget's terms, Vygotsky distinguishes between two kinds of concept, *scientific* and *spontaneous*, and contrasts them in three ways:

1   Scientific concepts are consciously taught, whereas spontaneous concepts we pick up automatically in the course of living
2   Scientific concepts depend upon their verbal mediation, whereas spontaneous concepts depend upon our contact with reality
3   Scientific concepts provide systematic, general structures, whereas spontaneous concepts provide the substance of experience which can make the former more than just empty symbol categories.

Analysis of a science lesson

These contrasts can be illustrated clearly by a science lesson with a mixed class of nine- and ten-year olds. The class was to see a television programme which set out to show how mountains (in particular Mount Snowdon) are made up of certain kinds of rocks, and how such rocks determine both kinds of industry and modes of transport. In the lesson before the film, the teacher wished to introduce the children to a basic classification system for rocks, that between *sedimentary* and *igneous*. On the way to this distinction, he drew attention to the differences between *molten* and *solid* and took in the three states of matter, *solids*, *liquids* and *gases*. (See transcript on page 128.) In Vygotsky's terms, all these are scientific concepts.

Contrast 1 is really a rough-and-ready contrast, because in one sense there is only an accidental difference between what we are taught deliberately and what we pick up automatically. For example, if our father happened to be a geologist, we might have classified rocks as *sedimentary* or *igneous* as early and as easily as we categorize cats and dogs. In normal circumstances, we are familiar with rocks in all sorts of ways – things to climb, to throw into the sea, to build houses with, perhaps even things with fossils in them. Generally, it would be unlikely that *sedimentary* or *igneous* would be part of our concept system unless we had been taught to use the words.

Contrast 2 points to a defining characteristic which has some psychological significance. Scientific concepts under this heading are those which depend upon other verbal concepts for their definition. Once the definitions have been grasped, however, the concepts do not divide up language, but the world of things to which they refer. *Sedimentary* rocks are those formed under pressure from sediment, and *igneous* rocks are those formed as a consequence of heating. Spontaneous concepts are those we pick up from our mother's knee as we take over her language. The rock on the beach is *hard*, because it makes a dent on my knee, and I need a plaster. It is a *rock* rather than a tree, because it is a dead thing, whereas trees live.

Vygotsky, in *Thought and Language*,[1] describes contrasts 1 and 2 in this way:

> The child becomes conscious of his spontaneous concepts relatively late; the ability to define them in words, to operate them at will, appears long after he has acquired the concepts. He has the concept (knows the object to which the concept refers) but is not conscious of his own act of thought. The development of a scientific concept, on the other hand, usually begins with its verbal definition and its use in non-spontaneous operations – with working on the concept itself. It starts its life in the child's mind at the level that his spontaneous concepts reach only later . . . The inception of a spontaneous concept can usually be traced to a face-to-face meeting with a concrete situation, while a scientific concept involves from the first a 'mediated' attitude towards its object. (p. 108)

Contrast **3** is more difficult to understand, although of great importance. Vygotsky says:

> In working its slow way upwards, an everyday concept clears a path for the scientific concept and its downward development. It creates a series of structures necessary for the evolution of a concept's more primitive and elementary aspects, which give it body and vitality. Scientific concepts in turn supply structures for the upward development of the child's spontaneous concepts towards consciousness and deliberate use. Scientific concepts grow down through spontaneous concepts, spontaneous concepts grow upwards through scientific concepts. (p. 109)

This suggests there is not only a difference between the two kinds of concepts, but that they are also essentially related. (A similar point was made by Kant, in another context, when he said that 'concepts without intuitions are empty, intuitions without concepts are blind'.) In terms of our example, the suggestion is that by acquiring the concepts of *sedimentary* and *igneous* we will have acquired an organizing structure for our spontaneous concepts of rocks, and that our spontaneous concepts will become part of that network. Bruner is saying something very similar when he asserts that the 'structure' of a subject or topic makes each individual learning episode easier to master. He starts from the hypothesis that most things can be taught even to the younger children, but points out that we cannot move them on in their understanding by 'presenting formal explanations based on a logic that is distant from a child's manner of thinking and sterile in its implications for him'.[2]

The acquisition of a new technical vocabulary involves more than just getting some words to say. It means acquiring an interconnected set of words, and making connexions between the meanings of these new words and other meanings which you already have. In terms of our example, it means acquiring something like the following system:

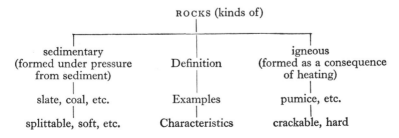

ROCKS (kinds of)

sedimentary (formed under pressure from sediment)	Definition	igneous (formed as a consequence of heating)
slate, coal, etc.	Examples	pumice, etc.
splittable, soft, etc.	Characteristics	crackable, hard

Perhaps also it means connecting it with this other system:

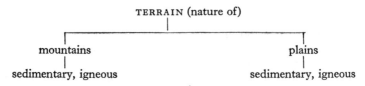

TERRAIN (nature of)

mountains   plains

sedimentary, igneous   sedimentary, igneous

The two systems are a mixture of the two kinds of concepts described. 'Slate' and 'coal' are both spontaneous concepts. But here they are brought into new relationships with one another, because this system allows it. The system provides what James Britton has called 'a specific and general criterion'[3] for sorting – specific, because the qualifying conditions are clearly laid down; general, because rocks that might differ in almost every other respect are alike in this.

The lesson included a mixture of the two kinds of concepts. And that raises the teasing question of how we connect one set of concepts with another. The transcript below is of the closing moments of the lesson.

TEACHER Now let's get back to where we were with our mountains – well how come this boiling up then? Of the inside of the earth erupting out in volcanoes, how in the past, and we're talking about millions of years, what did this do? How did this make mountains?

PUPIL Um . . . the war?

TEACHER Come on, it's almost the same – what about you, Martin, you haven't said a word, at the back. David? How do you think? Well it's obvious, isn't it? (*Constant indistinguishable answering from pupils*) Ssh. You think about the earth, right?

PUPIL Er, it's the centre of it.

TEACHER Right then, we boil up from inside. What's going to happen, what's going to boil up? (*Pupils answer together*) – you erupt! And as it erupts, it will go out of shape won't it? And there, maybe, it will go out of shape. So what's one way, then, that mountains were made?

PUPILS By eruption.

TEACHER By eruption.

PUPIL By things crushed at the bottom?

TEACHER Ah no, that's the other way.

PUPIL . . . Pushed up by the centre of the earth.

TEACHER Good. So it's made by eruption and this rock is given a special name, which you'll probably guess.

PUPIL Earthquake?

TEACHER Well, an earthquake is similar to this, except that . . .

PUPIL Cracks.

TEACHER Well really they're not in mount . . . well they may be in mountain-ous ranges, but they're in fact the opening up of the earth in various parts of the world that are open to such earthquakes. A volcano, here, is more in hilly parts where there's the eruption and the lava. Well, what's this rock called, these mountains called when they're made from this molten rock? Does anybody know the word? Barry?

PUPIL Limestone.

TEACHER No, limestone is one rock and it isn't this type of rock. I'll tell you this, because it'll probably be mentioned in the broadcast, I don't know whether I've spelt it right, it's probably not a . . .

PUPILS (reading) Igneous.

TEACHER Igneous. And the other one, Roddy, how did yours, your rocks, how were they formed, your mountains that you were talking about?

PUPIL Squashed together.

TEACHER What was squashed together?

PUPILS Trees in the undergrowth. Leaves and soil.

TEACHER And layers of . . .?

PUPILS Rocks . . . soil.

TEACHER Soil, rock, and gradually they were pressed together.

PUPILS And made rocks!

TEACHER And so they came out like this, in layers. What's a good example of this kind of rock?

PUPILS Rock. Mineral. Slate.

TEACHER Slate's one that's been pressed out very hard, yeah. One that's near here?

PUPIL Coal-dust.

PUPIL Coal.

TEACHER Because as they go down and dig a shaft through, they are in fact attacking the face . . . What's this rock called? Put down in layers, it's called . . . (various inaudible suggestions) . . . sed . . . i . . . men . . . tary. I'm sorry I've run those two together. Sedimentary. Now your two types of rock are igneous and sedimentary. (General chatter.) Yes? Pardon?

PUPIL (Inaudible.)

TEACHER When were they formed?

PUPIL I thought they were formed in the Ice Age?

TEACHER These? Well there have been movements all the time, the earth's surface, haven't there? The time when there was this mighty explosion in space and our solar system was started, then from the moment the earth was formed, there have been movements of the earth and laying down, the movements which would give you igneous, and er laying down of layers of mud to give you sedimentary. So when you're approaching rocks, you've first of all got to decide whether they're igneous or sedimentary ones.

The teacher was inhibiting all but those spontaneous concepts which he considered relevant to the distinction he wanted to make. He was not concerned with the frameworks which the children, in their different, individual ways, already possessed. In this respect he was interested in volcanoes only because they provided key examples of the heating of rocks, and not in how volcanoes might be a rich source of fantasy for the children in that class. He was interested in coal only because it was an example of sedimentary rock, and not in the fact that most of the children's fathers worked in coalmines. He commanded the system, and had the criterion of relevance at his disposal. But how does the learner decide relevance?

With something like this question in mind, we asked two pairs of children from the class to tell us all they knew about rocks and mountains. Each pair talked for about a quarter of an hour. The flavour of the talk comes over in this short transcript of part of one of these discussions.

PUPIL 1 There's some rocks on telly we seen, a film I think it was, there was some big rocks, looked like men and that.

PUPIL 2 Probably . . . I know . . . I've often wondered, you know, when they're they um . . . they've died, th . . . when they've died they might have been pressed and made, y'know, pictures of a man's face and that, probably . . .

PUPIL 1 Yeah. You might find that – something like that would be . . . very lucky. There was er another programme on the telly and er there was this er big rock in a museum and er . . .

PUPIL 2 It's nice to go into a museum, isn't it?

PUPIL 1 Yeah . . . there was like a witch thing in the museum and he pinched half of the . . . half of the . . . rocks.

PUPIL 2 They can do lots of things, though, to rocks, y'know, can't they? They, if you just put it under a bit of paint it can come in a little – you know, pottery.

PUPIL 1 Yeah. Like when the pottery's, you know, moulded, it sets hard.

PUPIL 2 Mm. I wouldn't like to go down into one of those old castle dungeons.

PUPIL 1 No, it would be funny . . . funny you said that because you know I've got the reader book, book nine, you know, and it's got about castle dungeons where prisoners used to be hung.

Looking at what one of the pupils said throughout the whole discussion, the following references to rocks were made: rocks to climb, to find fossils in, resembling men, in museums, resembling pottery, to construct dungeons with, which are nice to look at, with skeletons inside, you slip on, you drop on your toe, you hurt your hand on, imitated by painting wood, which are heavy, Stone Age men use, you enjoy hearing about, under water, which look pretty if you hold them up to the sun, which provide the twist in the plot of a particular story, you make field walls out of, illustrated in books, in lava form coming out of volcanoes, which kill people, you build houses out of, you can feel like. There was no mention of *sedimentary* or *igneous*, and the reference to rocks in larva form coming out of a volcano was a reference to a Tarzan film. In the girl's talk as a whole there appear to be no scientific concepts. This is not to say that she does not have such systems, but only on this occasion, on this topic, with this task, that she did not show any. Our impression was that this particular pupil had not succeeded in making the relevant scientific concepts part of her network. Even if she had remembered the words she had not mastered the system.

Too little is known about the difficulties children face in their learning at different ages and stages. One thing is clear; more than verbal definitions are needed if we want to help pupils master new concepts; we have to pave the way if new learning is to be fitted into existing frameworks. We do this by drawing out relevant spontaneous concepts, and using them to help meet new scientific concepts half way. Here we have spelled out the problem. In the second part of Chapter III, 'Moving towards systematic learning: how can teachers help?', we discuss the work of pupils and teachers making headway in bridging the gap between common sense and school knowledge. But first we need to take a closer look at the spoken language and its special contribution to the learning process.

References and notes

1. L. S. VYGOTSKY, *Thought and Language* (MIT Press, 1962).
2. J. S. BRUNER, *The Process of Education* (Vintage Books, Random House New York, 1960), chapter 3.
3. JAMES BRITTON, *Language and Learning* (Allen Lane, Penguin Press, 1970).

III. Talking to learn

The theoretical framework

The eight-year-old has a highly developed speech system with which to cope with his curiosity and needs, a system he has learnt without formal instruction but with much support from parents and siblings, other children and other adults, and with much effort on his own part. He knows, without being able to articulate the category differences, that he can use language: **1** to satisfy his material needs; **2** to control the behaviour of others (more often, since he is young and often of low status in the groups of which he is a member, language is used to control him); **3** to get along with others; **4** to give expression to the self; **5** to learn about and explore the natural world; **6** to pretend; and **7** to tell others what he knows.[1]

The list shows the range of options a child uses in his speech in a social context, basically as a matter of necessity for making headway in what is mostly a verbally organized and maintained reality. The first two items need not give us pause. We are very familiar with the ways children (and adults) ask for or demand the necessities of life. We easily recognize, too, a range of verbal strategies used to persuade or order others to do what we wish, and how others seek to control our behaviour.

The third and fourth items proclaim the fact that speech is used in group situations as a means of person-to-person interaction. For the young child, such interaction through talk enables him to discover how other people tick, and provides him with a context in which he can reveal and present himself, and thus define and discover himself. Within the family, with mother a constant companion, every word spoken by her reveals an attitude, expresses a framework of expectations, which the child has to meet. Every next occasion of speech adds to that framework. Thus in time the child builds up a notion of the many-sidedness of his mother. Side by side with her words to him, he begins to take up the mother tongue of the tribe, and by joining the conversation adds his loaded commentary on the world. He presents himself, and soon becomes adept at reading off from his mother's verbal and non-verbal behaviour how he is perceived, how understood. Speech fs critical for him in articulating his consciousness, and without the personal feedback from his audience, he can in the early phases of personal growth make little progress. In this way his identity as a person is embedded in the behaviour of others.

His social world spreads beyond the family to other adults and other children, and within that confrontation of self with those who people his world he builds up a picture of himself in society. Children also invest their dogs, dolls and teddy bears with human properties, and have imaginary conversations with them – and with fictional characters they create, people they meet in stories read to them and favourites from television. Imaginary replies are constructed from the internalized responses of their human social groups, and also from their growing sense of what a sympathetic or angry 'other' would say. These contacts immeasurably increase the range of options in terms of which the child can see himself.

The fifth item lists speech as the tool for making requests for information. The young child is inveterately curious to know the what, how and why of the world around him. If he were at the mercy of what facts and explanations others chose to give him, unsolicited by his own initiatives, he would make uncertain headway in comprehending the world. At best, most facts would be at a tangent to what he wanted to know. Information unrelated to any reason for finding it out tends to be fodder for the crosswords of our existence, not for the living of our lives. (At the same time, however, information of no immediate relevance can sometimes be remembered and used later.)

The sixth item reminds us that many children repeat the jingles, verses and stories of others, as well as make up their own, as easily and as often as they enter into any other language activity. Clear influences are the stories and poems read to them, the songs and jingles mother sings to them, and the whole lore of fairy-tale and make-believe which is part of all childhood environments.

With the seventh item we come to communication proper, or at least the sense of the word most people have in mind when they talk about speech as communication, namely the expression of propositions. 'The child is aware that he can convey a message in language, a message that has specific reference to the processes, persons, objects, abstractions, qualities, states and relations of the real world around him.'[2] We might designate this use as the transmission of content, intentionally meant, because speech in context is notoriously apt to be used in propositional form to serve other functions. Halliday points out that this use of language is not a dominant one in the young child's language behaviour – although, as the final two contexts in Chapter I clearly show, it is expected to be so in much work in the later middle years at school.

In using speech in these ways, the child interprets reality. Every word he learns to use gives him a new category, a new generalization with which to type-cast similarity and difference. Every relationship he expresses in a sentence puts those categories into juxtaposition. Every successful meaning he makes leads towards a more complex and more subtle understanding of what happens to him, and what the world is like. The range of possibilities in terms of which he can act is inevitably enlarged.

The most comprehensive account of 'language as an interpretative system' has been given by James Britton, who seeks to show, through the distinction he makes between *language in the role of spectator*, and *language in the role of participant*, that man (child and adult) characteristically use language for two general purposes.[3]

The distinction rests upon the notion that man acts in the world of events through the representation of it which he has put together from what he has done and from what has happened to him. Britton draws on the work of Sapir:

It is best to admit that language is primarily a vocal actualization of the tendency to see realities symbolically . . . an actualization in terms of vocal expression of the tendency to master reality not by direct and ad hoc handling of this element but by the reduction of experience to familiar form.[4]

Langer:

The material furnished by the senses is constantly wrought into symbols.[5]

Cassirer

. . . we should define him [man] as an animal symbolicum.[6]

And, more recently, Kelly:

Man looks at his world through transparent patterns or templates which he creates and then attempts to fit over the realities of which the world is composed . . . without such patterns the world appears to be such an undifferentiated homogeneity that man is unable to make sense of it.[7]

Britton argues that the experience of a person is not given by an influx of data, although that provides the basis, but by acts of processing whereby the data is reduced to familiar form. Man does not carry events round with him, but only their symbolizations. Further, if he is to make anything of his accumulated experience – the past as he has met it – then those symbolizations of particular experience must themselves be ordered into something of a coherent totality. That ordered totality – the accumulation of interpreted experience – Britton calls 'a world picture', or world representation.

In every new confrontation with reality, the individual draws upon that representation to make sense of the new. The distinction which can now be drawn is described in an article by Britton and Newsome as follows:

> If we accept that man operates in the actual world by means of his representation of the world, it will follow that two courses are open to him. He may do just that – operate in the actual world *via* his representation, or he may operate *directly upon the representation itself*. This is a non-participant activity: let the world's affairs look after themselves while I contemplate my own past experiences, other people's experiences, imaginary experiences – probable, possible, or merely conceivable – and in doing so *improvise upon* my representation of the world. In daydreams I improvise situations that flatter my vanity; in gossip I may improvise upon the lives of my neighbours to satisfy my spite. In reading a novel I am also improvising, drawing upon the raw material of my past to give to it a new shape in relation to the events of the story. I do so, normally, because I am not satisfied with the one and humdrum life I have to lead.
>
> All these are uses of language in the role of spectator: a spectator may be deeply involved, deeply participating in the illusion, but to be in the role of participant in the way we are using the term he must participate in the affairs of the actual world. I may, to take a simple example, engage you in a discussion of my plans for the future: if I seek your help, your permission, or merely your good opinion of me, I am in the role of participant and am involving you as participant. If, on the other hand, I invite you merely to *enjoy* with me the prospect of my future – then we are both in the role of spectator.
>
> We take up the role of spectator of other people's lives – whether in chatting about last summer's holidays or in reading a novel – mainly for the reason already suggested: we enjoy tasting experiences at second hand that we have never had at first. We are, moreover, interested in the *possibilities of experience*, the unfamiliar and unlikely patterns that events may assume.
>
> We take up the role of spectator of our own experiences sometimes for similar reasons – to enjoy them, to savour them perhaps in a way that we could not while we were caught up in their happening: talking round the fire in the evening we enjoy the ardours and excitements of the day's walk,

for example. But at other times we go back over experiences as spectators for other reasons – from need rather than for fun. If an experience proves too unlike our anticipation of it for us to adjust while it is happening, we may need to go back to it in order to come to terms with it. We do this ordinarily in talk, but of course many stories and many poems are evidence that their writers have turned to writing in order to deal with recalcitrant experiences: and in so far as our needs overlap theirs, we may sort our own problems in response to their words: or, more accurately, we may adjust our own predictions in line with the writer's adjustments. When a child responds to a poem, this is a crucial process, for he is likely to be making his adjustments in accordance with the values of our pattern of culture, values we have derived by giving currency to the most mature and sensitive adjustments our society produces, those in fact of the poets and other artists.

As participants, we use language to get things done: to explain or persuade, to buy and sell, to acquire or pass on useful information, to pass examinations, to co-ordinate joint activity – and a thousand other ways of interacting with the environment. The point about language in the role of spectator is that it is disengaged from practical activity. When we take up this role, then we are freed from certain responsibilities, and we use this freedom to do other things: in particular, we attend to the utterance itself, *as a form*, or as a set of forms. We attend to the forms of the language, its sounds and rhythms, to the pattern of events in a story, and to the pattern of feelings embodied – the changing kaleidoscope of tension and relief, fear and hope and love and hate. When we are participating in actual affairs, feelings tend to be sparked off in action: as spectators, we are able to savour feeling *as feeling* and perceive the forms it takes. (We savour, for example, the miseries and anxieties of the long walk as we sit by the fire and talk it over afterwards.) We use our freedom for another purpose also. As participants we evaluate situations in order to regulate our own behaviour in them: often enough we are aware of the need to go back over these events and re-evaluate against a broader frame of reference than we were able to use at the time. As spectators, we typically re-evaluate our own experiences and evaluate other people's in the full light of the attitudes, beliefs, values we have derived from living. Language is, then, a means of shaping experience, modifying our representation of the world, whether we use it as participants, in our stride, or as spectators, going back over experiences or going out into other men's lives.[8]

This distinction suggests two different relationships between what is being said (or written) and what is done. It has been used as a basis for 'function' distinctions at the practical level of language utterance. The purposes of talk, writing and reading may be plotted along a continuum roughly divided into three main divisions:

Transactional————————Expressive————————————Poetic
(participant role)   (spectator role)

The Schools Council English sub-committee in their paper on English in the middle years of schooling described the three functions as follows:

> *Transactional language* is language adapted to the manifold purposes of getting things done in the world. Adaptation to different kinds of task (or transaction) sets up formal differences as striking, for example, as those between a running commentary on a race and an electioneering address, or a recipe and a psychiatric case-study. In general, its form is such as to articulate at any point with the practical, professional or intellectual concerns of those to whom it is addressed.
>
> *Poetic language* is the medium of an art: it is language adapted to constructive, artistic purposes, to the production of objects of contemplation. Thus, its form is such as to *resist* piecemeal articulation with the practical, professional, intellectual concerns of a reader (or listener) and strive for internal relations that give it a unified structure and make it a unique object.
>
> *Expressive language* is language close to the speaker (or writer). It verbalizes his current preoccupations, displays his mood of the moment. Centrally (i.e. in its purest form, for as we noted the line on the diagram represents a continuum), it is utterance at its most relaxed, utterance as free as possible from outside demands, those of a task or of an audience. It is informal, intimate language and the person addressed (if there is one) is regarded as an intimate. What is said is likely to reveal more about the speaker's opinions and feelings about the world than it reveals about the world itself. Much of what is said would be ambiguous or meaningless to a listener who did not know the speaker, his general circumstances, and the circumstances of the utterance. Expressive language at this central point moves easily from participant role into spectator and vice versa. (If in talk with a friend I share in retrospect the pleasures of my summer holiday, this is talk in the role of spectator: however, a part of his response may be to consider the possibility of going to the same place for *his* holiday – that is, to slip over into the participant role – and he may indicate this by interrupting my retrospect with some such question as, 'How far did you say it was from the sea?') Expressive speech is important as:
>
> (*a*) The principal means by which we approach and meet each other in all our separateness, each declaring his unique identity, and (at our best) offering and accepting both what is common and what differentiates us.

(b) The first tentative formulation in words of most plans for action, most new ways of construing our experience of the world.

(c) The principal means by which we influence each other, as the functions described in (a) and (b) converge. (The quality of the expressive talk – in homes and pubs and church-porches – that follows, for example, a national crisis has a major effect upon public opinion and political action.)[9]

At a general level, the participant/spectator distinction throws light on the divisions within the curriculum of the eight- to thirteen-year-old. The former picks out those areas of the curriculum which are concerned with the public domains of knowledge – for example, solving problems, explaining, organizing information to show historical, geographical or scientific relationships. The second focuses on those aspects of living and learning unique to the individual, which in specialist curriculums are parcelled together within subject English (or more broadly within the expressive arts as defined in Chapter I, Context 11).

At the level of language utterance, the expressive function captures the way in which the young pupil moves between these two roles, and his shifting consciousness finds its embodiment above all in expressive speech. This function is allotted a pivot position in the scheme, from which the transactional and poetic functions develop as the participant and spectator stances become separately dominant. The differentiation in speech towards the poetic function at a highly structured level is relatively rare. It takes a real hold only in improvised drama which naturally introduces the notion of performance, or when, in narrating an experience, the teller begins to shape his utterance to tell a story, and so pattern the events to hold his audience. For most children telling an anecdote or narrating an experience within expressive speech seems satisfaction enough. The significance of this and of dramatic improvisation is considered in the last part of the chapter.

The differentiation from the expressive root to transactional uses of language takes place by inhibiting the self and the organization of feeling, or at least its expression, and starts as soon as systematic instruction begins. There are inherent dangers in this movement.

Moving towards systematic learning; how can teachers help?

Teachers have to take responsibility for providing the context in which talk occurs. The social context for the development of speech and its accompanying functions has up to eight years old been the small group of family and friends, and that has two advantages. The first is that in the large group talking time is strictly rationed – if the group exceeds four or five some members are confined to a listening role for considerable stretches of the conversation, and therefore cannot learn by talking. The second is that the small group provides the face-to-face contact between speaker and listener (in dialogue this relationship is continually changing) which enables the speaker to read off the effects of his language on the 'other', thus gathering the essential data for building up his language and for forming some notions about the appropriateness of his reaction to reality. In the earliest stages of learning, and later when in unfamiliar territory, he has to depend upon the 'other', an other who ideally is interested in what the speaker has to say and is willing to respond at the verbal and non-verbal level. The teacher can take up this role by engaging the young in talk, but no one would ever suggest that the ideal (or even plausible) situation was a ratio of one adult to thirty children.

The essential complication arises because teachers individually and schools generally are held responsible for what a child learns. This immediately raises questions. What should the talk be about? Are there contents which are necessary? If so, who should decide them?

Two points of view, stated as extremes, influence the solutions schools look for. The first, derived from looking at the way in which children have already developed, suggests that the starting point for school experience lies in what the child wants to find out, a base which naturally promotes individual contact and support for small groups. The curiosities of the individual child have to meet the interests of other children, and are moulded by the range of opportunities the teacher can provide. But under this central impulse the school experience cannot be dominated by the presentation and interpretation of bodies of knowledge which adult society deems it worthy to know. In so far as this approach has a 'centre' for learning, it will be the development of reading, writing, artistic and mathematical abilities, encouraged as necessary accomplishments for the deepening of curiosity and providing the possibilities of new horizons. Within such an approach the teacher has to be something of a parent, trusted adult, social mentor, artist, craftsman, mathematician and scientist, adept at the language arts, and committed to support investigation and speculation.

The other point of view, derived from the objectives of upper secondary and tertiary education, is that the contents of schooling must be related to the broad bands of specialist bodies of knowledge which represent man's accumulated wisdom – the literature, history, mathematics, science and geography which is there to be inherited and investigated. The main functions of the teacher are to present materials derived from these sources suitable to the intellectual and social maturity of the children, and to help the children interpret them. The teacher sees himself as a specialist, adept at the appropriate skills of the discipline, familiar with the range and quality of the materials falling within its scope. He sees himself as an instructor on the one hand and a consultant on the other; in the first role he is likely to give lessons to whole classes, and in the second, to use group and individual work where he has laid down what the task should be.

Few schools exhibit either of these patterns in a pure form, but the curriculum framework at the lower end of the middle years of schooling is influenced by the first pattern, and the second clearly influences the upper end, even in the integrated studies programmes which have been developed. The talking environment is markedly influenced by the viewpoint of the individual teacher.

The following paired examples establish the two poles. Both examples concern teachers and ten-year-olds. Beyond that they diverge in almost all respects. The first example is a geology lesson, given to a full class by a teacher who is himself an expert. (This teaching style resembles that of the teacher in Chapter II although the school is a different one.) The teacher is at the blackboard, the children in their seats. The excerpt we quote is some way into the lesson.

TEACHER You can also get further larger crystalline structures with larger shapes making it up instead of being very fine where you can't see what is making it up, you'll find very large shapes joined together, for example, felspar and quartz. So those are the first sorts of rock. Igneous rocks formed by fire. The second sort related to this is through processes called metamorphism, producing what are called metamorphic rocks. The spelling of that is m–e–t–a–m–o–r–p–h–i–c. You'll see this in any books that you start to look at when you're studying your geology. Now metamorphic rocks are formed again during this process of the earth cooling down, but, as well as heat and fire, there is also pressure involved. Now how can pressure be involved? Can everybody think about this? What is pressure first of all?
PUPIL The pressure would first of all come out from the centre of the earth.
TEACHER This is partly to do with it.
PUPIL Could be the rocks on top of it – things on top of it, pressing it down.

TEACHER Good. Now as the earth cools, the outer layer of it, if you think of an apple, you put it in the sun, the outer layer goes dry, and becomes hard. This hard outer layer forms what was called our crust of the earth. Within the earth there was tremendous pressure being exerted by the hot molten material; now whenever anything is hot what happens to it?

PUPILS (*indecipherable – alltogether*) . . . sparks.

TEACHER Sparks. What else is given off?

PUPIL Gas.

The teacher does almost all the talking. His utterance is an extended monologue, that of his pupils short answers to his questions. This pattern comes about in an obvious way. If a teacher is an expert on the topic under discussion, and the pupils relatively ignorant, the simplest course the teacher can take is to give a structured lecture, testing from time to time by questioning that the pupils are following the sequence. (Clearly, the teacher could have explained 'pressure', and moved on from there to 'gas' without any spoken response from the pupils.) The teacher has chosen this strategy, with the result that the pupils are confined to a listening role. They are also confined to a pupil role. This packaged deal of structured information is seen by the teacher as objective material, having little or nothing to do with subjective response, calling for no shift of perspective from that of learner to that of person. It is an example of a tight instructional situation; the teacher's job is to instruct, and reciprocally it is the pupil's job to learn. The whole sequence has a clear and defined objective, which both pupils and teacher know well enough. It amounts to this: if the pupils have not gathered the information and understood it by the end of the lesson, the lesson has failed.

Both the structure of the information – definitions and explanations – and the language by which it is mediated, are preformulated. That is to say, prior to the lesson the sequence in which the material is to be presented is already well formed, and the sequence of utterances therefore already mostly determined. To the specialist this material is old ground, already highly structured and assimilated. When it comes to the point of utterance he is in no conflict – his pathways are clear, and he has ready access to prior language formulations. The sequence of definition, explanation and example through the main kinds of rock, and the language abstractions, 'larger crystalline structures', 'processes called metamorphism', 'hot molten material', etc., are ready-made.

What of the pupils' expectations? If the teacher's game is embraced, they must be something like this. It is our job to speak only when asked questions; we must listen carefully to the language so that we can follow the sequence of ideas, and thus give sensible and relevant answers; we are not responsible for the choice of topic (even if we choose 'geology' as an option), nor is there space to investigate our interests – we must stay on the pathway. We must not: propose interesting diversions; introduce new topics; ask questions with unknown answers; refer to our own experience. These, strictly speaking, are irrelevant to the particular learning activity. If we succeed in all this, we shall come to where the teacher is now. For the children, all the options are defined.

A maximum contrast is provided by the next example. The group, a teacher and ten-year-old pupils, are out on a field expedition. A student teacher with them finds a caterpillar and the group gather round her.

STUDENT It's very, very prickly . . . bristles.

K They're awfully quiet, aren't they, when you touch them. The other one curled up in a ball, but this one doesn't, does it?

STUDENT It doesn't really need to because it's very prickly.

K Ah, it's clinging round the grass now. Isn't he lovely? Yes, look, he hasn't got all the short little short soft ones – big spiky ones like a porcupine.

STUDENT He's got soft ones underneath.

K Yes

A (*referring to reference book*) Well, it isn't in the book . . . caterpillars.

TEACHER It isn't in the book, did you say?

A Yes, it isn't in the book. It must be a rare one.

M Come here, let's have a look. Let's have a look.

TEACHER Well, let's remember what it looks like. How can we describe it – what did we notice about it?

C Black, spiky, and ugly.

STUDENT It's got a white patch on the . . . top of its back.

TEACHER ⎱ Oh yes.
C ⎰

W It's spotted . . .

C Does it bite you?

W It's spotted with white . . .

TEACHER What about its underneath part?

W . . . or silver.

TEACHER Can you see how many segments it's got?

M Has it got little red things by its feet?

TEACHER Has it?

C What?

M Little red spots by its feet, because otherwise that wouldn't be it.

TEACHER Oh yes, oh look.

(*Pages turning over.*)

M Is that anything like it?

A No.

C Yes, that's it.

TEACHER Yes, that's it, isn't it?

C Yes.

A Has it got fur underneath?

STUDENT Have you got . . .

A Yes, but it hasn't got the white spots.

STUDENT Have you got a magnifying glass?

TEACHER You've got the magnifier, haven't you?

C He's coming out.

M (*still trying to identify caterpillar in the book*) Yes, he has, he's got little red pieces. Yeah, that's it. But what is he? Two-twenty. (*Looking up in index.*)

A It isn't because look there's lines – look, Mrs —— there's lines going across there. (*Pointing to illustration in book.*)

TEACHER Oh that's true.

A (*still scrutinizing the book*) It isn't . . .

TEACHER Yes, it is orangey rather than red, isn't it. No . . . Bright yellow things at the ends of his segments.

C Shall I squash him and put him in my book?

TEACHER *No.*

M (*coming up*) Look at his prickles.

C Ugh.

A There's the sting, Mrs ——, look, a little hole.

M Yeah, Mrs ——, look he's got – turn him upside down. Kind of flick him off.

C Hello. Hello. Put it there (*by microphone*). See if he talks.

TEACHER Does he speak?

M Does he speak?

C He doesn't speak. Say hello.

K He might come out on the tape-recorder.

M (*in caterpillar voice*) Hello.

C (*also in caterpillar voice*) Hello. I'm Mr Caterpillar.

TEACHER Look at his eyes. Look, can you see his eyes?

K Isn't it horrible?

M (*referring to book again*) Yes, that's it. Mrs ——, look, he's got those big eyes, look.

TEACHER Oh yes, so he is, so he has.

All the members of the group talk; in the first 250 words, comparable in length to the previous example, there are thirty-seven utterances by seven speakers. In this quick-fire, short sentence dialogue, talking is a joint enterprise. Compared with the last example, there is no defined topic. There is, however, a centre of interest, and that focuses the group. But no defined sequence can be laid down in advance.

It is typical of such open situations, that more than one interest is taken up, more than one kind of response appropriately made. A close look at the transcript reveals three main sets of interests and responses of which the first is the interchange between the student teacher and the pupil K which initiates the episode, the second is the ongoing interchange between the teacher and the pupils A, M and C, commencing with 'Well, it isn't in the book', and the third is the excursion into fantasy, commencing with M's 'Hello'.

The second of these is relatively easy to describe, relatively easy to understand. A, who initiates the sequence, is consulting a reference book, an activity which we recognize as likely to arise from school-type pursuits. This provides him with a highly selective focus – he must accurately describe the features of the caterpillar, and match it with a description in the book. The teacher joins this enterprise, and asks of the group, with every justification, one of the few teacherly questions: 'How can we describe it — what did we notice about it?' C, who joins in, can hardly be said to advance their intent. 'Black, spikey and ugly', 'Does it bite you?', 'Shall I squash him and put him in my book?', provide a dimension which is idiosyncratic and personal; his remarks implicitly categorize his response to the caterpillar as much as they describe it in any neutral terms which would be of use to A and M. In this respect, he has more in common with the student teacher and K who begin the dialogue.

The student's and K's contributions may appear from the written transcript to have mainly descriptive import. However, it is clear from the intonation of their speaking that the words serve at least equally to express the feelings they have towards the caterpillar. Explicitly this appears in K's remark, 'Isn't he lovely?', which refers to a framework of feelings and attitudes which she has, but to a listener the whole of this sequence has an equivalent reference – for example, 'Yes, look, he hasn't got all the short little short soft ones – big spiky ones like a porcupine.' Clearly sympathy, wonder and concern are there. It would, for example, be inconceivable that the student or K would contemplate any hurt.

The final sequence, by contrast, is an excursion into fantasy. The speakers move aside from reality-adjusted thinking in order to enact a possibility which in a serious sense they know cannot be actualized: caterpillars do not talk. This excursion into physical and verbal play enables them to engage their joint sense of the ridiculous, to rehearse in a fragmentary way what it would be like to be a caterpillar-human.

These three elements are worth noting because they suggest that a group at work can encompass more than one activity without losing a sense of direction. The caterpillar itself is the centre of interest, and everything revolves around it. However, within the dynamics of the unfolding event, the teacher herself plays a major part, albeit a very different one from the teacher in the previous example. Quantitatively, she says more than anyone else. She takes part in the identifying activity, partly in a teacherly role, partly in being, like the children, genuinely interested in pasting on the right label. She takes part in the fantasy element, both by utterance and laughter. She also gives free rein to her own personal response – her 'no' to C's question is not a 'no' of authority but an expression of 'What an awful thing to do to a living thing', and her 'Look at his eyes. Look can you see his eyes?' is almost equivalent to saying 'Horrible'. By behaving in this way, she declares her own expectations concerning the group – namely, what it finds worth doing is worth doing. She thus sanctions their activities and talk. She neither ignores nor discards anything said to her. She also puts herself alongside the children as a person, willing to share her own responses, willing to partake of theirs. She accomplishes this without negating her role as a teacher to their role as pupils. Reciprocally, the children have their expectations as to what is appropriate behaviour. They know they can follow their noses, and expect her help and support. They know they can be themselves, openly declaring their interests and responding individually, and expect her to enter sympathetically into their world. Each child knows he can make his contribution towards her as a trusted adult, without risking rebuff.

In this particular situation, there can be little pre-planning. The nature of many of the questions is of critical importance. Almost all the questions cannot be answered by the asker, and arise out of the need of the moment.

Thus both asker and answerer have to be responsive at the moment when information is sought. As their attention and interests shift, so must their language. A table summarizes the points made so far.

	Example 1	Example 2
Who talks?	Teacher	The group
Pattern of utterance	Extended monologue	Short-sentence dialogue
Topic	Determined in advance	Evolves
Teacher's role(s)	Instructor	Guide, supporter
Pupils' role(s)	Pupil/learner	Person/responder
Teacher's expectations	The pupils shall learn presented material	The pupils shall inquire
Pupils' expectations	Lessons are for listening; learning happens by following the experts	Lessons are for saying what you want to; learning happens by inquiring into what you yourself determine
Learning situation	Closed	Open
Character of talk	Preformulated	Formulated at the point of utterance
Function of talk	Transactional	Expressive

Obviously both teachers could have done other than they did, and so could the children. Indeed in both cases in other parts of the sessions they did so. In the first, the teacher ended his lesson talking with interested individual children as they handled various specimens of rock; in the second, the teacher talked with some children about how they might order their observations when they committed them to field notebooks. We have been looking at the dynamic structures of these lessons, but such a structure can only be understood if it is shown in its entirety. Thus the excerpts cannot be used in evaluating the lessons as wholes. We use them here because they *can* be helpful in isolating specific examples of the use and misuse of language in school.

The geology lesson appears to have a serious educational content, but it is so one-sided in favour of the teacher, in both thinking and speaking, that it is doubtful if the children's capacities to handle such information, and fruitfully to expand *their* thinking and language horizons, are much enhanced. The pupil is denied choice, interest and curiosity, as well as opportunities to rehearse his own experience and to get his own language round this 'new' knowledge. He is being asked to use someone else's relatively abstract language in a context in which no attempt is made to mediate between the teacher's language and his own, between the teacher's highly structured formal concepts and his own informal ones. Even teachers who mostly work within tight subject boundaries, with a high content profile, have to note that to deny the pupil access to language in order to structure the information is to fail most of the pupils at the very point where the teacher most wants to succeed. The pupil should do more than remember parrot-fashion, he should be connecting new experience with past experience, be internalizing complicated patterns for structuring new knowledge, so that he may approach new situations with greater understanding and more comprehensive strategies.

On the other hand, in the second example all the children in the group are encouraged to talk and there is free rein for the children to exercise choice, interest and curiosity, with the teacher supporting their activities. But some would remain uneasy at the progress they make in formal learning. On the face of it there is much specious activity and speech to achieve the identification of one caterpillar, if indeed that was the aim. Some would claim the whole episode is, relative to the first example, aimless wandering, and that the all-round looking of the children needs to be channelled immediately into more disciplined acts of thought and language – what we have befits the playground, but not the classroom.

We can respond to both kinds of anxieties. How can children be supported in their curiosities, in their capacities to be interested in all manner of things, in their impulses to explore for themselves, coupled with a wide opportunity to use their own language, and at the same time grow towards achieving mastery in knowledge and ways of construing experience which their teachers possess and wish to share with them?

While there can be no prescription, we do not believe the problem will be resolved by increasing the kind of speech activity represented in the first example. The children must not be denied expression, and if their curiosity and motivation to learn is to be properly harnessed, they must be given opportunity to exercise what they already know, and encouragement to bring themselves as persons to the task of learning. It is in expressive speech that even the thirteen-year-old will want to approach new knowledge. We therefore believe that the basis of operations must be of the kind represented in the second example, where the children can shift easily from one interest to another as they give voice to what engages their attention.

This does not mean, though, that that is where the matter rests. The teacher cannot merely leave the child to his own devices. He has to support the child's endeavours to become more at home in the ways of thinking required by different specialisms, which often enough can only be introduced through verbal means. The teacher has to conceive his role as something more than that of a dictionary. At the very least, he has to lead the children towards asking more fruitful questions than they would if left to themselves, to design more cogent inquiries than their present understanding of the world might suggest to them. He has to engage the children in conversation, and through that encourage them to frame their own hypotheses, even if those hypotheses are finally rejected by both teacher and pupils in favour of a more objective and codified form of knowledge and thinking.

In the two following examples we can see teachers at work on just these tasks. The first is a conversation overheard in the laboratory, where a teacher helps eleven-year-olds towards understanding the formal notions of weight and density:

TEACHER Why do you think copper's heavier when you've taken the same sort of amount of it?
PUPIL Miss, the copper's a metal.
TEACHER A metal?
PUPIL . . . and it's solid, Miss, and it's bound to be heavier.
TEACHER We do not say – well are the pieces solid?
PUPIL Miss, 'cause usually metals are the heaviest.
TEACHER You think metals are the heaviest?
PUPILS Yes.
TEACHER Well if I took . . . um . . . if I took a metal pin . . . er . . . and I took a great big basin of feathers, which do you think would be the heaviest?
PUPIL The basin of feathers.
TEACHER Why?
PUPIL 'Cause there's more.
TEACHER More of it. So it depends on how much of it you take, that's why you have to fill it up to certain marks so that you're taking the same amount – hmm?

Here the teacher resists the impulse to say too much too soon – 'We do not say [heavier, but denser]' – sensing that such a move might well end the conversation. Rather, she chooses to stay with their own understanding of weight, moving towards the technical notion of density by getting them to note the relationship between size and heaviness. She is helping them to think. In Vygotsky's terms (see Chapter II) she is helping them to make links between networks of spontaneous and non-spontaneous concepts.

In the second example, we see a teacher inviting thirteen-year-old pupils to construct their own hypotheses about why the Great Wall of China was built as wide as it was. The context is more open that the last, in that some freedom of interpretation exists, but such freedom is still circumscribed by the facts. First, the teacher poses the problem and elicits two answers:

> TEACHER Twenty foot seems like a pretty interesting and pretty big size. Can we, I mean it's not just a wall. This looks like quite a wall and this is two foot. Why twenty foot? Any suggestions? Lesley. Why go to the enormous trouble of making it so big? . . . Karen?
>
> PUPIL So no one could climb over it very easily.
>
> TEACHER Well, what do you think of that? Anyone agree or disagree with Karen's suggestion?
>
> PUPILS (*Answering together.*) Disagree!
>
> TEACHER Why, somebody, Brenda?
>
> PUPIL Because of the roads . . .
>
> TEACHER Pardon?
>
> PUPIL The roads go through the middle of it?

The teacher could move straight from here to discourse on the interpretation given by the second pupil – the road on the wall provides a quick means of transport between one defence tower and the next – but he senses that any feasible answer requires consideration. He therefore treats the first pupil's answer seriously, and by so doing reinforces the habit of constructing hypotheses even if they have to be rejected in the light of evidence.

> TEACHER Ye–es, the, yes, wait a moment, surely the point Karen made about climbing over it. I mean, there's still only a fairly narrow area for climbing over, and once they're over, it's easy. Yes? Because to jump from this side on to the ground, once you've got there, is probably quite easy. So I don't think that can be the reason. It's not as if they've got to climb over twenty foot of barbed wire. The bit they've got to climb over is still fairly narrow.

He then turns to the other answer and, once having accepted it, encourages the children to explore that answer by inviting them to put themselves in the shoes of both the Mongol invaders and the wall defenders.

> TEACHER . . . Yes, so it's a road. Let's have more on this road idea. You're right. Yes?

PUPIL If the soldiers want to get to a site of trouble they have to go along the road.

TEACHER Yes. Right, let's put it in a let's reverse it, put it up on its head. Michael. You are the leader of a dastardly crowd of Mongol, Mongolian invaders. (*Laughter, cries and warlike hoots.*) And how would you attempt to take the China Wall? Hush! I can't hear Michael's brain churning over in this.

PUPIL (*inaudible.*)

TEACHER This needs a tremendous lot of men doesn't it? If you've got enough to attack at lots of places, OK. What if you've got 200 and you know that along the defended part of the wall there are 20 000. All right? You've only got 200 but you decide to jump.

PUPIL Take one of the towers.

TEACHER Take one of the towers. Are you concentrating all your strength on one particular tower?

PUPIL One or two.

TEACHER One or two towers. All right?

Both these examples occupy the middle ground between the 'geology' and 'caterpillar' extremes, and illustrate that even when the demands of the topic are fairly clearly defined and the outcomes predetermined, both teachers and pupils can together make common cause in thinking their way through a problem by formulating their speech at the point of utterance. There is no loss in taking the starting point to be where the children stand, and no loss in postponing instruction until the problem has been investigated.

Spectator-role talk, personal anecdotes and improvisation: what is their contribution to learning?

We have argued that all information and knowledge is integrated at a personal level; it is by accepting and using what pupils bring to the classroom that we can help them move forward. Learning depends not only on accommodation to new ideas but also on absorbing new ideas into existing frameworks. Thus assimilatory activities, speculative talk, improvised drama and storytelling are appropriate as a means of learning in many areas of the curriculum. It is nevertheless true that traditionally the English teacher has had a special concern for what the individual child perceives, feels, imagines and thinks; for what we possess individually rather than for what we hold in common. Of course, we want pupils to enter sympathetically into the predicaments of others. One of the points of listening to other people's anecdotes, or in reading fiction and poetry, is to confront ourselves with 'chapters in the lives of other men'. But when the thoughts, feelings and preoccupations of the pupils are at the heart of what goes on, the need to accommodate to outside criteria of relevance and appropriateness is less strongly felt.

We would expect to find more opportunity for speculative, assimilative conversation, more attention to the total concerns of the individual, in the English classroom than in other lessons. Special value is given to the anecdotes children offer as a contribution to whatever is being considered. These can be thought of as small segments of lived experience, and become the touchstone for much of the work. Experience is, however, a somewhat slippery term and we use it here to cover more than what actually happens to someone. What happens in the mind, in the imagination, is also significant and worth sharing with others. To some extent all experience is something we structure for ourselves rather than something that is given. In sharing anecdotes in discussing a poem or story, or some issue, pupils often find that in the telling they have managed to assimilate something, some loose threads in their thinking have become integrated. In the following example a twelve-year-old boy pulls out of his own past history something which helps him to enter sympathetically into the predicament of a character in a story. The tale, which the teacher has read to the class, turns on the disappointment of an old lady who receives money instead of presents on her birthday.

> GARY Sir, there used to be . . . when I was younger, sometimes whenever I got a present or something I remember when it always came in an envelope and it was money. Sir, and I remember it was my birthday and I was waiting and all for everything to come, presents and all and anyway half of it was money, Sir, and I was kind of disappointed . . . whenever I opened envelopes I put all the money in a pile and when I'd finally opened all the presents it was nearly all money. Sometimes I'd have a stack of money and nothing to do. Sir I'd just throw it on the floor and pick it up again. Sir that's the way it is, just pick it up in my hand and drop it again, nothing to do with it . . .
>
> TEACHER Yes . . . Gary's feelings are much the same as the old lady's feelings in this situation.

This story, fact or fantasy, is relevant to the pupil's conception of the old lady's predicament. It is his individual perception and is valued by his teacher as such. It involves others, for by sharing in his experience they see him a little more clearly, and by putting his experience against their own, they see it in a new light. This anecdote was in response to the teacher's invitation in a class situation, but such contributions are often shared in peer-group conversations.

The role of such contributions is strikingly shown in the discussion analysed in detail in Context 10 (page 87). Here some lower secondary-school pupils are discussing old people and, in particular, their grand-parents. The children test the acceptability of each other's comments against their own experience. Each seems to be asking of the others' contributions – does this ring true according to my view of the world? And of his own offerings – is there an observation or an incident I can quote from life which will make this insight more convincing to the others? Frequently in spectator-role talk we look to our life experience for support for what we say. The boy whose poem is the focus of the transcripted part of the discussion, realizes that some of the others think his poem is sad. He tries to explain that because someone has a thoughtful, philosophical approach to life it does not necessarily mean they are unhappy, and gives a vivid picture of his grandfather deep in thought, unaware of immediate practical matters. '*I* don't think it's sad. You see, he does that. He's think-ing and the milk boils over. He always has his eggs boiled hard. I don't think he ever had a soft-boiled egg in his life.'

Speculating in this manner with people we feel comfortable with (this was a self-chosen group – see page 87 for a thumb-nail sketch of each member) provides an ideal setting for the integration of many thoughts and feelings. There is no doubt that these pupils have assimilated something about the human condition, the predicament of the old, but they have also discovered something about the nature of poetry. When asked to explain the image of 'wrought-iron bridges' in his poem, D says, 'Well I suppose, I suppose I did kind of well write it or it kind of came; but I think it is right.' This is just it – we do not build up a poem in the way we construct a rational argument; the laws of the imagination work in quite a different way. But when challenged by the group to say why it feels right, he is able to articulate what he previously knew intuitively to be true. 'Well the main thing about him [his grandfather] is he is like a bridge . . . made kind of, well bridges you see across, between things, between us, too. Do you see?' He goes on to say, ' "Wrought iron" was because he does everything well and because in his day bridges were made of, well were made of wrought iron not cement.' This boy has helped the others to make some progress in judging the worth of an image used by a writer, and has confirmed to himself the power of his own image.

Such speculations are valued in English lessons. Truth is measured against our experience of the world. Younger pupils particularly swing quite easily in talk from a participant-role to a spectator-role stance, and in every lesson the teacher has to see relevance partly in the pupils' terms. In the following example the pupils, nine- to ten-year-olds in a school in Northern Ireland, are applying themselves to a specific task – planning the presentation of a story about St Patrick to the younger pupils in the school – but the conversation is the richer and more fruitful because the teacher welcomes a speculative element.

There has been some talk about dates on which events occurred and we break in at the point at which a pupil protests about this preoccupation:

PUPIL 1 What I mean is we've got to try to get the people in the hall interested and I don't think history's interesting if it's all dates . . . I mean if you just say basically how old he was, that'll be enough, you don't really need to know when and where he went.

PUPIL 2 He stayed in Ireland six years and then he left when he was twenty-six years old.

TEACHER To let them know the framework of the stories we have to have a general outline.

PUPIL 1 I'm sure the little ones, say in P3, wouldn't know what AD means . . . or BC or any of those things.

PUPIL 3 . . . and they'll be shuffling around . . .

PUPIL 4 You could say, um, a few hundred years after Christ's birth, um, Patrick was born.

PUPIL 5 Do we *have* to do it all reading – couldn't we do a bit of drama as well? I was watching a drama programme the other day and I think we can put a bit of drama in or something like that.

PUPIL 4 This is beside the point, but do we know his second name?

TEACHER Does anybody know? Did people have second names in those days?

PUPIL 6 Shouldn't think so.

PUPIL 7 Must have, cos when Jesus was born there was Judas Iscariot, and that was his surname.

PUPIL 1 Some people did then. People like blacksmiths would be called just Smithy or something like that.

PUPIL 8 There was Ben Hur too.

TEACHER I think people tended to be known by the name of their occupation. You would be known as – someone suggested Smith – so Patrick the Smith.

PUPIL 1 My grandad's grandad's grandad a long way back . . . suppose they were hunters that would be how their name like or Skinner might be someone who took animals' innards out and their skin or something like that.

TEACHER Can anyone think of any other explanation for second names, surnames?

PUPIL 1 You don't really need a surname . . . cos it would sound funny to the little ones you know – they would be used to call him Patrick or St Patrick. Cos if he was called say Wilson – Patrick Wilson would sound very funny to the little ones. Wouldn't sound famous or well known.

PUPIL 6 Patrick Wilson wouldn't sound right.

Here we find contributions being valued, not only because they approximate to some given notion of the truth, but also because they are what a pupil is able to offer at a certain stage in his development. These pupils show that they are able to put themselves in the position of others – 'I'm sure the little ones, say in P3, wouldn't know what AD means.' They wonder also if too much reference to the dates will bore the audience, but the teacher remarks that some sort of general framework is needed. She is not dominant, she always takes her cue from the pupils, often inviting members of the group to take up a pupil's point. Because she is able to see relevance in the pupil's terms, this teacher is helping their progress. She does not cut off contributions which some would consider to be off the point, but takes up interesting speculations and ensures they are not overlooked by the others – 'Does anybody know? Did people have second names in those days?'

Pupils often have to accommodate to ideas and information organized by others, but learning is also to do with assimilating what comes to us from many sources. Talk that is on the expressive to poetic part of the Britton continuum, talk arising out of a spectator-role orientation towards the world, facilitates the organization of knowledge into existing frameworks. The assimilatory nature of this kind of talk is clearly illustrated in the following discussion. After a term's work on the Aztecs, a group from a nine- to ten-year-old class are asked to discuss the following proposition: 'Put Cortez in Montezuma's place and imagine how each would have behaved.' The task the teacher has set demands much more than a consideration of the known facts. We find the children using the sort of sympathetic insight that we associate with the careful consideration of a novel or poem.

J Well I think Cortez would be much crueller than Montezuma in lots of ways.

A The thing is that what Cortez was doing to Montezuma, Montezuma was doing to other tribes . . . so he was doing exactly the same thing.

J Yes . . . but I still don't think Montezuma would have done it as cruelly as um . . . Cortez . . . in his place.

A Why not? Why not?

J Well I think Cortez had a much crueller spirit than Montezuma . . . I think if Montezuma had wanted to take over he would have taken his time over it . . . so that the people would have liked him.

A What do you think Christine?

C I think Cortez would be very, very cruel in one other way . . . he would um . . . try you know to abolish their religion and their way of life . . . by stopping all their sacrifices . . . all their . . . their whole point in life, trying to stop their religion and their sacrificing and all the other things.

P I think if Cortez had been Montezuma I think Cortez would have taken the initiative to attack and um you know destroy completely . . . destroy Montezuma's army. I think Cortez was more ruthless than Montezuma and so I think you know . . . that where Montezuma didn't attack Cortez would.

S When Cortez didn't know about . . . um . . . what it would be like at the beginning . . . it was only towards the end that he knew he could reign over Montezuma.

A Montezuma treated Cortez kindly because he was a god . . . he thought he was a god – that's the only reason Montezuma treated Cortez kindly.

C Ah yes . . . but the point there . . . halfway he treated him kindly but I think Cortez realized he was a god (in Montezuma's eyes) and I think Montezuma sort of realized later that Cortez wasn't a god. So then I think he started treating him kindly so Cortez wouldn't fight him.

A Well the only reason Montezuma treated Cortez kindly was because he was a god and no other reason.

C There can be.

A Well tell me one then.

C I've just told you. There is one because . . . well he knew that he was more powerful . . . He had a white skin. He had a lot better weapons. He had lightning sticks. So that's why. Montezuma treated him kindly because he thought he was going to fight.

A Christine said lightning sticks. I don't think some people will understand what that means, now will Christine tell us what lightning sticks means.

C Well lightning sticks to the Aztecs were their guns, their muskets and Cortez's cannons. I think they called the noise the cannons made thunder.

S Yes, they called it thunder.

J They probably called the spears Montezuma had lightning sticks because they went like lightning, they looked like lightning. If they got caught in the sun then the blades caught it.

The teacher could have asked the pupils to write on this theme. In choosing a talk context he has obliged pupils not only to put forward their own view but also to respond to the hypotheses of others. They also have to 'think on their feet' in a way avoided in a writing task when there is more time to consider. The question which provided a starting-point is a fairly sophisticated one, and the pupils' resources are challenged by it. As expected, such young children tended to judge the behaviour of the individuals by contemporary standards rather than in terms of a particular cultural context. Notions of moral relativity might have begun to emerge if the teacher had suggested several children take up the point of view of each individual, trying to enter his mind and defend his actions, while another element in the group acted as 'us, now, in the United Kingdom' and judged those actions.[10] We cannot, of course, be sure that this would have produced a better discussion, and indeed parts of the talk suggest that a pupil has been moved on in his understanding. ('I think Cortez would be very, very cruel in one other way . . .') hits on the insight that the most effective way to undermine a people is to inhibit their culture and religion. Running through the whole conversation is the impression that some aspects of history are a matter of informed speculation, and we need not, therefore, feel afraid of offering our own view if we can support it with appropriate evidence.

Here then were pupils using their knowledge and imagination to begin to come to grips with an interesting proposition. Now we turn to improvised drama, that unique method of learning and teaching in which pupils act through incidents and situations. In this, speech comes nearest to a poetic function. The pupils make something which exists in its own right and they enjoy presenting their improvisations and seeing those of other groups. But it is the learning aspect we are most concerned with. By taking up the roles of individuals in particular contexts and predicaments pupils encounter times and incidents which might otherwise seem remote and inaccessible. This is shown convincingly in the drama work described in Context 6 (page 52) Improvisation generates a particularly rich and varied range of language activity and we observed with interest the planning talk which so often precedes and follows dramatic episodes. Here are some ten-year-olds assessing their first attempt at improvising the story of the three wise men.

HEROD But they weren't at the stable, were they?

WISE MAN 1 The king, Herod, would ask them to speak when he wanted them to, not by themselves really. But you asked us what business had we, and we told you. But you wouldn't be saying it in an angry voice, because you only just knew about it.

WISE MAN 2 But there were three things that we forgot. One of them was a merchant . . . but they weren't all kings.

WISE MAN 1 They weren't all actually kings – they were just rich travellers . . . trying to find the place . . . saying the star told us . . . the angel told us . . . they were Melchior . . . Balthazar.

WISE MAN 3 I can't pronounce any of them. (*Laughter.*)

WISE MAN 2 And Caspar.

WISE MAN 3 We'll have to think about our places, and how we should come in, and all that . . . and what mood Herod would be in. The three travellers would be tired, worn out with the journey.

WISE MAN 1 You'd be surprised, as you're Herod, because you didn't know this, so we just told you.

WISE MAN 2 You'd say that . . . um . . . you do have rooms, but they are very small. Instead of saying we have some rooms, you should say we have some very small rooms.

GUARD They weren't very big, were they?

HEROD Then I come in, and all my high priests. Then I call my chancellors and all my high priests in, and all that, and they discuss it – they haven't heard about it – and then we ask certain people to keep an eye on them.

WISE MAN 1 Yes, but some people in the village might believe them . . . there might be some people in the village who are on their side . . . but you (Herod) don't really like this king who might take over our place.

WISE MAN 2 We have to make up our minds if Herod would believe them or not believe them.

(*Several pupils talking at once. Comments like: 'There'd be trouble when you heard about what we'd said; You'd probably be angry'.*)

WISE MAN 1 Yes, you'd pretend to be kind, but in your own self – yes – you would be angry and do everything to stop him.

HEROD In the village some people believe it and others don't.

WISE MAN 1 And then they wonder what's going to happen to you . . . and then the king has a dream.

WISE MAN 2 Does he have a dream?

WISE MAN 3 Yes . . . they made connexions with the stars. In that film we saw, they'd gone to visit Mary, Joseph and the baby, and they were sleeping somewhere, weren't they? And they went to settle their horses, and one king was late, and one king said to another, 'Where is he?' and then he rushes out and he says he's had a dream, and that's when they start to discuss it.

WISE MAN 2 Wouldn't there be guards to stop them? Wouldn't Herod question them first when they were leaving? Or wouldn't he know about it?

WISE MAN 1 He would know about it, because he wanted to know more about Jesus . . . to find information about him.

WISE MAN 2 He would call all his counsellors and priests and things. If he was a puppet king, he would have to have help off somebody.

WISE MAN 3 And when the guard comes in, he wouldn't just say, 'Follow me'. He . . . he'd say something more, and go and fetch you. He'd go and ask for your permission, whether you wanted to see them or not.

GUARD Yes, because of course we don't know whether they would talk slang or posh, do we? The Romans, I mean.

WISE MAN 3 Well, Herod would be quite ruthless, but a king couldn't be all that rough and ready.

WISE MAN 1 But they would be tired, and they wouldn't bring forward answers straight away – they would be hoping you would give us a rest.

The group recognize two challenges. First they feel a need to make the details of the story ring true to themselves, and here their endeavour is similar to the group discussing the Aztecs – what were things like for people in this particular predicament in a far off place and a far off time? Second, and this takes them beyond the scope of the other group, they want to help each other to reveal these insights in the course of the improvisation. How, they wonder, can they make it clear that the wise men were almost incoherent with weariness and that Herod was concealing a raging anger under a façade of calm? They have confidence in their ability to work out theories and ideas, drawing on impressions they have built up over time – it is after all a well-known tale – and integrating these with fresher insights and ideas which have emerged in talk with the teacher, and from filmstrips and books about the period of the Roman occupation. They ask questions, 'Wouldn't there be guards to stop them? Wouldn't Herod question them first when they were leaving?' Sometimes they proffer advice; one of the wise men points out to Herod that at first he wouldn't sound angry, 'You wouldn't be saying it in an angry voice, because you only just knew about it.' They ponder on the way they should present the drama. 'We'll have to think about our places, and how we should come in and all that . . . and what mood Herod would be in. The three travellers would be tired, worn out with the journey.'

These pupils are used to working in this way and have become able to evaluate what is emerging without the constant presence of the teacher. Pupils less experienced in drama work do need help from the teacher. In the next example we look at the way a young teacher perceives her role in helping a first-year secondary school class make something of a story about a fourteenth-century port threatened by an epidemic. The pupils are clothing the bare bones of the tale in their own way. They agree that they need a narrator to provide continuity between the scenes.

NARRATOR This is an English port in the fourteenth century. An old woman comes with the news that a great epidemic is spreading towards this country. There (*pointing*) is the market place with the various stalls, this is the docks here and there is the town council with the mayor there.

OLD WOMAN (*Comes into the market place singing and muttering.*) There is a terrible disease spreading towards this country . . . buy my lucky charms to wash away this sickness.

CITIZEN 1 Listen to me everybody – do not let her make you spend your money on these foolish charms – they can do nothing for the sickness, even if there is a disease.

CITIZEN 2 Yes, go away you silly old woman (*turning to the group*) . . . these old women are always telling these stories to try to sell their charms.

(*The crowd in the market mutter, some agreeing with the citizens who spoke out against the news, others expressing fear that a dock is particularly vulnerable to outbreaks of this kind being brought from abroad. An official from the docks comes hurrying past the market place towards the town council. Some of the market crowd follow anxiously.*)

CITIZEN 3 Perhaps the old woman was right – they say someone working at the docks is ill.

(*The mayor appears.*)

MAYOR (*to dock official*) Come tell me exactly what has happened.

DOCK OFFICIAL One of the workers felt dizzy – no one thought it was serious, but now we have heard news of an outbreak of disease coming close to our shores.

WORKER (*running in from the docks*) The man has died and two others are ill as well now.

MAYOR We must burn the bodies and lock up all those who have been in contact until we know they have not got the disease.

The pupils now pause, and the teacher says, 'I think we need to be aware of this edict and show you see the implications. Have any of you relatives working in these docks? You have? Well let's see if you can show us in this how you feel about their plight.' The pupils decide to have a town crier to give news of the epidemic and of the mayor's edict. The plan is that a crowd should gather near the town council to heckle the mayor.

> (*Outside the town council.*)
> PEOPLE (*all talking at once*) We want the mayor to come out and speak to us; we want an explanation (*and so on*).
> TOWN COUNCIL OFFICIAL People, be silent, your mayor is going to speak to you.
> MAYOR Listen. Yes these people have some strange unknown disease and the rest of us have to keep away from them. (*People muttering*: 'Yes we know that already.')
> CITIZEN 3 It's your job to protect us, and what about the people who have got it – what are you going to do about them?

The improvisation goes on in this vein – the people against the officials – for some time. Then the teacher breaks in – 'Do you want this play to be about the clash between the people and the mayor and council, against authority, or do you want it to be about the effect of the epidemic on particular families?' Most of the pupils say they want it to be about the human angle and the teacher asks them, 'How then can we direct this back to show the emotional impact on the people? How can we get away from the political angle and look at the individual suffering an epidemic of this kind brings?' One of the pupils suggests they explore the plight of a widow whose only son works at the docks and has to be locked up as a contact. All agree to develop the improvisation along these lines next time they meet.

Here we have some pupils trying to recreate a slice of social history. Interestingly the activities in various areas of the town, the docks, the market and the town council, are going on simultaneously as they would in reality. This made it a difficult improvisation to transcribe, but gave the activities authenticity and distinguished them very clearly from more audience-centred drama. There is much we do not know. We were not there when the story was read, nor did we see the earliest attempts at improvisation, or the follow-up to this session when the pupils planned to show the story from the point of view of individual families. But there is enough to show how this teacher and her pupils work together. They look to her for direction and help in the planning. She acts as a sympathetic audience to their efforts, breaking into the work at key points to comment on how things are developing, and the different ways in which they could direct the work. In articulating the issues and choices, the teacher is opening up the possibility that pupils will internalize this way of looking, and become more autonomous in their work. Pupils like those in the wise men transcript have been engaging in this kind of activity long enough to be able to do this job for themselves by the time they are secondary-school age, but most children need the speculative, flexible but partly directive kind of help exemplified here.

Improvisation is a unique way of learning, integrating as it does so many different ways of knowing and feeling. Insights from all manner of sources inform the work – from books, from the teacher, from maps and photographs, but above all the children's own commonsense notions about what it would be like to be this person in this particular predicament. It creates unusually rich opportunities for language work. Apart from the improvisation itself and the planning talk which precedes and accompanies it, the children are often able to produce lyrics for songs and ballads which are incorporated into the drama, and pieces of writing in the role of the characters, which give the work some permanence. All this makes a powerful case for including improvisation as a major method of teaching and learning in the informed middle-years curriculum.

What then have we been trying to say? Expressive talk – talk to make things clearer for ourselves, talk to sort through developing ideas, talk to test out our insights against those of others – is a potent means of learning. Writing, listening and reading can sometimes play an assimilative role but, particularly for the middle years age-range, it is above all free-wheeling, speculative talk which helps pull together ideas and integrate new information into larger frameworks. The subjective element is uppermost in the expressive mode in that the learner is organizing things for himself. This personal perspective has always been valued by the English teacher, traditionally dealing with the broader concerns of the human predicament. All that we have observed supports the theme explored in *Language, the Learner and the School*,[11] that the personal element has a contribution to make right across the curriculum, particularly in the early stages of coming to know and understand a subject. This means extending notions of relevance. If a science teacher wants to look at electricity, salt or oxygen, all common themes in science for pupils in our age-range, he might begin in an open way inviting pupils to talk either as a class or in groups about the pheno-

mena, sharing their existing commonsense notions, before leading them
into more systematic study. The conversation about the caterpillar during a
field trip (page 142), could prove a good forerunner to the careful study of
the life-cycle of caterpillars, and their place in the insect world. The teacher
has made the pupils feel they have something sensible to say; they are
actively involved from the start. Where the gap between everyday ideas
and school learning becomes too great, boredom can set in. Talk is one
crucial mediator between the two kinds of knowledge. We want pupils to
become increasingly able to deal with ideas and information beyond their
everyday, commonsense experience. We begin by welcoming their spontaneous notions and stories, but we want to help them develop discussion
beyond an anecdotal level towards more general comment and later towards tentative conclusions. Talk sometimes becomes circular and tedious.
We welcome the increasing incidence of small, teacherless talking groups,
in which pupils feel confident enough to share their difficulties and help
each other, but we know that the teacher often has to provide direction. In
Context 12 (page 119) the teacher helps pupils to struggle with the parallels
between the Indian caste system and social class divisions in European
countries. This teacher thinks aloud so that pupils can hear his thought
processes at work; he recognizes this as one factor in helping the pupils
become more articulate. He also appreciates that he must listen to the
pupils to find out what their conceptual difficulties are. Progress in becoming able to discuss and understand such difficult issues is made in small
moves as we see from this example. In spite of the difficulties, we believe
the teacher was right to confront the pupils with this topic, for it is in
facing such challenges that we become articulate.

The teacher's role is partly as the provider of an array of imaginatively
organized talking situations: carefully planned class discussion, small group
discussion with or without a teacher present, larger groups reporting the
fruits of their discussion back to the class, the teacher talking to individuals
– all these deserve a place in the programme. Over a period of time we
would want to find pupils engaging both in talk to solve a practical problem
and in talk to come to terms with complicated ideas. Apart from providing
the range of contexts and presenting lively material and absorbing issues
to form the basis of discussion, are there any other ways in which teachers
can help? Some teachers do seem to acquire the knack of knowing when and
how to intervene helpfully in talk situations, sometimes seeing things in
terms close to the pupil as we see in the discussion on density (page 148), on

other occasions moving a pupil on in his understanding by a question about the validity of his argument (see Context 12, page 120), thus successfully challenging the pupil to find new evidence and perhaps a new synthesis of that evidence. It need not always be the teacher who poses the question; the peer group can also provide an important audience for developing ideas. Some pupils find that the small group without a teacher present is the ideal situation in which to raise and explore an idea.

And what about spectator-role talk – why have we been so insistent that this kind of talking activity should be regarded as a priority? Pupils exist and have their being apart from doing science, physical education, music and all else that school offers, and there should be adequate opportunity for cogitating on the wider, more total concerns of the individual. English lessons have provided a haven where such integration of all the things that are happening and what we are feeling about them can come together. Talk of this kind makes it possible for us to shape for ourselves a mass of input and to be reflective about it; it also provides a context for sharing such special insights and comparing views and experience. Of course some teachers are operating in difficult classrooms where they fear that offering small group discussion of this kind and improvised drama might result in chaos. Success with pupils who have come to feel that school has little to offer them is going to be relative, and nothing will bring about an immediate breakthrough. We believe, however, if teachers even in such circumstances as these can create a space for talk where the particular preoccupations of their pupils are paramount, perhaps followed by some short episodes of improvisation, pupils may gradually come to regard the spoken language as a means of sorting ideas out for themselves. This really is the point, whether our stance is participant, geared towards getting things done in the real world, or whether our stance is the spectator role, concerned with speculating and improvising on our view of the world – our talk is first and foremost to work things out for ourselves; the sharing of insights comes second.

References and notes

1. M. A. K. HALLIDAY, *Explorations in the Functions of Language* (Edward Arnold, 1973), p. 17.
2. Ibid., p. 16.

3. JAMES BRITTON, *Language and Learning* (Allen Lane, Penguin Press, 1970), chapter 3.

4. E. SAPIR, *Culture, Language and Personality* (University of California Press, Berkeley and Los Angeles, 1961).

5. S. K. LANGER, *Philosophy in a New Key* (Harvard University Press, Cambridge, Mass., 1960).

6. E. CASSIRER, *An Essay on Man* (Yale University Press, 1944).

7. GEORGE A. KELLY, *A Theory of Personality* (Norton, New York, 1963).

8. JAMES BRITTON and BERNARD NEWSOME, 'What is learnt in English lessons?', *Journal of Curriculum Studies*, 1 (November 1968), 68–78. The extract is reproduced by permission of the *Journal of Curriculum Studies*.

9. These divisions are explored in greater detail in the report of the Schools Council Written Language of 11–18 Year Olds Project, JAMES BRITTON, et al., *The Development of Writing Abilities* (11–18) Schools Council Research Studies (Macmillan Education, 1975), and in JAMES BRITTON, 'What's the use – a schematic account of language function', *Birmingham Educational Review*, 23 (June 1971), 205–19.

10. I am indebted to my colleague Geraldine Murray for this suggestion.

11. DOUGLAS BARNES, et al., *Language, the Learner and the School* (Penguin Books, 1969).

IV. Writing

Learning to speak is seldom a struggle for a child living in a talking community. Learning to write is more difficult, if only because what a child can say outstrips by some five years of mental development what, when he first begins, he can write. It is as though someone who can walk from home to the corner shop has suddenly to travel that same distance pedalling a bicycle he cannot balance through an obstacle course designed to slow him up.

Is the obstacle course worth negotiating? Looked at from an adult's point of view – not all adults, to be sure, but certainly most teachers – writing offers the message-maker special advantages. Among them, a permanent means of communication would rank high. In speech, the talker is mostly restricted to the here and now, to his immediate social group, in which his saying serves the present moment. Without a tape-recorder or an unusually good memory no accurate record remains. It is also true that the accurate retention of the uttered words is likely to serve no good purpose, for speech is the medium for serving the needs of the moment, not to be divorced from the context to become independent of the situation in which it occurred

Writing offers a means of thinking through by oneself the complications of and justifications for a point of view, the subtleties and intricacies of states of feeling. As a result of such endeavours, the writer can make a deliberate presentation. This, shared with others, stamps the public world with his own mark without the need to be present to certify it.

To children the case is different, especially for the beginners, but probably for many thirteen-year-olds as well. Given their speech performance, initially they are unlikely to see advantage in the permanent recording of what they think, or find delight in the careful pursuit of subtlety and consistency of thought with which the endeavour to write confronts them. In the initial phases they are much more likely to see in writing a struggle for minimum competence to handle their thoughts at a deliberate level. They are probably sufficiently satisfied with making their loaded personal commentary for that teacher and those friends who accept their statements at face value. It is only those who battle through the stage of minimum competence who are likely to find in writing a personal satisfaction, without which writing in any of its kinds can be no more than another skill which schools demand.

To grow towards competence, it is of paramount importance that the writer comes to see the writing act as purposeful behaviour. Two conditions contribute to this. Firstly, the writer must come to see that what he writes is seriously received by the reader. This can only happen if his writing is a genuine communication. Secondly, each act of writing should enable the writer to know more about what he thinks, feels or supposes, and this gain has to be won against the competition of his already developed speech. If both conditions are to be met, the writing task must offer an invitation to tell, explore or state, and suggest a real purpose, rather than an exercise or mere practice. Perhaps most important of all, the writing must fulfil the pupil's purposes before it can fulfil the teacher's.

This should not be taken to imply that children should write if, and only if, they choose the topic. In the early stages of learning to write, many children might never voluntarily take up a pen. But it does suggest that if teachers choose for the pupils, they can only do so in a limited sense. They can choose the target area, or they can provide a set of starting points, but they cannot, as an exercise of will, make the pupil take over the task for himself, and this must happen if the writer is to see writing as important for him. He may well start off writing because he trusts the teacher's judgement that the suggested topic has potential for him, or because he fears the teacher's wrath, although that could hardly be recommended. Yet in either case, if the writer sees himself as merely fulfilling a mechanical duty, rather than searching for meaning and significance, that particular piece of work will be merely an exercise, an exercise in which he can find neither joy nor satisfaction, and it will be a task from which he can learn little. Every such experience contributes to an expectation that writing for him is just another school demand.

Teachers who operate from the assumption that they know which tasks are worth doing always run the risk of an empty result. But the other extreme – write on what you wish to write, and when you want to – may be appropriate only for those who have already found a personal satisfaction in writing, and may not be a sufficiently stimulating invitation for those who are struggling towards competence. Further, if that invitation is genuine, there can be no comeback by the teacher if the pupil says, 'I have nothing to write about'. On any single occasion such a response is of no great import. But we do know that many children, not wishing to display their inabilities, or to expose themselves to possible ridicule, often make such a disclaimer, and if left wholly to themselves they would not write.

The problem for development is how to achieve authenticity in the face of inadequate command over the written language. What is good practice here?

In Chapter I, which traces what some teachers and children do, three features stand out. The first is that in the early stages, the tasks are often based on the child's first-hand experience, whether the task originates with teacher or child. The second is the compelling nature of story-writing and poem-making, at least for most of the children we saw at work. The third is the halting progression of writing in the curriculum as a whole. Each of these deserve special comment.

First-hand experience

The very young writer sees his experience from his own perspective, a perspective from which there is no need to spell out the context of what he does, a perspective from which what he did, what he felt, what he thinks can exist together in a complex of its own. He cannot easily dissociate himself for long enough, nor get sufficiently far outside himself, to perceive what others might need to know in order to understand him. He is likely therefore neither to anticipate what will puzzle his reader, nor be able to tell what he needs to elaborate in order to make himself clear. When he is in a speaking context, these limitations are never severe, because he can rely upon the immediate feedback from his talking companions to encourage him to be more explicit. With writing, however, he has to learn to be both writer and reader to his own productions.

It is not surprising, therefore, that first-hand experience is a good quarrying ground for the beginner, because with it he certainly knows the context and is aware of what he did and how he felt. With the encouragement of the teacher who can accept what he offers, and appreciates at this early stage that experience is likely to be presented as a matrix of fact and feeling, rather than as clear and coherent statement, the writer can get himself down on paper quickly without having to be wary of the result. Karen (ten) writes:

> Rams, sheep, horses, all the iron barrs separating different kinds of livestock. Men and people – bying men, people bidding. Horse boxes reving up pounds and pounds being payd for lovely wooly little lambs. Why are men so cruel. Now the summer has come they must be sold and shawn. What is this an enormous cart full of bullocks. Now some snortie smelly pigs ah a bidder how much oh £15 he's sold. Snort snort says mother pig to her piglets now to be weighed oh gosh half a hundred weight you will have to go on a big diet.

This running commentary jotted down on the spot during a visit to a farmer's market is about as close as the writer can get to that matrix of happening and response which together make up experience. This record does not take the writer very far, nor would it bring to the reader's attention anything startlingly new. Its interest lies in its transparency, for this is expressive writing at its simplest.

One step further away from such closeness to actuality is narrative. Here is an eight-year-old's account of a summer outing:

> On Wednesday we went for a walk to Harborough. We set off on the road and then we went into a field. In the field the grass was swaying, it was very hot. I wanted to sit down. We were still walking on and on. I got so lazy that I fell down. Everyone was puffing and panting. At last we stoped and had a rest. I was sweating like a dog – it was hard going. I heard planes and cows quite close, I saw spiders eating insects. When I sat down the grass was cool and I ran my fingers through it. Maureen and I got Beasty and David to carry our bags because we were too lazy – so they carried them. When we reached the church everybody was tired out, and we all flopped down on the grass. On the way back it was not quite so bad – the boys were still carrying our bags. We were very hot when we got back I took off my shoes and socks and sat down.

Narrative is a selection from all that happens, a selection governed by the purposes the writer has for the telling. In this narrative, the writer intends to go no further than to share an experience with others, an experience in which events and feelings keep hand in hand. The little personal details and asides mean that we see the summer walk very much from the young writer's perspective. Sometimes, however, such accounts show signs of diverging towards transactional purposes. This trend is clearly seen in the next example by Sarah aged eight:

The Langton Way nurseries

On the 18th May 1971 we went to the Langton Nurseries and we met Mr S—— and Colin they took us round the nursere and we looked at lots of flowers and then we went into some green houses and inside we saw some pine trees we saw some cinearia and saxifraea and Gladiolus Plants and then we went and saw some outdoor plants like bamboo plants and colceariar. The green houses were heated because the flowers came from hot countries. Water ran under the green houses because they used to wash and water the flowers. Some flowers needed special treatment and needed their leaves to be washed. The plants were grown for decorating the town hall. The plants were resting on stones because if the plants got too much water they would drown but the stones would help the water to drain away.

A picture of a plant appears at this stage in her work.

This plant comes from the hydrangea it has four petals. The green houses were made of wood and glass. The roofs of the green-houses were painted because if the sun got at the flowers too much they would dye. The names of the plants that grew outside were bamboo, and irises and hydrangeas. You can tell the monstoro plant because it is shiney and it has lots of wigorly wagerly things coming out of it and you can tell how old it is because it has a certain number of holes in it.

This narrative has gone a step further than the example which precedes it. In addition to telling us what happened on the day of the visit to the nursery, Sarah includes a great deal of information about the exhibits, information which was given in answer to the children's questions as they progressed round the nursery premises. In terms of the language function model described in Chapter III, the account has moved a pace or two from the expressive towards the transactional. This trend is what we would expect to see increasingly as pupils move through the middle years. It is partly a function of developing maturity, partly the result of the situation the teacher provides as a starting-point for writing.

Narratives can move in the other direction, towards the poetic end of the continuum as we see in this rather unusual piece by nine-year-old Mary:

My pet

When my hamster died I was very sad all that day. When I got home from school Mummy told me I had better clean out the cage, which was in the workshop. I was just about to pick up the cage when I saw a note on it. I read it and it said

Dear Mary,
Your mother told me that Hazel had died and that you were very sad. That makes me sad too. May I introduce myself? My name is Horace, which was always a favourite of my mother's. When I was born she was so anxious to use it she immediately christened me without waiting to see if I was a boy or a girl. So I don't know either. Until today I have been living in Mr M——'s pet shop in Belfast in a rather crowded little cage with my brothers and sisters. I love them very much, but as you know, we hamsters would rather have a place of our own. So if I may live with you I promise to keep the cage tidy always. May I stay?

Yours affectionately,
Horace Murphy

I looked into the cage and there I saw a tiny little hamster looking very scared indeed. So I took him inside. The hamster seemed almost magic. His fur was a lovely dark golden colour and it shone like gold. Everybody loved him and whenever you went to his cage he would go round in his wheel for you.
One morning I went to his cage before school and he was lying at the bottom of his cage dead. I stood for a moment not knowing what to do. I just couldn't believe it. Then I ran upstairs to Mummy and Daddy's room to tell them. I was very miserable for a while. We buried him beside Hazel. We didn't have another pet for a long time afterwards. Now we have another hamster called Coco.

This tells something of the attachment to pets which is often so strong a feeling in children in our age-range, it tells also of the relationship parents can have with their offspring, and of grieving for loved ones and making some kind of recovery. It seems likely that in writing this Mary sorted out something important for herself. She was moved on in her understanding of herself in relation to the things that happen in life. Her stance is firmly rooted in the spectator role and her narrative falls some way along the expressive/poetic continuum; she has begun to select those elements from her experience which make a good story.

In general it is expressive language in which individuals are likely to rehearse the growing points of their formulations and analyses of experience. It is language which, by being close to the self, by following closely the contours of thought, can carry the tentative and exploratory thinking which is a necessary part of the digestive process. This is true whether the problem is one of assimilating new and challenging data, or of restructuring one's interpretative framework to make more of, or to understand better, what one encounters. The speculative writing of this eleven-year-old shows how the expressive function can serve this kind of purpose:

Watching the world go by
Many times I have sat down on a gate, or lain on the grass, and just watched the world go by and the birds singing, and I began to think about a lot of things.
One such time when I watched the world going by two old women passed by with a little black poodle. They always passed by on this road, almost every day and I wondered if I would ever see them again, would one of these old ladies die, or would they perhaps just not come back, but for as long as I can remember these two old ladies and their dog passed by this road on nearly every day.
Then a car flew round the corner, brakes screeching and I said to myself, 'What kind of idiot is that, anyone could get killed by him', and well I knew that a few months ago my pet dog was run over by a similar affair when another driver just flew round the corner the driver never even looked to see if anything was there, and the result was my dog got killed, but the worst part of it is that the driver never even bothered to stop, but he just went on, and it made me think that some people don't care for any form of life. After all it could easily have been a child that he ran over.
Then my attention turned to the sky. I saw the birds singing and chirping to each other and then I looked at the sun, and thought that all life depended on that big mass of fire, and I also thought of God and how he made these things and gave us life in the first place.
Then suddenly I realised time was creeping on and I got up and made my way home.

What has been called 'expressive' writing, then, is not an early mode to be discarded when pupils master other modes; we continue to use it for learning throughout life, and writers develop in the expressive mode as in others.

Story-telling and poem-making

We collected a vast number of stories, poems and dialogues, and we believe children experience a very special kind of satisfaction in making something for their own pleasure, in giving their thoughts and feelings a shape which completes their meaning. In the right classroom climate they enjoy sharing what they have made with the teacher and the other children. As mentioned in Chapter III, the poetic function is rare in spoken language except in improvised drama. It is mainly in writing that children can develop in this direction. The first stories, as we would expect, have an expressive flavour; Mary's story about the hamster is a narrative with an expressive/poetic function – 'expressive' in that it brings together (in a speech-like way) some significant feelings and understandings, and 'poetic' in that the narrative form is the result of some conscious reflection and shaping by the writer. Kerry on the other hand found that she could most powerfully convey the immediacy and atmosphere of a shipwreck by writing a poem (see page 192). In these examples the young writers were becoming able to undergo the discipline that writing in a special form or pattern imposes, but both pieces retained some elements of an expressive function. If poems embody the kind of insights, implications and nuances which are less readily explored in other forms of writing, there is a strong case for making a place for reading and writing them in school. A poem is by definition an artistic construct, something that exists independently of its creator, but we must appreciate that for children poetry-writing is also a special way of learning. In the case of younger pupils the emphasis is less on producing something that the audience considers 'good' according to some generally agreed aesthetic criteria, and more on the pupil's own perception of his success in matching language to the segments of experience he is trying to crystallize.

All writing is creative in the sense that we have to organize and shape what is to be articulated. Even a narrative about what happened in the park yesterday involves the writer in selecting what to include and what to leave out, in deciding how to order the events, in planning what to highlight and what to hint at; it is not a question of simply recording the facts. The more fanciful stories are even less directly related to 'actual' experience, and we do not pretend to understand the intricate processes which go on in the mind in drawing out a fantasy from remembered events and our feelings about them at the time and in retrospect. We do believe, however, that even the strangest fantasy emerges from a writer's experience both actual and imagined. The imagination needs basic materials to work on – nothing comes out of nothing.

Some pupils seemed to choose a fantasy theme whenever they could, while others preferred to remain in the world as we know it. We found the following classification helpful in sifting through stories and poems:

Actual – based on actual happening but may be elaborated (*Down my street*, Bruno, 10 years).

Possible – involves events which might well have taken place but which did not (*It was super*, Edwin, 11 years).

Improbable – events unlikely but no natural laws are contradicted (*England* v *Brazil*, Lee, 10 years).

Impossible – events incompatible with the natural world as we know it, yet the best of these tales are self-consistent and deserve willing suspension of disbelief (*The blue flower*, Jacqueline, 8 years).

From a vast array of work from children of different ages and abilities, four examples are reproduced here – the examples which are mentioned above and which fall roughly in each of the categories. In the first example, eleven-year-old Bruno has considerably embellished his tale, but it is based on an actual incident.

Down my street

Bill Jones was the boy down my street, he's moved now, but while he was here it was fantastic. When he first came I was eight years old and pretty square but it didn't take long for him to change me. One of our first adventures was called 'Skinheads Retreat'. When this adventure took place I was nine years old and Bill and I had formed a gang with some other boys who lived in Rob Street. Set up H.Q. in a remote part of a common near my house. Bill was our leader but I was in charge of military strategy and arms, the reason we had weapons (catapults, shields, bows and padded arrows, etc.) was because of a gang of skinheads who made repeated attacks on our H.Q. This is the story of one of our greatest victories. The whole gang was seated inside the hut which we had made our H.Q. when there was the familiar sound of bovver boots clomping across the grass outside. Quickly we ran to our stations where pieces of amunition (i.e. clods of earth) were waiting. Soon the air was full of angry sounds from the skinheads as clods of earth hit them full on their faces. We too had been hit but so far looked like winning. Soon the skinheads retreated but came back with an old log. It was obvious that they were going to use it as a battering ram, quickly we pushed a table in front of the door and went back to our places waiting for the skinheads to come in range of our catapults. Suddenly Bill had a brainwave which you will hear about in a minute. Bill ran over to the door pulled the table away and laid it down on the top towards the door. Bill waited for my signal . . . Now!! Just as the skinheads were about to hit it Bill threw the door wide open. They ran full pelt into the table and were so bruised and battered that they had to surrender!!

Bruno's story tells us something of hero-worship, and of what it means to children of this age to belong to a gang. It is also an illustration of how the facts can be shaped and presented to make a readable story.

Moving along to the 'possible' point on the continuum here is a story which seems not unlike Bruno's in flavour. However, the teacher describes Edwin as a quiet, amiable boy, who never hurt anyone in his life. What follows is, therefore, a construction of a possibility, rather than a reflection of actuality.

> *It was super!*
> We had gone down the street because we had an appointment with some fool after school. It all started because this kid had blocked a kick of mine which surely would have been a goal, a little earlier. I had warned him and a few other kids that if they did anything that annoyed me I would bash their heads in. Well he didn't heed my warnings and blocked the kick so we made an appointment. It was very unusual.
> The afternoon was fine that day – I didn't get any headaches like I usually do and the only time the teacher got mad at me was when we had to write a poem. So I did. The teacher did not mind – he was just enchanted that I was finally doing something. It was only when he saw the poem which started
>
>> As I was walking down the street,
>> I heard a kid shouting names at me
>> He said 'Youre the dirty bloake who knocked my brother down'
>> So I walked across the street and knocked him into the gutter.
>
> Well the teacher was just furious he shouted at me across the room 'Can't you do anything without the subject of force?.' I just can't understand why he didn't like the poem.
> After school I went to the appointed corner, but you would never guess what had happened the boy who had bravely stood up to me that morning was now so scared because of what his classmates had told him that if I touched him he would have collapsed to the ground dead, and then I walked up to him and knocked him down he tried to stand up and run away but I picked him up and knocked him down and I kept doing this until he lay on the sidewalk a sobbing piece of crumpled flesh.

A lot could be made of a story like this; one could suppose that it is the wish fulfilment of a quiet boy who in reality has no high status with the peer group at an age when this is important. Terms like 'sidewalk' and 'mad at me' suggest the influence of certain kinds of American film. We can only speculate about his reasons for writing it, and if the violent element worries us it did not seem to worry the boy's teacher who knew considerably more about him.

Edwin's story is a fantasy, although a casual reader would not recognize it as such. The next example is a fantasy of a different kind, the projection by a young writer of himself into an unlikely, glamourized adult role, and it would be placed at the 'possible but improbable' point on the continuum.

England v. Brazil

The teams

England		*Brazil*
Hatton	1	Crolly
Meager	2	Tis
Pyle	3	Poizi
Smeludes	4	Wogy
Reece	5	Bilado
Mason	6	Grendal
Delaforce	7	Jarihldo
Payne	8	Ale-Tomi
Cole	9	Pilhard
Flitton	10	Crolly
Babbington	11	Tomuzzi

As we walked onto the Wembly turf we should easily win on paper but my nerves told me it would be tense and close. Brazil took centre and straight away Crolly made an impressive run down the left flank. Crolly crossed the ball Pilhard headed against the bar, the ball came out to Grendal who shot fiercely but Hatton clung onto the ball. Hatton booted a long ball up field which reached Payne. Payne crossed beautifully and Flitton headed down to Cole who just slipped the ball into the net to put England 1–0 in the lead. This time Brazil's centre forward played the ball to his inside right Ali-Tomi who was immediately tackled by Mason. Mason passed to Babbington, Babbington played to Delaforce and Delaforce done another beautiful cross. Cole headed the ball Brazil goal keeper Crolly saved brilliantly but couldn't prevent the ball going to Flitton who with the last kick of the first half put England in the lead 2–0.

In the second half England were pressurising Brazil but failed to score. Babbington was crossing the ball it was about to go to Payne's head when all of a sudden Wogy pulled him down this was a penalty which Wayne Flitton scored his second goal and put England 3–0 up. There was still 15 minutes to go England were pressurising Brazil still Cole shot it was a certain goal but Wogy handled it it was another penalty. Wayne Flitton settle and

scored his hat trick score 4–0, five minutes to go Cole popped up from no-
where and scored 5–0. We were in injury time Delaforce past to Cole who
scores.
Final score: England 6, Brazil 0.
Scorers: Cole 3, Flitton 3.

Lee Cole's piece was the result of an invitation to write a story of his own
choice. Most of the players are imaginary, and he no doubt derives great
satisfaction from placing himself in the star role. This kind of story is by
no means untypical from boys of this age.

Eight-year-old Jacqueline's story is a delightful fantasy finding a place
at the extreme right of our continuum. The teacher here found his pupils
reluctant writers on the whole although most were fluent talkers. Jacqueline
was not among those finding most difficulty with writing; nevertheless, this
fairly sustained tale was something of an achievement for her.

The blue flower
It was a warm day the park was full of plants and flowers I picked up a blue
flower and I began to chew at it. Suddenly I knew something was wrong. I
looked round everything was very very small. I couldn't understand what
had happened. I grew bigger and bigger I felt dizzy I took a step and found
myself at the other side of town. Then I walked and walked, then I saw a
tiny little girl going across the road and a car was coming I just grabbed her
the tiny little girl. She said thank you then I said you should run across the
road then I left her across the road everyone looked at me I said to myself I
wonder why they are looking at me like that. Then I saw people fighting so I
shouted at them to stop. When they knew how big I was they run away. I
walked along a bit and I saw smoke coming from a window and people were
calling out but because I was so big I was able to reach out my hand and
break the window and then I blew hard and the fire went out. Then I helped
the old people and the children and the young people and all the people
across the road and then I went back to the park and took a bit of the
flower and grew small again but I was pleased that I had done something
good.

The story was a result of the teacher asking the class what would happen if
they ate something magic, and as several of the other stories mention eating
a blue flower it seems likely that this idea was suggested during the talk that
preceded the writing. This class was asked to write a fantasy, and comparing this writing with other work they had done there is evidence that
this appealed to them.

Looking at our sample of stories as a whole a pattern emerges, especially where choice of theme was left to the children. Many children can and do make almost any starting point develop into what they would like to write. The under-tens, particularly girls, write many stories which would fall towards the extreme right end of the continuum. The stories of older pupils gather further towards the left. This no doubt reflects changing interests and new ways of confronting the world. It may also be connected with the older child's capacity to tackle his problems directly rather than in terms of symbols. Eight-year-old Jacqueline perhaps feels still the vulnerability of the very young child, unable to make much impact on the world, and enjoyed taking up the teacher's invitation to imagine herself in a role of power. Elizabeth Cook[1] believes that eight- to ten-year-olds delight in creating magical worlds where people can be impossibly tall and incredibly strong. Similarly we were not surprised to find the older boys choosing themes centring on aggression, power and status-seeking for these things are, rightly or wrongly, presented to them as being part of acquiring a male identity.

In make-believe it is not perhaps the credibility of what we pretend that matters most. Story-telling is one important means by which we can have more lives than the often hum-drum one which is our daily lot.[2] In a story we can rehearse and explore possibilities without having to pay the price of actuality – this is evident in the stories by Edwin and Jacqueline. It is through stories that the symbolic transformation of important experiences takes place which enables us to deal with threat indirectly. The writer may write out of need, a need to sort out a personal difficulty. Perhaps the most telling example of this is the following poem written by a thirteen-year-old girl in school in one of the troubled areas of Belfast:

The riots

i

The evenings so quiet
Everything so still
Suddenly a shot
Then another.

ii

No longer do people sit by the fire,
and feel the warmth of a home.
The sound of doors opening
People talking

A crowd of men come up the street
    shouting fierce language
to the women and children.
            iii
I am told to go into the house
    and watch the children
Who are crying with fear,
    I shake with fear too, but try so
hard to hide my tears.
            iv
Hear men shouting 'he's hit'
    and running out to the street to
    my father I wonder
'God is it he who is hit and what has he done to deserve this.'
            v
Trembling with fear I push my way through
    gangs of men.
No longer can I hide my tears,
    for in the distance I see my father,
Lying in front of the barricade with
    men and women shouting orders
Of what has to be done about him.
            vi
At once one of the neighbours seen me
    and shouted 'Get this child out of here'
As two men grabbed my arms
    I seen my father being took away
    On a stretcher.
'Father, father' I squealed and as I set
    myself free from the men,
I run to my father
    And his last words to me were
'Don't cry now, you look after your mother
    and brothers and sisters because
you are the oldest,
be proud of me
    for this is a good way to die.'
As my heart broke
    He my father faded away.

The work is not based on an actual experience, but the vividness of the language suggests that the piece arises out of some preoccupation deeply felt by the writer. It tells us something of the powerful effect on children of the social environment. Some of the work in this chapter arose out of need, out of an eagerness to think through and give form to disturbing experiences. However, children also like the opportunity to write for fun. There were many lively examples, but here are just two typical pieces: the 'Owley Growley' a nonsense rhyme, showing occasional strain because of the rhyming scheme chosen, but nevertheless greatly entertaining to the writer's fellow pupils; and Sarah's vivacious 'Slipper plant' story. Children should be able to write 'from need' and 'for fun' at different times and it is the teacher who judges the right moment to invite each kind.

The Owley Growley
The Owley Growley was shiney and fat
He sometimes did this and sometimes did that,
But he always eventually managed to say
I'm going to while all my time away.

One beautiful, wonderful, marvellous day,
The sunshine was shining as if it was day,
The Owley Growley was having a nap
When up came a kitten and gave him a tap.

O please Owley Growley, I wondered if you
Could find any beautiful Haggis the noo?
For I am a Scottish cat, hungry indeed
And cannot find all of the food that I need.

The Owley Growley was there on the spot.
He thought that the kitten was talking such rot.
He went to the larder to get out some meat
So the poor little kitten would have it to eat.

This is the end of a very strange tale
And after all this the poor Owley went pale
We had better leave him to go to the vet
But tell him that you are so pleased that you met.

The dancing slippers
One night when i was watering my slipper plants which were yellow with red spots my mummy called me and said it is time you were in bed dear so i put my nightdress and got into bed i closed my eyes and went to sleep i had a

dream and this is what i dreamt. I dreamt that my slipper plant had grown as big as my feet and they had pulled me out of bed and they had put them selfs on my feet and had started dancing down the stairs. I had just maniged to grab my dressing gown and shut the door behind me. I went danceing down the road crying out somebody help stop slipper plants stop by they would not stop suddenly they started danceing up into the air oh no somebody help. The slipper plant went flying on withing takeing any notice of me. Now there was knowone to help me. Suddenly we started going down and down untill i suddenly went bump on the ground as soon as i had stood up of i went again danceing and danceing danceing and danceing then i came to a large cave the slippers kept on dancing they danced down a tunnel in the cave i quickly opened a door just before i bumped into it and just guess what i saw well i saw about a million pairs of slipper plants dancing round and round the room twirling and wirling round and round with spots and dots pink and brown red and blue and pink and purple. Suddenly the slippers started danceing with all the other slippers, round and round went twirling and wirling round and round and round went colers wirling bright and twirling round and round then all of a sudden the slippers started dainceing out of the door and right to the house where i woke up and found myself in bed with the slipper plants on the window.

It is the teacher's role to create a sympathetic climate in fostering the progress of individual pupils and in receiving their work. For some pupils the opportunity to write can be enough – in Context 2 (page 32) the sudden thunderstorm coming in the middle of exploring ruins during a field trip was a strong impetus for writing. On other occasions a more direct invitation seems appropriate; the teacher gave the children in Jacqueline's class a firm nudge into fantasy (see page 176). Music, paintings, extracts from literature, anecdotes offered by the teacher and various physical phenomena can all be fruitful starting-points.

Teachers need to avoid the kind of starting-point which is likely to produce a superficial response, a stringing together of contrived phrases. Although we have seen (and have given ourselves) many fruitful, self-contained lessons where pupils have been invited to respond in writing to a starting-point initiated by the teacher, it is our impression that it is when we give story- and poem-writing special names like 'creative', 'intensive', or 'imaginative' writing, and when we devote special short sessions to it, that we run most risk of an empty result. Much of the most satisfying writing we saw had its roots in thematic and project work. The shipwreck poems in Context 3 (page 32) and Paul's two pictures of decaying trees in Context 7 (page 68) are examples which immediately spring to mind. Good results seem most likely when pupils and teachers are involved in something together, when they enjoy each other's anecdotes and listen to pieces from literature that they want to share.

Once the pupils are engaged in writing they look to the teacher as a sounding-board for their first drafts. Mature writers assume that they will often have to revise and amend, to change lines and phrases, to restructure a poem. To welcome this careful approach in young writers is not to contradict what has been implied about not concentrating too much on the code, but on what is to be articulated. Once we have given basic shape to our idea, some rearrangement to achieve greater impact will help us feel more satisfied with what we have made. In poetry, as the pupil in Context 10 noted, in talking about his poem, some lines just come to us, but others are less obliging and have to be struggled with. Where a teacher has managed to create a warm and constructive classroom climate, pupils and teacher can listen to a writer's effort and give their view about parts which do not satisfy the writer. This is the atmosphere in which the devices writers use can be considered. When the pupil feels satisfied with what he has produced the teacher can show his enjoyment by reading the poem or story aloud, displaying it on the wall, in a class book, by inviting a group of pupils to present their stories and poems to the others.

Finally, how do we see development in this mode of writing? In our study of the writing of Kerry and Cathy (page 190) we note that Kerry, the younger child, is very much at home in what we have called the expressive/poetic kind of story and poem. Some of her work, however, is just showing signs of mastering the shaping and moulding which are characteristics of the maturer writer. We think this movement reaches completion in fourteen-year-old Cathy's poem, 'Alone' (page 200); it exists in its own right as an artistic construct: form and meaning fuse. Pupils find great satisfaction in this kind of achievement as we see from Michael's feelings about his poem, 'The wreck' (page 39). The paradox is that if we *try* to achieve 'good' work from the children we miss the point. Particularly in the case of the younger ones, writing which takes on a shape is a special way of making sense of what confronts them.[3] We will give the right kind of help if we understand the implications of this.

Making progress in writing across the curriculum

Many pupils approach much of the writing in school with little enthusiasm, and this seems connected with the way in which writing tasks are set up. Very often the pupil is asked to struggle with a kind of writing, a prose style, which he finds too difficult to handle. In trying to accommodate his ideas to the style, all freshness and originality is lost. The pupil suspects that there is a model of 'how it should be done' in the teacher's mind, and that success will be judged more on how closely he makes his piece resemble the model than on what he has to say. Of course each school subject has its own technical vocabulary and particular ways of presenting information and structuring arguments; in later stages, success in the different fields depends partly on mastering the conventions. Perhaps we have not always recognized just how difficult some writing tasks are. We show in the next section that even an able fourteen-year-old has limited success with the more difficult kinds of transactional writing; for example, in 'Young, gifted and black' (page 202) Cathy is unable to sustain the argument she has begun by continuing to build up a series of logical points towards a coherent conclusion. We have to face pupils with the challenge of the more difficult tasks, but progress towards becoming competent is made in small stages.

Making a good beginning

Clearly much depends on the earliest years; if pupils view writing as an enjoyable and useful activity from the very beginning, many of the later problems may never develop. Many primary schools now base talking and writing on what teachers and children do together. Then there are practical activities in the classroom where writing tasks can arise out of an absorbing activity tackled with enthusiasm. We noted that where the writing was liveliest, the teachers tended not to see themselves only or chiefly as assessors; often they showed that they enjoyed sharing the child's ideas or acted as a sounding board for developing thoughts. They also recognized the peer group as an important audience.[4]

Success also seems associated with the teacher's capacity to welcome a varied response in writing to a learning activity or situation. As is evident in the first few contexts in Chapter I, topic and project work can give rise to a rich array of writing. We find in Context 3 upper primary-school children unearthing a wreck on the seashore and assimilating their experience in many ways, including writing. Interestingly the fruits of their research in the public library and the local archives is reflected in some of the poems and stories. John's piece, 'Grounded' (page 40) depends partly for its success on his knowledge of how the vessel is constructed. He has been able to provide an answer to the question – how would a vessel of this kind break up if it was driven by the elements on to rocks? So factual information can be assimilated through poems and stories.

Not all knowledge can come from direct experience; for much information and understanding we need to turn to secondary sources. Books have always been an important source, but teachers are increasingly recognizing the impact and immediacy of film and pictures as a way of learning. For many pupils the visual image is more accessible than the printed word. In the example below a teacher uses a visual experience as a starting point and seizes a special opportunity for helping pupils to handle writing. A class of ten-year-olds had seen a short film on the kangaroo and were eager to talk about how the young find their way into the mother's pouch. After looking at pictures, and making their own sketches and paintings, the teacher suggested they might write about this particular episode in the kangaroo's life. By choosing this topic, in which they had invested a lot of interest the teacher has limited the writing task to something they can do well. She also recognized that to reorganize visual images into writing is generally easier than to make something of what is written in a book. Most of the children managed a short narrative like this one:

> A Kangaroo is a beautiful animal. Its front legs are quite short and his back legs are very long. It has a very strong tail and can hop around at thirty miles an hour. When a baby kangaroo is born it is only about two centimetres long. It has no back legs when it is born and to get to its mother's pouch it has to climb to it. It takes about twenty minutes for it to climb into the pounch. A kangaroo is an amazing animal, but a beautiful animal.

The children have not just taken up what they have seen. The film commentator, the teacher and the other pupils all made their comments and there was also much painting and drawing between the film and the writing. Other pupils chose to shape their observations in poetry:

> *The struggle*
> It's just born,
> Only two centimeters long,
> Amazing –

A twenty minute climb,
It's quite a bit for a baby kangaroo,
Only two centimeters long,
Climbing up,
Only by its front paws
It's in!
Oh dear!
That was a struggle,
It stays in its mother's pouch,
Even when it's quite big,
It's just amazing.

Here again writing a poem seems to have helped learning as much as writing a narrative ought have done. Both examples reflect the vitality of the children's talk. Given that these pupils cannot see kangaroos in the wild, the teacher has shown them the next best thing. She has supported the film with pictures and provided the right climate for talking and painting. These activities have got the assimilation process going before the pupils face the more difficult activity of writing. She makes it more likely that the pupils will succeed by inviting them to write about a part of the film which she knows has captured their interest. This narrowing down ensures that all the pupils are faced by something manageable, but she welcomes a variety of writing response, recognizing both poetry and prose as ways of handling experience and information.

If the visual image as a help in learning is becoming established in practice, we are slower to recognize the special contribution of improvised drama. Improvisation is, as Context 6 aims to show, a powerful way of learning in its own right, but it also creates the context for a variety of written work. Obviously when pupils need to know how Saxon monks lived, what their daily routine was like, they have, as Context 6 shows, a powerful impetus into research and writing to inform their drama. In turn the improvisation puts flesh and bones on the stark information. Improvisation and writing can be complementary ways of working through the concepts and ideas explored.[5]

Some of the factors then in making a good start with writing include the welcoming of a variety of writing responses, (poems and stories can be ways of assimilating information as well as prose accounts); there are dangers in imposing difficult prose styles too soon and, as we argue later in this chapter, in stressing conventions of grammar and spelling. Where it is not possible to explore at first hand, visual and dramatic approaches can help make involved information accessible. Most of all we want young writers to feel confident that their own everyday language is appropriate for learning; the 'expressive' touches which are more to do with the needs of learner than of audience are a sign that the learner is managing to make his own mark.

Going beyond narrative

Hopefully in the early years we have created a climate in which pupils have come to view writing not as a death knell to all enthusiasm and commitment, but as a useful way of sorting out all that is happening around them and how they feel about it. But how do we lead them beyond narrative, to writing which demands the building up of an argument and making general points? In the next section, 'The work of two able writers', we find Kerry at nine writing very uncertainly when she has to try to build up an argument. Arranging information in hierarchies of points and marshalling a coherent argument are beyond her. Indeed even the older child still has difficulties at nearly fourteen. Perhaps such reasoning is among the most difficult of tasks for us all, and for most of us success will only be relative. Improvement is partly made possible by providing sensible contexts, learning situations which give rise to a need for this kind of writing, but all-round intellectual development and increasing maturity also have a part to play. The teacher might also help in some cases by narrowing down the writing tasks, as illustrated in the previous example. In the case of older pupils engaged in humanities or topic work there is nearly always an opportunity for thinking and writing to centre on a controversial issue giving pupils the chance to grapple with different points of view. A group looking at communities and factors which encourage or inhibit them, might be invited to present an argument for or against high-rise flats or for or against institutions for the old. Class or group discussions are a useful forerunner, but writing offers the opportunity for careful consideration of the points to be made and their relative importance, without fear of interruption or having to turn to a different point made by someone else. Not that writing tasks should be contrived – rather they should emerge as useful ways of deepening understanding. As Nancy Martin makes clear, it is not so much a matter of learning to write (and talk) but of becoming able to write (and talk) to learn.[6]

 Pupils can so easily remain unabsorbed and uncommitted. It is up to the teacher to use his ingenuity to bring the work alive. One teacher hoping to generate some interest in a social theme, old age, began by accepting the pupils' anecdotes, used pictures from Age Concern, drew attention to newspaper reports of the plight of individual old people and, once interest had been aroused, felt able to challenge them with the more difficult writing tasks. For example, the pupils considered how humane or otherwise we were as a society. We seem to be kinder than the Netsilik Eskimos, for instance, who allow their old to fade away in the snow, but are we cruel in more subtle ways? Discussions on such themes preceded and went alongside writing where the emphasis was on presenting an argument. Fairly late on in the topic work each pupil was invited to write a piece in which they took up the role of an old person with a housing, health or other problem. The 'old person' wrote to a problem-page adviser explaining their difficulty. The second half of the writing task was working out a helpful reply. This was intellectually challenging, but the pupils found it an engaging task and many of them willingly read out their work in class. In general they seemed to find presenting the two viewpoints easier than some of the main general arguments.

So often we have obliged pupils just on the brink of becoming able to support a viewpoint or justify an opinion to write huge chunks of the 'showing what we know' variety. The examination system tends to make teachers anxious to be reassured that something has been absorbed. It is much more satisfying for a pupil to tackle a writing task which enables him to *use* rather than just report what he has learnt.

Using books

Although many teachers now use books as only one source of information among several, print assumes a more and more dominant place in learning as pupils move through the secondary years. Pupils in their middle years at school find difficulty in writing syntheses of what they find in books, so how can we help? In looking at project work which relied entirely or partly on book information we pinpointed two main difficulties. Available books are not often pitched at the optimum level for pupils using them, and most pupils need more help in finding their way round reference books. How can teachers give this help when the class is large and most of the pupils need a guiding hand? We would not like to see opportunities for individual topic work disappear but a carefully chosen and prepared class project for younger children, or integrated studies theme for older pupils, within which group and individual work is arranged, make it more possible for a teacher or team of teachers to gather together a range of suitable material for the pupils. Work-sheets and cards can help to ensure that each pupil covers the main core of information before choosing to explore a particular aspect of the topic. Work-cards can be used to suggest the range of possible choices and direct pupils to particular books, sometimes even to particular pages; they may also guide the reader in getting the essential material from a particular source. In a well-organized topic lesson, groups often report back to the whole class and invite questions from their peers. It is by talking through and comparing insights, and becoming able to justify a particular viewpoint, that new information is sufficiently assimilated for pupils to feel able to commit some of their findings to the written word.

Burrowing into reference books is most absorbing when we are trying to solve a compelling problem. The pupils who had uncovered a wreck had a strong reason for wanting to find out about the old coal-carrying vessels (see Context 3, page 36). Finding out from old papers, documents and books was the logical next stage after their practical work. As Peter Medway[7] puts it – we need to know what we are going to do with information when we have it. Poems, stories, folk legends and novels have an important contribution to make as well as reference books.

To avoid wholesale copying, and to make writing more active and enjoyable for the pupils, some teachers suggest that they take up the role of a character in the past or in a distant country. Information from books and other sources can then be used and adapted to the writer's requirements. We saw a great deal of writing on the lines of the following:

> I am a stone age girl. I live in a cave. One morning as I lay in bed, which was really two deer skins, and the small log fire glowed in the corner of the cave and mummy was making the breakfast, daddy who is the leader of our little village came in and said, 'Pack up your things because the deer have moved to another place and where the deer go we must go.' Mummy started to gather up all our animal skin blankets and to put them in an animal skin bag which was sewn up with sinus [sinews]. An hour or so later the village people started to follow the herd of deer. All the women and children carried the belongings so that the men could hunt animals. In the evening we came to a nice little spot. Here we camped for the night and we were lucky that a herd of deer had sported here and while the men ran to catch them I and some other girls made the first animal trap. Here is how we made it. First

we dug a deep hole then we stuck sharp knives into the trap and we covered the trap with grass and animal skins. In the trap we caught a deer.

As we might expect her conception of how things would be is at an early stage of development, but she is beginning to make intelligent speculation about how it might have been, against the backcloth of book information and drawing on what the teacher and other pupils have said.

From studying examples of pupils and teachers working together we have compiled the following generalized comments on good practice:

1 Stories, poems and personalized accounts of the past are all ways of assimilating ideas and information, and have a place alongside more factual writing (and reading).

2 Expressive touches, personal asides and observations, should not be inhibited but should be recognized as evidence that pupils are making headway in 'getting on the inside' of the material. Particularly in the early stages when attitudes towards writing are being formed, children must be encouraged to feel their own everyday language is a suitable vehicle for learning.

3 Invitations to write have a greater chance of success when pupils have shown a special interest in an area or when the information to be garnered and organized is needed for another activity, or will be used to solve a problem.

4 The power of a visual approach should be exploited. For many pupils who find difficulty with books, a sophisticated response is possible where pictures, films, photographs and slides are used. Subtle understandings about relationships and predicaments can sometimes be shown powerfully and the impact is often sustained in subsequent writing.

5 Improvised drama can play a vital role in making remote events and situations accessible, and often promotes writing of particular vitality and commitment.

6 Books are important sources of information, particularly for older pupils, but most pupils need considerable help in using them. Novels, poetry and stories can impart information but in a different way from the more obvious reference books.

7 It seems wisest not to insist on a special structure in the early stages of writing, but to be open to a variety of writing responses.

8   Often, but not always, writing is best introduced after the assimilation process is already begun through talk or art.

9   Sensitive teachers do not see their role only as assessors. They welcome and enjoy sharing their own and their pupils' ideas, and they encourage the peer group to be a receptive and sympathetic audience.

The work of two able writers

In this section the writing output of two pupils, near the extreme ends of the age-range, is considered in terms of the language functions described in Chapter III. Their work demonstrates how two able writers cope with normal school assignments; it illustrates the range of function available to them at their respective ages, and gives a sense of the journey which the eight- or nine-year-old has to take in writing development to become an accomplished writer at the upper end of the age-group.

Both children come from that section of the pupil population that enjoys writing, reads widely, and has adequate home support and encouragement. Both children, for their ages, are among the best overall writers we observed. Kerry, aged nine, is represented mainly by her work in the project, 'Ships', which took up the best part of a term. This project relied heavily upon secondary sources, and perhaps because of that there was no work with a directly expressive function (there was, however, a great deal of expressive talk). We have therefore supplemented the project work with another piece of Kerry's work. Cathy, aged fourteen, just beyond the age-group proper, is represented by her English work connected with two projects, 'Alone' and 'Groups', and by work in various subjects in the traditional secondary-school curriculum. This work was done in the first term of her third year in the secondary school, and represents the pinnacle of what might be expected from the ablest thirteen-year-old writers.

The English work in Cathy's class is structured round projects, although there are opportunities to take up individual themes. The 'Alone' project had its roots in a Nuffield Resources for Learning Project anthology, 'Alone', consisting of a collection of poems and pictures, and was supported by poems and stories drawn from other sources. Most of the material focused the pupils on their own preoccupations – self-identity, relationships with the family and the peer group. The pupils mostly worked in small groups, the teacher supporting each as the occasion demanded. Each group had some work-card assignments. There was much reading, talk and writing. The range of writing tasks was a wide one, and in addition each pupil was expected to compile an anthology drawn from established literature and the writing of other pupils. 'Groups' was a similar project, but did not draw so heavily on personal knowledge and personal exploration.

1. Kerry

Example **a** is a piece of occasional writing; the rest of the examples, **b** to **h**, are from work on the project about ships (Context 5).

a *Function: expressive*

The visit
I was waiting anxiously to see the Wall's house (that was the name of the people we were going to) and at last dad halted to a stop. Jillian and Roger Wall, and Mrs Wall, were waiting at the door, and Jill ran out to me. She is a very pleasant girl with ginger hair and freckles, an image of her brother, well, he has freckles and ginger hair too. I carted a suitcase into the house up into Mrs Wall's (we call her Aunty Beral) bedroom. Jamy (his proper name, James) who is four was slightly shy but that didn't surprise me. When everyone and everything was in (including Simon) Jillian and me started playing but we were soon interepuded by a call, to say it was dinner time. It was a lovely dinner and I said so. Mrs Wall seemed very pleased as well she might be. Uncle Mike (Mr Wall) is a very comical man but also very pleasant. Jillian annoyed him slightly at dinner I think for she wanted to go to Bantek park and was annoyed when nearly all afternoon the boys (Ian and Peter) and Uncle Mick watched rugby and taped it. So it was late before we went. It was too late for Jamy to come out (much to his annoyance) but we really had a super time, well I did. We didn't go to Bantock but to Treetok for Roger wanted to go there and Jillian wanted to go to Bantock but Roger won. I went on nearly everything and half of the time I played football with the boys, and I got yelled at by Peter for missing a goal or two, but girls aren't very good at football. The time simply flew and then we had to go home. Aunty Beral was looking after Simon. I was really whacked, but I watched telly for a bit until it was about nine o'clock. Then for an hour we played cards. It had been a most interesting day.

We learn a good deal about Kerry from the abundance of expressive signals, signals about her judgements of people, her reactions to what is taking place around her. The piece is as much a portrait of herself as it is the record of a visit. While the account follows the chronology of events, the selection depends upon what strikes her as significant. Experience comes to her as 'I', and is put before us in very much that spirit. She is to some extent, though, aware of the need to make available to her readers aspects of her private knowledge of who's who and what's what (see the bracketing) so that they can gain a foothold in her world.

b *Function: expressive/poetic*

The secret of the deep-sea wreck
Dawn breaks with a cool breeze, the sun gleaming strongly down onto a huge handsom house, 'Gwinline', a great clammer rose from the lawn, panting loudly a stubby dog ran exhausted after a group of boys, a great crowd of them. A deafening noise. Oh! What a terrible din. A elderly lady appeared at the door of 'Gwinline' come in boys dinner's ready. Pity I was enjoying myself, a noise rose up above the din, by see you this afternoon! A wiry boy separated himself from the crowd, curly ginger hair, and a football in his hands. Me better be going to Goodbye. A tiny fellow disappeared through the huge black gates. The lady was still standing. Nice fellows, Peter, weren't they. What's the tiny fellow called, oh you fall over him Mum, his names Gwen and that wiry fellow is Frank. Come on it's dinnertime. Well have you wondering what name the dog has got, his name is Shadow. The house is silent but not for long, Frank and, where was Gwen, Frank was bouncing his ball up the long track to the house, beautiful Gwenline. Peter looked out the window, Mum where is Gwen, Frank is there but – Gwen isn't. Golly Frank looked worried. Finish your breakfast cried Peter's mother. I have, by mum, I'm off! Where are you going, but Peter had gone. Frank looked worried, Frank what is wrong? Where is Gwen? Before he's dinner, Frank stutted, He went down on the beach, on a boat, I watched him. He disappeared, he is dead! He's dead, cried Peter, well i think he is sobbed Frank. Don't waste time with questions! They ran so fast they collasped on the beach exhausted. Can you swim, they both said. Yes! Like a nightmare, I must say! Down down and still down, lucky they were both good swimmers where is Gwen? Is he died or is he alive? Where is Gwen? Suddenly Peter who was leading, stood motionless at a sight, a great sight. A huge everlasting wreck. Don't stare, we are looking Gwen you know. Oh Golly where is Gwen. Gwen Gwen it was Gwen suddenly cried Frank, lying still in the wreck. It was. Without a word they made their way into the deserted wreck, fear gripped them. A noise made them tensed. Come on or you will get hurt, it was Gwen, Yes it was Gwen. A rough man behind him. Now for heavens sake shush! He put his finger across his mouth for a sign of silence. Go on

boy. A rough voice echoed. Keep you here, don't needa guard, nobody ever comes round ere. You won't have a nice time tomorrow, your father will be poor before you know, and if he ain't you shall die, I will hold you as hostage tomorrow, lad you going to be in trouble tomorrow. Do you hear. He grabbed Gwen by the collar and threw him roughly on the stone floor. I will go now. Leaving him unconsciously on the floor he left. Immediately Peter stepped forward, lucky he is unconscious, he hates swimming and we will have to swim. Lucky he's light too, said Frank. Up, up, to the surface. Gwen was safe. Suddenly a plice car roared past, he stopped it, trouble down there sergeant. I will deal with them thieves. Thanks kids, have a medal. What an adventure. Gwen is safe!

In presenting this kaleidoscope of imagined events, Kerry draws upon her experience of children's adventure stories, the stately home belongs to one genre, the policeman to another, and the rescue of one child by his friends is a frequent theme. When an author has to 'invent' events which have no counterpart in personal experience, he may turn, albeit unconsciously, to available models. Such a derivation per se does not undervalue the story; it becomes a stumbling block when the writer can merely imitate. Kerry does much more than this. The events tumble on top of one another in a series of cameos, and the writing is like an unpremeditated, expressive speech monologue, rapidly shifting from one picture to another as it comes to mind. If she had attempted to shape the narrative to make more of the episode, she might well have sacrificed some of the vitality gained through the expressive treatment.

c   *Function: expressive/poetic*

> *The shipwreck*
> The impatient waves
> lashing against the
> straining boat, the sky
> looking heavy with rain.
> Feet skuttling anxiously by on deck.
> Terrified, disaster has befallen us, torrents
> Of rain falls heavyly.
> The waves now pounding roughly against the swaying boat.
> Were done for, finished.
> Given up hope of every living!
> All hopes have gone.
> Brave minute boats, help is coming,

Through all the dangers of the sea, help is coming,
We're safe now, safe!
Out of danger now.
Help is on its way.
A miracle has come.
Safe, safe from the dangers of the sea.
Safe!

This has something of the same characteristics as the story; the same personal voice, the same impulsiveness, although here there is a greater attention to the shaping. The verse form is one contributing factor to that shift, because a discrete incident is more easily moulded into separate lines. This mechanical feature, while important, is not nearly so significant as the capacity of a poem to support implicitness in the context, a dynamic feature of which many writers in the eight- to ten-year-old age-range can put to good advantage. We can see Kerry doing just that in the last half of the poem.

d *Function: poetic*

> *The elegant mermaid*
> The elegant mermaid sitting on her throne,
> her locks of hair swaying behind her,
> Her tail coiled behind her.
> Her voice ringing like bells,
> Sweet and charming.
> But her eyes filled with evil.
> Death to all men who dare to enter her kingdom.
> The waves iridescent, rocking gently.
> Creatures jumping to attention at her orders.
> It's her kingdom!
> All hers!
> Every rock, every wave, is hers!
> every man is hers!

The shaping of the construct reaches its height with Kerry in this poem. The expressiveness of the previous pieces has here undergone a change, becoming part of the subtext of the poem, rather than part of the poem itself. It informs the pattern of feeling, but is not part of the texture.

e   *Sources: secondary – experience mediated by books; principle of organization: chronological; function: transactional*

Ships
Victory, a very famous ship, is the fifth ship of the Royal Navy to bear this name. The first Victory, launched in 1559, of 800 tons was the flagship of Sir John Hawkins at the defeat of the Spanish Armada in 1588. In 1778 France entered the war on the side of the American colonists and Victory was hurried to Portsmouth and in May she hoisted the flag of Admiral Keppel in command of the Channel Fleet. And Nelson soon left England, later Victory led his people into battle, but Victory was damaged, so very damaged she had to be towed to Gibralter to be repaired and soon with a crew on board she sailed for Portsmouth and soon she had battered sides and creaking masts. On December 22nd she arrived at Sheerness and here she had the proudest flag she was ever priveleged to wear.

The difficulty of restructuring material gleaned from books, which in her notes is probably not much more than a collection of data, is not one she can easily overcome. One ready-made principle is that events occur successively in time. To this principle she remains faithful, which gives the report a certain overall coherence. Still, certain details obtrude – how and why Keppel gives way to Nelson remains a mystery; what flag is 'prouder' than Admiral Keppel's is left unexplained.

f   *Sources: secondary – experience mediated by books; principle of organization: classificatory; function: transactional*

A powerboat is made from fibreglass, its heavyier at the back than the front. The shape of the ship enables it to move. It skiddes across the water. Once they had a powerboat race. They started at Portsmouth. The sampan is like a floating market, it is a flat boat and it is moved by a pole. The pole is stuck in the ground under the water and above the water the boat moves. It is like a floating market with about five boats (sampans) moving along the water with food stored in the boat. It is a lovely sight! Aircraft carrier is a ship that carrys aircraft. It is made from steel. It has a jetty leaning out from the side. A river barge is transport for Africa. The bottom of the river barge is wood. The other parts are steel. It takes people across rivers. It is a good transport. It is build like a raft. It carrys oil. A passanger liner carrys passengers. It is made of steel. It is a very tall ship. A racing yacht has a huge sail. Well two huge sails. It billows out in the wind. The racing yacht is made of fibreglass or wood.

In structuring this information which has no chronological sequence she is at a loss. Here the problem lies in not being able to make generalizations which impose an order, and make the selection of critical details possible. Without such generalizations, a random collection of data can become nothing else. With Kerry, as with most writers of her age, the problem is almost insuperable in extended composition. She has no difficulty in giving relevant answers when the questions on a work-card structure the inform-ation for her.

g   *Sources: part (i) secondary – experience mediated by books; principles of organization: part (i) chronological and classificatory; function: part (i) transactional, part (ii) poetic*

Old Father Thames
i   Queen Elizabeth's palace was at Greenwich, she was often to be seen in her royal barge as she travelled from Whitehall. Charles II was a keen sailor, he soon started a fashion, by having a yacht for racing, a pretty thing, says Pepys.
Gilded barges were for the King and Queen, they carried the Queen and King. Merchant ships carryed cargo. Light skiffs carrys one passenger. Wherries are used for taking passengers across and round the river, a rowing boat. Slow barges were loaded with coal and grain. Racing hoys are speedy little ships, Charles II liked racing and so they had these racing hoys. Queen Elizabeth I and Charles II were often seen by the river. The river was like a road because they liked the river. They had to go by river for Whitehall was on the river and they went there a lot.
ii   More nearer the sea the larger ships were seen, sovereign of the sea, great barges and so on. A ship would be used as a taxi. The buildings tower-ing up, our small little wherry straining, pushing her way to safety. The engine rumbling away, the waves lapping gently against my boat, the boat floating swiftly across the water, night is here, lights vanishing, one by one. The lamps gleaming, like cats eyes on the peaceful water. All is silent. Every-thing is motionless.
Silence follows.

Kerry's difficulties illustrated in **e** and **f** are shown clearly in this piece. She begins with the marshalling of material in a chronological order. She then shifts to a classificatory principle. Neither principle carries her very far. Then, in part **ii** she shifts altogether to make a poetic construct of a high order. It is difficult to believe that the same writer is responsible for the piece as a whole. This example dramatically illustrates the strength and weakness of the nine-year-old writer.

h *Sources: primary – her own standards of moral behaviour; and secondary – experience mediated by books; principle of organization: classificatory; function: transactional*

Wreckers
It is not right to say Wreckers are in the wrong. For if you had a choice, let your children die or steal. And I don't mean hunger, I mean starving. So they have a difficult decision. So they row out to a lighthouse and signal a false alarm, so that the ship walks into danger instead into a safe harbour. And the people who don't die and drown in the terrible waters are killed. The ship is smashed against the rocks and all the goods are thrown out. They kill the survivors for they would tell the police about the disaster of the ship and crew.

It is beyond her powers at the age of nine to sustain an explicit argument for more than an utterance or two. It is a much later stage in the thinking and writing of children which would allow a detailed, explicit argument such as the following:

It is not right to say that wreckers are in the wrong. Given that a parent is responsible for the well-being of his children, and given that he has no means of support, so that his children starve, it is perfectly understandable that the parent – in this case, a wrecker – should steal, even though stealing is wrong. If you believe that it is a greater sin to let one's children starve than to steal in order to feed them – I feel this way – then one can condone the theft.

2. Cathy

a *Private writing: diary entry (concurrent with work on 'Alone' project); function: expressive*

Dear Diary,
I often wonder why I am two people, when really I am only one . . . Today, when I woke in the morning I was angry and snappy, and acted like a two year old. I don't know why. Perhaps it is because I am at the most difficult stage of growing up, as at times I am quite capable of being a sensible and responsible teenager. At school I felt slightly better, but as always I had the feeling of being inferior to the other girls. They still appear so childish to me, although sometimes I am just the same and even worse, especially at home.

Life seemed dull and uninteresting in the morning, but later today I was full of new and good ideas about it. It might seem strange to you, but once at school I usually put on a happy and cheerful face, but you know, as well as I do, that I'm normally unhappy and depressed underneath. Why, oh why! I feel I want to escape from myself, to start a new life, to move away from here, to know different people; I just can't understand myself . . .
This evening I went to a discotheque and I felt a completely different person. Not that tense, serious schoolgirl, but instead a lively and free teenager. I didn't care a damn about life, all I wanted to do was to be happy and independent. At home, I wanted to be part of the family, wishing never to be separated from them, but this evening I didn't care about them. Who wants them? They don't want me . . . I danced with various people as the loud music played. My friends were among the many people there but they seemed different, not the people I knew at school. Are they *all* two people?

The occasion is one for gentle, speculative rehearsal of the contradictions in the adolescent's stance towards herself and other people, towards school, home and the society of her peers. Cathy cannot resolve the contradictions by a mere determination to behave in one way or another – in order to sort out her behaviour she has to rehearse first what is at stake in a free-floating way. (If the sentiments appear mawkish to an adult, it is as well to remember that those who have passed through this phase of identity crisis can afford to take a tougher, more realistic, line.)

The audience provided by the silent and sympathetic ear of the diary – a kind of second self – enables this 'soul-searching' to be as honest as she can make it. Feeling and fact are inextricably intertwined, and they are presented as such. The writing thus has a powerful expressive core.

b   *'Alone' project; function: poetic*

Those first days
As we entered the heavy iron gates of my new boarding school I felt closed in like a lion in a cage . . . alone in the world. Then my mother left me I suddenly realised that I was really alone and not just thinking about it. I knew I had to make the best of my new life, but I wasn't at all certain of how to approach the girls, who seemed so different from my other friends. My first night was the worst . . . I felt so shy and afraid of the girls who seemed very uninterested in me. They weren't even prepared to show me how boarding school life should be led. As I lay on my hard, uncomfortable bed, waiting for the lights to be put out by the housemistress I looked out of the barred windows at the fading sky and the beautiful sunset which brought

back all my memories of my earlier days in Hong Kong . . . I was happy there, but now in the dismal dormitory I felt lonely and in despair. I had no support, no mother to give me comfort, but instead a new life to learn to lead in a place which I already hated.

.   .   .   .

Finally the lights went out . . . but I couldn't sleep . . . I watched the girls walk silently to each other beds wishing everyone good night, except me. A certain group caught my attention particularly . . . they were all sitting on the bed of the 'Head of the Dorm', called Jackie. She gave me the impression of a rather self-centred person, but the girl I liked least was Helen . . . she put on a kind and sweet front, but really underneath she was sly and stupid as I was yet to learn. I heard them whispering about me, saying how odd and difficult they thought I was. I was upset then, but now I know they were really speaking the truth.
At last they went to sleep and I was left alone, lying awake, watching them, as they moved restlessly in their beds. The room was damp and I shivered, not only because of the cold, but probably because I was nervous and tired. It had been a long day and I learnt several new ways to look at life. I had found out that I enjoyed being by myself sometimes and I thought about the weeks ahead of me when I would have to share my life all the time with other people who hated me. I would have no privacy, the girls would always know what I was doing and I would always be 'alone' in myself, with no one to confer with.

This piece has an autobiographical root, a brief spell in a boarding school when the writer was eleven. In turning back to those events she perceives them afresh in her present framework, which promotes the incidents of isolation and insecurity above those of excitement and challenge.

It is in this sense a one-sided recall, an adolescent's view of what was then taking place, and of what is relevant in those events to present concerns. This supposes that the author is telling the truth. It is equally likely that this is not so – that remembered events are often falsified in the details, in the overall pattern of feeling, in order to update them, and shape the piece into an ordered whole. Our impression is that Cathy the adolescent and Cathy the writer, are equally involved. It is autobiography with a poetic function.

c   *'Alone' project; function: poetic*

The final visit
The journey was long and tiring, and as the luxury coach continued, the winding country lanes, and swaying cornfields, which had at first been a joy

to me, were making me dizzy with depression. The previous train journey had been bad enough, but this was even worse as it seemed I would never reach my destination – Wintleborough.

At last the bus turned into the small but pleasant village and it dropped me off outside a rather battered old post office . . . the street was deserted with the exception of a dowdy looking pensioner, who hobbled helplessly along the pebbled pavement. I didn't know which way to go . . . I couldn't remember where the 'home' was, as I had only visited it once before. I cautiously walked up to him and asked him if he knew, but he was deaf so it didn't help at all.

    .   .   .   .

Finally after walking around for an hour or so, I found a signpost pointing to the 'home'. At last I cheered up . . . I was happy and the thought of the prospect of being under a roof was bliss. The rough pathway to the home was stoney and uncomfortable as my thin soled shoes crunched over them . . . I now remembered my previous visit and as I saw the large authoritative building looming ahead of me I clearly memorised the day that I had been before . . . It had been hot, with a most beautiful sun in the deep blue sky but now it was winter and it was cold . . .

I marched through the frightening iron gates . . . I don't know why but 'iron wrought gates' give me the impression that any building with is like a prison. I wasn't far wrong where this establishment was concerned . . it was a miserable place.

I rang the bell at the entrance of the house, and the two large doors flung open soon after, bringing me face to face with a stern looking matron. I explained carefully to her about my business there and after a long ordeal she eventually remembered who I was. I was shown to a waiting room where I sat for quite a time. Nobody else seemed to be there and I felt a slight chill about the whole atmosphere. A grandfather clock stood in the corner of the room and every quarter hour it chimed in a low depressing tone. I watched every minute pass with slow industry and I became more and more nervous as the time ticked on.

At last I was collected by a beautiful nurse with most lovely legs I have ever seen. I felt so sorry for her to be captured in such a career, especially in that old, outdated building. She took me quickly to a small dark room at the end of a corridor which was cold and poorly lit. Then she opened a door with a sign on it saying 'critical'. A man lay in a special bed, covered in blankets – he was my father, an old man with a haggered face, wild and glassy eyes deeply set under his eyebrows. Naturally he didn't recognise me, and I found it difficult to visualise him as the man I was brought up by. He had changed so much and he lay on his bed staring madly at the ceiling . . . I didn't know where to look – I had never seen a human being in such a mentally deficient state. His mouth lay agape and he kept making sucking noises with his tongue. When I inquired about him the nurse told me that he hadn't eaten for several hours – a certain sign of death . . . she seemed very concerned about him and I could see she was quite attached to him, after the many years of difficulty with him. I tried speaking to him, but he didn't even notice I was there, so after kissing him on the forehead and saying goodbye I left. The visit was short and sweet and I felt like leaving it that way. I had had enough for one day, so I entered the fresh air again and started my struggle back to the village. Before I was half way down the path, I heard a shout coming from the house and I saw the nurse running towards me.

I knew at once what had happened and as she broke the news to me my thoughts were far away. I didn't wait for more explanations . . . I just walked on, holding my head high and lifting my feet correctly. It all seemed so sudden and yet I was still to realise the true facts. Then, I thought it was only a dream, but now I know that it was my last visit. I ran into the wind.

Here the relationship between what has happened to the writer and what is constructed in the piece as experience is much more problematic than in the last piece. Indeed, that may no longer be a central concern. Cathy has entered into the task of composing a story, in which the 'I' referring personally, has been transmuted to an 'I' of a persona. While the distinction between real happenings and constructed happenings is difficult to draw at every point, this piece has moved into the realms of what Langer calls 'virtual experience'.

The story contains what we might call the 'full and relevant' picture. Events are detailed from both the writer's point of view (all that is necessary for the making of significant patterns is here) and the reader's (all that is necessary for the reader to grasp the context is considered). The 'I' in part stands outside the events – a commentator, reflecting upon the significance of what is happening. (It would put too strong an emphasis on this aspect to call it an arbitrary device, since it is absolutely controlled and appropriate and there are no fracture lines.) This gives to the events a richness of texture unusually compelling.

d *'Alone' project; function: poetic*

> *Alone on the beach*
> Sand . . . miles of it,
> Warm and soft.

Water . . . fathoms of it,
Sharp and cold.
Sun . . . streaks of it.
Tempting and bright.
Man . . . feet of it,
Flabby and white.

This, in our view, is a complete making, and needs no further comment. It stands as a poem in its own right.

e '*Alone*' *project; principle of organization: classificatory; function: expressive/transactional*

Can we live without people?
When the day has been hard and tiring, when people have been cruel and nasty, when I myself have been irritable and unknowing I feel like dying . . . sometimes I think that I really could die, just to get away from the system of the world . . . I feel that all my trouble would be solved then . . . no more would I be happy, no more would I be depressed and no more would I feel alone . . . I would be dead – a negative body in the earth . . . I would do all this just to be away from other people when I 'hate' them.
Although I often feel that other people are a hindrance to me, I know at times of relief from depression, that I need them more than ever. I want to find somebody to talk to, I need someone to help me sort out my life of tangles and muddles. I do not endure or enjoy sympathy as I am a very hard person, but I do need other people to help me, when I feel I can go on no more. I am not the only victim here . . . everyone needs other humans or animals to confide in and trust in.

This is the beginnings of an analysis of the social needs of a human being still very much tied to the here and now of her own social predicament, her own feelings and needs. She recognizes she is not unique in needing other people, but it can hardly be said that she argues towards this. It is very much the case of the individual presenting an analysis of the personal which has to be conceived by the reader as representative. Risking herself with her audience in this open way is perhaps all that could be expected of her – indeed, the honesty of personal truth is often preferable to the sometimes empty tautologies of a sociological argument which pays scant attention to what loneliness and conflict are really like.

f *'Groups' project; principle of organization: classificatory; function: transactional*

Young, gifted and black (the brackets show Cathy's crossings out)
Today the white people hate the blacks and vice versa. We look on the blacks as though they were people from a different planet. Many of us feel that they shouldn't belong in the world, and therefore exclude them from national games and decisions. If this is the situation it proves that many blacks are much nicer and better than any of us . . . a race which can be trodden on! This is twentieth century and people have progressed so much in the past ten years, by inventing new machines and discovering several (new) good necesities of life, (but) that if all that it has bought us such things as more racial discrimination I consider all these great and marvelous machines a waste.
In the 'future' people might be more concerned with the peace of (people) the races, instead of making luxurious comforts of life which aren't really necessary anyway. A pill to turn black people white might be used if we can't accept that whatever the colour, we are all equal. These pills will make the blacks look a sallow white, (but if this will) and although it won't be very attractive it might help to make the world a peaceful race.

Whereas **e** is pursued from the personal standpoint, this is an attempt to write from a more representative position. This movement away from the personal in an area in which strong personal feelings are involved is very difficult for even as accomplished a writer as Cathy. What, for example, is the explicit argument? Impassioned as the writing is, it is probable that she is not clear on this. Given that there is a conflict situation in which tolerance, understanding or reflection is involved, and one in which she wishes to support one side, what realistic solutions can she propose? The actual solution she proposes we can hardly take seriously – we suppose she does. Given that she had both of these aspects clear, would she have been able to present them in a completely coherent statement? The conditions for this happening do not exist independently of the previous two points. To work out your position is already to be half way to presenting it, and this piece can be considered as a first step to such a working out. There is the additional fact of being able to sustain in language a set of generalizations, relating one to another, and supporting them with examples, which remains a problem in all forms of writing when attempting to classify. This problem reaches a height of difficulty when you are not sure what your position is.

This kind of writing, in the area of personal opinion and commitment, is very difficult to carry out successfully.

g *History; sources: secondary – books and lessons based on books; principle of organization: chronological; function, transactional*

Martin Luther

Martin Luther was born on the 10th November, in 1483, in a small town called Mohra. His parents were poor peasants, but they decided to name Martin after a famous Saint, when he was baptized in the church of St Peters. His father Hans was hoping to find work in the local copper mines but he wasn't very successful so a year later he took his wife and child to Mansfeld, where he wanted a worthwhile job, preferably self managed. Luckily he went into partnership and after seven years he was elected town counciller. A very good and high position! Because of this and his business Hans bought in quite a good pay every week, which made the Luther family reasonably wealthy. They needed to be though as they were a family of eight altogether, which was a large number of mouths to feed. Martin went to school in Mansfeld, where he learnt to read and write thoroughly. Even at that age he appeared quite a bright boy. At the age of fourteen he was sent to school in Magdeburg . . . it was a monks school so, therefore, very religious. He had a special gift for music and he earned his board by joining the choir and going from house to house, singing to earn money. People were quite generous and this kept Luther going . . .

In 1525 he was married and thereafter he spent his life in solid isolation living in several castles as time went by. While he was staying at Wartburg he began and completed the German translation of the Bible and revised it over twenty-five years. As the Bible was originally Greek this was a great achievement. It was a Vulgre edition – approved by the Roman Catholic Church.

In July 1543 Luther was sixty . . . he now had six children and with two of them he returned to his birthplace, Eisleben. When he arrived there in 1546 he was very tired and had obviously found the journey too much for him as he fell to the ground and died.

This extract is from a piece twenty-four pages long, with many illustrations. The length of the piece, the writer's persistence in carrying it through from beginning to end, may indicate either that the author is very attracted to the story of Martin Luther, or that she is very concerned to show the teacher what she knows. Whichever it is, it is clear that the writer is in command of the material. In this function, she can make use of all she has learnt in the many narratives she has written in the past, probably mostly reports on her own actions and life. The shift here to another's life, remote in time and space, is probably for her only a shift in memory. To marshal together the necessary 'facts', to hold them together in the required order, to be able to summon the little details at will – all this points to persistence and a retentive memory. If you have those, and are not concerned to evaluate the *significance* of one period in a man's life as against another, then the facts of a man's progression through time determines the sequence of events as reported.

Quite a different kind of report, still depending upon a chronological principle, is this typical example of writing up an experiment.

h   *Chemistry; sources: primary – observations; principle of organization: chronological; function: transactional*

Experiment to find out what pigments are present in spinach
The spinach was cut into small pieces and then ground with some acetone, with a mortar and pestle. Water wasn't used to be ground with the spinach, because the pigments in spinach are insoluble in water. A piece of filter paper with a thin slit cut in it was then placed on top of an evaporating dish with acetone in it. The paper from the slip had not been cut off completely, but was still attached to the filter paper so that it could bend back and reach the acetone in the evaporating dish. Four drops of the spinach solution was then added to the centre of the filter paper with a dropping pipette. Then it was watched for the results while the acetone soaked up the spinach solution to make it spread.
Results: One of the pigments in spinach is green which is chlorophyll and the other is yellow called xanthophyll.

The fact that this is recipe writing – the singular focus on the passive voice, which suggests that the writer is a detached, objective observer – carries with it an implication that the writer is engaged in presenting what *typically happens*, rather than *what happened*. That is to say, to report the succession of individual events as though they were unique is to do something different from reporting a set of events one ought to expect. If experiments are to have validity, we are told, then they must be repeatable.

i *Geography; sources: secondary – books and lessons based on books, and pictorial illustration; principle of organization: classificatory; function: transactional*

A village in India
Thaticara is a small village, situated near marshy land, south to south-west of Delhi. The main way of reaching it is by a rough cart track which seems very primitive.

The land. Most of the land is very flat. After the monsoons the land is marshy in the crop fields and extremely muddy in the hotter season, spring. The land is very dry, usually of a reddish colour and bushes and trees look dehydrated.

The village itself is very strange, compared to our well civilised establishments, with its white-washed houses often built of mud bricks and sometimes stone, clustered together along the numerous narrow lanes. The majority of the houses are very small with few windows and rooves of reeds, bamboo or straw thatched into a sloping style. The village walls are reasonably high and are also made of dried mud and painted in white to reflect the hot sun.

Farmwork and crops. Many of the peasants cling to their old habits and will not change them, but it is really the lack of money that keeps their farming methods very primitive. Both men and women work in the fields, but it usually is the men who use tools like pickaxes to turn the dry ground, over and over, to prepare it for farming. These 'pickaxes' are equivalent to our spades, but look much more useful.

The material organized here is in itself atemporal; the writer cannot depend, therefore, on any natural order of succession in time to sequence the material. The chief determinant is the headings, which guide her choice of the relevant. The material under each heading is not put together in a haphazard sequence. Each separate paragraph starts with a low-level generalization, to which the following generalized descriptions relate. The relationship, though, is not a tight one, and the presence of the generalization is perhaps more to do with finding a sequence than with making a major claim which she then proceeds to justify. The writer finds it possible, and appropriate, to present the reader explicitly with her judgements. This personal foothold should not be underrated when pupils are in the process of making unfamiliar material part of their own repertoire.

j *History; sources: secondary – books and lessons based on books; principle of organization: predominantly classificatory; function: transactional*

Spain and her attitude towards the Reformation

The foundation of the Jesuit order by Ignatius Loyola, a Spanish knight from Navarre was the first real Catholic attack on the Protestants, and because of it the Counter Reformation was strengthened. The first great leader of the Counter Reformation was also a Spaniard, King Phillip II (1556–98), the ruler of Spain, her colonies and possessions in Europe. He spent his reign attempting to suppress Protestantism.

At home he forced the Moslems living in Spain to become Roman Catholics, and put down their revolt cruelly. They were finally expelled in 160 . . . Philip made great use of the Inquisition which tortured heretics to bring them back to the Catholic Church.

For the first three years of his reign Philip was at war with France, but it was the revolt which broke out in the Netherlands in 1507, belonging to Spain, which brought the Spanish forces into Northern Europe and even threatened England. The war of the Netherlands was largely to prevent the Dutch becoming independent as they wished, but the Protestantism of the Northern Provinces brought religious conflict into the wars.

Bitter feelings developed between the two provinces and the North prevented ships reaching the old trading port of Antwerp which lost much of its trade to Amsterdam, and Rotterdam in the North. The Spanish Army of 20 000 men, commanded by the Duke of Alva, defeated the provinces led by William the Silent, Prince of Orange.

This account deals with events at a higher level of generality than the last two pieces. The writer is now handling classes of events, and organizing them into a series of generalization–exemplification relationships. To do that, she has to move out of a chronological ordering of data, although the fact that she is dealing still with an historical period promotes the selection of generalizations according to their time sequence.

These last four examples relate very much to the world of school, to the subject areas determined by the teachers and the curriculum, in which the tasks are defined, and there is a continuous pressure to meet the demands of official learning. Within these subjects, containing bodies of knowledge which are publicly verifiable, what is available to the *writer* to make these impersonal collections part of his everyday knowledge, part of his repertoire as a person? To put that differently, how far can writing be seen to achieve for the writer a personal insight, a personal knowing, in which his feelings become relevant and engaged, and he begins to explore issues in relation to himself, whether as historian, geographer, scientist, etc? With Cathy, this happens predominantly when she is invited to imagine herself as a person experiencing events, to see the meeting of man and his environment from the inside, which for a purely transactional task she would have approached from the outside.

Letters to friends are usually expressive utterances but in this one Cathy uses the letter form to get inside what it was like to be an Elizabethan Puritan, and to present data for a transactional purpose. This imaginative excursion is certainly a tour de force, and our scheme of functional analysis is not a fine enough instrument to deal with the complicated and subtle twists and turns of a very accomplished writer.

k　*History; sources: books and herself; function: poetic*

A letter from an Elizabethan Puritan to a friend
Dear Francis,
It is many years since I last met you, and indeed many months since I last wrote. The days have gone by at a slow pace and several new developments have occurred here in England. I, as an Elizabethan Puritan, would be most thankful if I could tell you exactly what has happened.
It all really started some time last year when Queen Elizabeth introduced a new prayer book, written by the late Archbishop, Thomas Cranmer. This prayer book was all part of the 'New Act of Conformity'. Elizabeth was made the supreme governor of our church in England which is under Protestant ruling at present. This settlement and prayer book are not as extreme as those of Edward VI, a worthy sovereign of his time, but they foretell a great deal.
In 1540 I decided to join a group of men who were also members of the church of England and many like myself were clergymen. We were by no means the only members of our society as there were also laity, who are people who have not been ordained in priesthood. We are extreme Protestants, but our ideas are quite different from those of the Elizabethans. Our group came to be known as Puritans, as we still are called.
We Puritans have many new ideas about the ruling of the Church. We believe that every word in our Holy Bible is true, and every night I read it with a serious note of importance it means a great deal to me. Throughout our group we feel that we are the elect. We are the chosen people of God, and everyone else are sinners – they have no proper station in life as far as we are concerned . . .
We have several ideas about how the church should be run, but two of our

strongest beliefs are that clergy should be re-elected and there should be no Bishops. In each level we think that people should elect others to represent them in the church. Each parish church should elect and vote themselves for their own priest. Unfortunately the Queen, Elizabeth, thinks differently as she is of the Anglican church which is governed by the Bishops chosen in Parliament. Oh, I am sorry to inflict all this onto you, but our country is in such a sad state of affairs I have to tell someone.

We also want all the congregations of our country to be independent – instead of having the whole country as an elected council. Because of this we're known as the 'independents' or the 'Brownists'.

Some time ago Queen Elizabeth appointed a man named Whitgift as her new Archbishop. He hates us Puritans and with the Queen's instructions he began a persecution against us. In the year 1593 she got Parliament to pass a law that said that us Puritans could hold no further meetings in this country. If we did so then it means our deaths and I am so worried that I will be wrongly accused of calling together my fellow brethren.

My friend . . . what shall I do? All these troubles make me weaker, not only in the heart, but also in the brain. I need support, but how to get it. Alas . . . I do not know. My only chance of freedom is to flee to America to found a colony with my friends. Perhaps you would like to come too. If you did it would console my heart . . . My best wishes and blessings will be with you always. Awaiting your reply,

From a true and loyal friend,
Walter

A general pattern emerges from this comparison. Kerry writes in the expressive and poetic functions with proficiency and control. In the transactional function she has great difficulty, especially when she is required to organize material on a non-chronological principle. Cathy has consolidated what is already powerful in Kerry, and has made dramatic gains in all the transactional kinds of writing. Her remaining problem is with those assignments which demand the presentation of a balanced and supported argument on controversial political and social matters. We hope that this is a useful indication of what pupils can achieve at different stages in the middle years.

Mastering the technical aspects of writing

Progress in writing is largely achieved operationally – we learn to write by writing. To a considerable extent progress depends on the provision of a rich array of situations, some structured, others more informal, giving rise to many different writing tasks for a variety of purposes. While accepting this, many teachers feel concerned about their role in imparting elements in a language programme which seem to need a more direct, systematic approach.

For example, during a visit to a teachers' centre we were asked if a knowledge of grammar as a descriptive and analytic tool was beneficial in developing pupils' talking and writing in our age-range. All the evidence suggests that a conscious knowledge of the rules of grammar seems to be of no help in improving children's use of language.[8] Adults speak as if they knew these rules. They may not be using the grammar of standard English, but their sentences will be constructed according to the rules for English. Young children sometimes make errors in grammar because they do not know the adult form, or they have made a wrong deduction, but it is through experience of hearing and using language and not through instruction in the rules that they acquire the conventional forms. We must make pupils feel that their own language is an appropriate tool for learning. Dialect in itself does not inhibit progress; making a child feel uncomfortable in the educational context does.[9]

Grammatical errors, as opposed to the use of non-standard forms, usually occur in the writing of older children as a result of muddled thinking. If the content is made clear, the grammar will follow. It seems best, in the middle years of schooling, to concentrate on meaning and on experience of using language in different ways, and to leave the abstractions of formal language study until the sixth form. (A knowledge of grammar may be helpful in learning a foreign language but English should not be a service subject for other departments.)

However, broader language studies, including the consideration of why some ways of putting things are more powerful than others, why some kinds of language are appropriate in particular contexts, and the mastering of certain conventions in writing, learning to spell accurately and to punctuate, are a different matter. What is the place of this kind of learning and how can it best be achieved?

Turning to the first of these questions we need to remind ourselves what is involved in writing. The writing which is produced from a spectator-role orientation involves the integration of ideas and feelings in a very special way. We do not pretend to understand how the laws of the imagination work, but we are convinced that the individual is learning when engaged in this kind of activity. The various transactional kinds of writing seem to be organized at a more conscious level. Pupils are involved in a careful sorting out and sifting of information, in selecting from first-hand experience and secondary sources the relevant elements, and then in ordering the facts and ideas.

This organization of thoughts, ideas and his feelings about them is, in the first place, for the writer himself. Often a first draft achieves this for him. Having managed this, the writer has to get the fruits of his thinking down in a way that helps him share his insights with his reader. It is here he needs to consider how to phrase what he has to impart, and to be able to operate the conventions in spelling and punctuation. Of course, a writer's awareness of his audience has some bearing on this. A teacher and the pupils in a class can nearly always understand what an individual pupil means in his writing, however poor his control over the conventions. Thus their role in helping communication in school can be overplayed.[10] Generally, in writing – as opposed to speech where phrasing is evident – we need to help the audience, and the proper use of commas, colons, semi-colons, speech marks, apostrophes, paragraphing and parenthesis plays a part in conveying meaning. Thus the conventions must be firmly placed in a position of secondary importance in a writer's development. They are not what writing as a way of learning is about, but they have something to do with writing as communication.

Teachers face the challenge of teaching these conventions, giving them the emphasis they deserve without distracting the writer from the enormously important activity of organizing, shaping and articulating what he has to offer. The guidance here is based on what seems to work for many pupils and teachers, though we recognize the danger in trying to offer general rules. In the end teachers have to develop an approach for the pupils they work with.

Most teachers in the schools we visited based nearly all spelling work on the pupils' own writing, working mostly with individuals but also with groups and the class as a whole. Some in addition offered the children spelling lists. The question raised here is – can we be certain there is any transfer between rote learning and using the words correctly in written work in general? There may be some benefit in looking at groups of words with silent or with double letters or some other common feature. Teachers who like working with spelling lists may be interested in the comments of the Bullock Committee on two recent lists produced by the Scottish Council for Research in Education and the New Zealand Council for Educational Research.[11] The Scottish list was compiled after examining a large number of pieces of writing by pupils in the seven to twelve age-range, and aims to reflect the vocabulary most likely to be needed. The New Zealand list allows the pupil some choice in which words he learns, based on his own perception of what he needs for his writing.

The most useful word-lists are those pupils make themselves, gathering together words they find troublesome. Pupils will need some help in alphabetical ordering, and this can be linked to dictionary work. Younger pupils enjoy games which provide practice in this skill. The outcome might be their own dictionary.

Short bursts of blackboard work on a group or class basis, the learning of helpful hints and rhymes, exercises for pupils who have a particular spelling problem, the testing of pupils by each other, work showing the details of word structure and letter order and the learning of four or five basic spelling rules – all these have a place. Each teacher has to get the balance right. To spend large stretches of time working laboriously through the older type of spelling book, and in a great deal of testing is to give spelling a status it does not merit. However, it is quite clear that, apart from a few naturally able spellers, pupils need more than incidental help to become accurate. A great deal depends on the attitude of the learner. As Peter Medway points out, where pupils are unconvinced about the necessity of learning to spell, the effort of persuading them otherwise must be weighed against other priorities.[12]

Many of the points made about spelling apply also to punctuation. We would feel some concern in cases where much time was given to blackboard work followed up by many repetitive exercises unrelated to anything else the pupil was doing, or where the approach was too vague, aiming to 'deal with the conventions where the need arose', so that some pupils might miss the help they need. Many teachers keep a checklist of points to be covered, an idea supported by the Bullock Committee.[13] Although in mixed-ability groups not all points can be made on a class or even group basis, teachers should have some general aim for a particular year-group. Just as individual spelling books can be helpful, so can reference jotters where pupils can write in examples of speech marks, apostrophes and so on. These self-compiled reference jotters reinforce the idea that writers should concentrate first on the substance, checking spelling and punctuation afterwards.

Other matters come into the area broadly termed language study. We certainly want pupils to show increasingly over the middle years in their talk and writing that they are able to read thoughtfully and to understand. But is it necessary to take arbitrary passages for comprehension exercises? When pupils and teacher are reading a story or novel together, a discussion sharing insights and impressions can serve the same purpose, and develop the same capacities without seeming an imposed chore. Such discussion can sometimes be followed by writing about an issue arising from part of the story. Pupils can be asked why a certain passage seems to have made an impact, and how a writer has achieved a certain effect. See Context 9, and Context 10 in which some pupils ask one of their group about the 'wrought-iron bridge' image in his poem. This is the right kind of situation in which to take a closer look at the devices used by writers. Pupils at the upper end of the age-range may benefit from some of the units in *Language in Use*,[14] which indicate how language changes according to the context. Some teachers may prefer to seek out their own materials to show the power and subtlety of language. We observed some interesting work on a study of the language of the mass media when teacher and pupils had together collected the materials for discussion.

Many secondary and middle schools are recognizing that every teacher is concerned with pupils' talk and writing. They are the means by which pupils learn in every lesson. There is a strong case for a team approach to planning a language programme.[15] Teaching the conventions should not be exclusively the job of the English teacher. The teaching of, for example, paragraphing might be successfully tackled where pupils are structuring a science account or marshalling some evidence in topic work. The teacher might begin by explaining that it is helpful to reader and writer alike if each idea in an account is developed in a few sentences which relate to each other enough to justify being in a separate unit which we call a paragraph. While mastering paragraphing, pupils may be helped by making a plan of their account, developing each point into a paragraph. Here we are thinking of the more difficult kinds of writing with a transactional function – to argue a case or support a point of view. It is unlikely that poetic writing could benefit from such a plan and it might well be hindered.

Where teachers are working together, paragraphing work begun like this can be further developed in the English lesson, perhaps by relating it to using speech marks. Once speech marks have been taught, rather than involve pupils in repetitive exercises they might be given suggestions for their own stories which provide an invitation to use dialogue. This helps them to feel satisfied that they have mastered the convention.

It is important that pupils should understand that writing is much more than acquiring a set of rules about spelling and punctuation, but that these skills exist to help them get their message across clearly to others. Traditionally the technical aspects of writing have been the concern of the English teacher and even where teachers work as a team final responsibility still tends to reside here; it is the English teacher who co-ordinates what has been learnt and who makes a broad plan of what needs to be covered.

Finally, how should written work be received and should it be marked? While marking in grades seems unhelpful to pupils not yet thirteen (the demands of the examinations system make it necessary after this age), they certainly appreciate a response to their effort. Sometimes this will be in the form of a conversation, on other occasions a written comment of a constructive nature or, in the case of stories and poems, an expression of appreciation and enjoyment. The nature of the response will depend on the kind of audience the teacher or the peer group (for pupils like sometimes to write for their classmates) provides on any particular occasion. These matters are considered in some detail in the Schools Council Research Study, *The Development of Writing Abilities*.[16]

In the middle years age-range the important thing is that pupils should see the teacher not only in the role of an assessor but as someone concerned with their overall progress, who wants to share in their discoveries and difficulties, and who is willing to be a sympathetic sounding-board for developing ideas.

References and notes

1. ELIZABETH COOK, *The Ordinary and the Fabulous* (Cambridge University Press, 1971).
2. JAMES BRITTON, *Language and Learning* (Allen Lane, Penguin Press, 1970).
3. For a helpful though difficult explanation of the differences in the processes which lead on the one hand to a work of art, and on the other hand to the logical statement, see S. K. LANGER, *Mind: an Essay on Human Feeling*, Vol. I (Johns Hopkins Press, Baltimore, 1967), chapter 4, and *Feeling and Form* by the same author (Routledge & Kegan Paul, 1953).

4. For a consideration of the sense of audience in the school situation see JAMES BRITTON, et al., *The Development of Writing Abilities* (11–18), Schools Council Research Studies (Macmillan Education, 1976), chapter 8, pp. 116–37.

5. For a study of the interrelationships between dramatic improvisation and writing, see MARGARET MALLETT, 'Improvised drama and writing', *Speech and Drama*, **25** (Autumn 1976), 15–20.

6. NANCY MARTIN, 'Stages in progress in language', in JAMES BRITTON, ed., *Talking and Writing* (Methuen, 1967).

7. PETER MEDWAY, *From Information to Understanding* (Ward Lock Educational, 1976), a teacher's booklet produced by the Schools Council Writing Across the Curriculum 11–16 Project (1971–76).

8. For a summary of the evidence, see ANDREW WILKINSON, *The Foundations of Language* (Oxford University Press, 1971), chapter 1.

9. See B. B. BERNSTEIN, 'Education cannot compensate for society', in B. COSIN, ed., *School and Society* (Routledge & Kegan Paul, 1971), and W. L. LABOV, 'The logic of non-standard English', in F. WILLIAMS, ed., *Language and Poverty: Perspectives on a Theme* (Markham, Chicago, 1970), chapter 9, pp. 153–87.

10. See N. MARTIN and J. MULFORD, 'Spelling, etc.', in A. JONES and J. MULFORD, eds., *Children Using Language* (Oxford University Press, 1971), p. 157.

11. Department of Education and Science, *A Language for Life*, Report of Committee of Inquiry appointed by Secretary of State for Education and Science under Chairmanship of Sir Alan Bullock. [Bullock Report] (HMSO, 1975), chapter 11, para. 11.46.

12. PETER MEDWAY, 'Spelling', *The Times Educational Supplement*, 28 May 1976.

13. *A Language for Life*, chapter 11, para. 11.21.

14. PETER DOUGHTY, JOHN PEARCE and GEOFFREY THORNTON, *Language in Use* (Edward Arnold, 1971), teaching material from the Language in Use Project, part of the Schools Council Programme in Linguistics and English Teaching (1964–71).

15. For a powerful argument in favour of a team approach, see DOUGLAS BARNES, et al., *Language, the Learner and the School* (Penguin Books, 1969).

16. JAMES BRITTON, et al. (Macmillan Education, 1975).

V. Implications for the curriculum

We have looked at how some teachers foster the developing language abilities of their pupils and help them to learn through talking and writing. Here we pull together the view of language and learning running through the report, and consider some of the advantages and disadvantages of different patterns of organization with accounts of how six schools approach their tasks.

English in the curriculum

Language in the spectator role
Whenever we reflect back over experience, ruminating on what we think or feel, improvising and reshaping what has happened, we have taken up a spectator-role stance. The spectator-role perspective and its associated language spans the whole range of utterance from expressive to poetic and has traditionally been the special concern of the English teacher. Stories, poems, dialogues, dramatic improvisation, anecdotes and narratives articulating a wide range of thoughts and feelings on many different themes find a home in the English classroom. In other lessons pupils are often required to accommodate to other people's ideas and purposes and carry out fairly narrowly defined tasks. In English lessons concepts of relevance are wider. Considerable weight is attached to what the individual perceives as important – his ideas and feelings about himself, his friends and his world. English has also tended to offer some respite from the world of practical action; things are seen in a larger context and there is room for chewing over and digesting experience. This assimilatory activity is of particular importance to pupils just entering adolescence, a time of searching for identity and coming to see oneself in relation to others.

English work thrives on flexibility and spontaneity and there is a strong case for preserving the unity of language activities, so that talking, writing, listening and reading interlock, each enriching and raising the potential of the other (see Contexts 9 and 10). This is not to say that a teacher will never read pupils a story for its own sake without subsequent discussion or writing, or that something a pupil or the teacher has brought to the class cannot sometimes be a strong enough impetus into drama or writing without preliminary talk. However, we do feel some anxiety about timetabling which splits off different activities. There is no context called 'creative writing' and this reflects our concern at the emptiness of much that went on in such sessions. Pupils struggled to describe flickering candles, the noise of liquids poured from one container to another and the colours and shapes of sprouts, shells and so on. When the focus is not on meaningful experience and one kind of writing is split off from the rest of the learning programme, the outcome is often a tendency to focus on the text, the words and phrases, rather than on the experience that language clarifies and makes explicit. Fruitful starting points are needed; but these are not ends in themselves. They serve their purpose if they encourage looking back, giving shape to what was previously unformulated, making possible new integrations of thoughts and feelings. Often in these short writing periods pupils were diverted from the authentic patterning of their own insights in an effort to meet what they thought was the teacher's expectation – that their writing should be peppered with descriptive words and 'plum' phrases. Matching language and experience is a difficult task, perhaps never perfectly achieved by any of us; we should make sure the experience is worth the effort. In general, the variety and richness of life makes it a perfect reservoir for starting points for writing.

We favour the provision of fairly long stretches of time for English work, so that talking, listening, writing, reading and drama can flow together, playing complementary roles in children's learning. Some aspects of English work should be free from the constraints of topic work and integrated studies. Several primary schools set aside part of the school day to enjoy what had come up unexpectedly – reading a poem a child had found and liked in an anthology, sharing a story written by a pupil, discussing something important to a child. This is not to underestimate the potential of integrated studies as a setting for stories, poems and personal narratives. Some striking and satisfying work arose in this way, for example, Paul's tree poems at the end of Context 7.

In many schools topic and project work gave rise to a great variety of ways of looking, knowing and assimilating, but in general, we felt the spectator-role perspective was undervalued. Stories and poems are important for pupils in our age-range as ways of learning. The pupils whose work is presented in Context 5 were learning by writing poems about mermaids and ships as well as learning by writing about the structure of ships and setting out the hazards that beset sailors. Improvised drama, too, is a way of learning in every lesson. When spectator-role activities are recognized as the potent instruments of learning that they are, as special ways of assimilating, they will be given their rightful place in the curriculum.

Language across the curriculum

Talking, writing and reading[1] are the instruments by which pupils come to understand all school subjects, and every teacher should concern himself with pupils' progress in language abilities. Concepts of relevance are narrower in lessons other than English. Pupils must learn the appropriate ways to organize, use and articulate information. However, a child's concept of what constitutes a subject, what chemistry or history is about, develops only gradually. Pupils cannot take over complicated systems of thinking and writing outright. Those who appear to have done so are often found to have acquired only a superficial understanding. To say that the basic concepts of a subject must be acquired before we can become active in our learning is to misunderstand the process. The activeness of learning from the earliest stages is stressed in Piaget's well-known model. The learner accommodates his existing framework to take in new information while at the same time assimilating and modifying this new information to make it digestible. If an idea or piece of information is quite unlike anything which he has previously encountered he will need some help in understanding it. The teacher must act as mediator between pupil and information. 'Starting from where the pupil is' has become a tiresome cliché, but where else can we sensibly begin?

Too little is known about how pupils learn, particularly how they acquire scientific, non-commonsense concepts, and how commonsense and non-commonsense concepts interrelate. Spontaneous concepts tend to be acquired from concrete experience, developing from the specific to the general; scientific concepts, embedded in the formal work of the school, are immediately presented at a high level of generality and need to be mediated by speech so that they can match the corresponding spontaneous concepts.[2] If the gap between the scientific and spontaneous concepts is too great no amount of direct teaching will effect genuine understanding. Many of us, like the teacher in the example in Chapter II, have not been able to help pupils make the link between what they already know and what we want them to know. In view of the difficulty of assimilating new concepts, it is clearly unhelpful to oblige a young pupil, struggling with a new subject, to take over new kinds of language – the impersonal uses of language which are the mark of mature writers in, say, history or chemistry. As pupils get a foothold in the new learning they must be helped to write in the new modes and to develop the capacity to become 'readers' in the discipline. But the younger pupil needs to feel that his everyday thought and language are valid instruments in his learning. When facing new conceptual frameworks, new ways of selecting and processing information, pupils need to explore in a personal way. In Chapter III we pinpointed language with an expressive function, language with emphasis on the needs and preoccupations of the learner, as the most appropriate language for learning in the early stages; later the job of linking what we know already with what is new can be done in our heads. In Context 8 (page 77) the transcript shows an eleven-year-old boy doing this thinking out loud. The teacher's role is to create the conditions for learning – to be a sympathetic audience to ideas in development as well as an assessor of what has been acquired.

Pupils do not take over concepts like feudal, revolution, igneous, sedimentary and refraction after a brief explanation from someone who knows. The verbal definition is the starting-point, but it needs filling in with a multitude of specific examples, much reading of the word and those with which it connects in context, so that an impression of the new word's meaning is gained from the general linguistic context.[3] Above all it is through talking and writing to explain these new notions to ourselves that we come to understand them. Impersonal uses of language are difficult for most pupils in the middle years age-range. In Chapter IV examples of fourteen-year-old Cathy's writing show her becoming more at home in some of the transactional functions. But for most pupils it is through the personal uses of language that ideas and information are most accessible. In Context 12 this is recognized by the teachers in the integrated studies team. The pupils attempt some straightforward accounts about China's history, in some cases structured by work-cards, but alongside this there is a wealth of personal writing (see pages 113–16). These examples are potent means of assimilating ideas, of matching scientific and spontaneous concepts. Thus the approach of English, which puts a premium on the subjective, on personal exploration of a topic or idea, an approach which values feelings about what we encounter as well as thoughts and ideas, has a considerable contribution to make to all learning.[4]

Implications for practice

New learning is integrated with existing knowledge at the point of personal response.[5] Speculative, open talk – so strong a feature of the English classroom – can also be the means by which all lessons are infused with vitality and meaning. Writing can become a means of learning, of pulling together and using ideas, rather than an exercise 'to show we know'. The English teacher is particularly favourably placed to convince the other members of an integrated studies team that we use language to learn.

However, we believe there are aspects of the English lesson which cannot be easily encompassed in an integrated programme organized round a topic or theme, and some time should be provided for spectator-role activities of a less controlled kind. Successful English work is recognized not so much by its content, but by the degree to which it helps children become more perceptive about their own experience, more sensitive and imaginative in relating to other people's experience, more able to understand patterns of feelings and emotions, thoughts and ideas, and the degree to which it helps children give shape to all these in talk and writing. The English teacher is a mediator between pupils and a wealth of literature, and in choosing books the teacher is aware of what pupils bring to each stage of their learning. Important and irreplaceable as stories and poems are, there is an increasing and welcome use of photographs, film, interviews and outings as ways of coming to know and understand.

Teachers should work together to plan a comprehensive and imaginative language programme.[6] Together they should map out the structure and content of the learning for each term; decide how the key concepts can be presented and then developed by the pupil; become aware of what needs to be included as a central core of work for all pupils and where there might be opportunities for individual or group choice; and plan a policy for teaching the conventions of punctuation and spelling.

Content: choosing themes and topics

During the middle years of schooling, teachers and pupils are relatively free from the constraints of examination syllabuses. On what basis then is the choice of themes and topics made for children at different points of the age-range? English work has a more flexible content and structure than most other subjects – there is no interrelated hierarchy of concepts to be mastered as, for example, in mathematics. Teachers of English are really trying to encourage certain ways of knowing and interpreting the world. Thus any theme which has potential for laying bare the human condition, or for throwing light on the struggles of the individual in his particular world, is worth consideration. The teacher's knowledge of the pupils will be a factor in the choice, and once a theme is established others tend to arise from it, and the work achieves its own pattern, its own continuity. There is an abundance of social themes which can provide an organizing principle for talk, reading and writing. Lawrence Stenhouse[7] believes that for humanities work we should look to themes containing an element of controversy, helping pupils to develop an informed argument with support and evidence from a wide range of resources mediated by the teacher. It is also true that we need to consider topics in which the pupils have some emotional investment – such as the plight of animals, and relationships between the generations. Other possibilities favoured by English teachers include a look at the world of fantasy, at imaginary worlds, a study of different kinds of story, a focus on narrative poems and ballads or a reflective theme like 'Alone' (see Cathy's work in Chapter IV, page 196). Some topics will be short term, and the group may move quickly on to something else; at other times the teacher may sense she has hit on something worth developing over a longer period. Careful planning and thoughtful presentation of resources to keep pace with deepening interest are necessary. Much depends on the quality of pupil–teacher interaction, and on the teacher's capacity to point to the potential of a particular topic. While an overall plan is needed so that all pupils cover a common core of material, we do not recommend an inflexible approach and believe pupils should have some opportunity for making choices, and carrying through the work on their chosen topic.

When the English teacher spends some time with colleagues in the other humanities subjects, considering possible themes is a combined task, and the English teacher has to ensure that the topic chosen has potential for the reflective, speculative stance. Since Bruner's argument that 'a curriculum ought to be built around the great issues, principles and values that a society deems worthy of the continual concern of its members',[8] many lower-secondary schools and upper-middle schools choose a humanities topic centring on the broad theme of man and his environment. (See Chapter I, Contexts 11 and 12, and examples 4 and 5 at the end of this chapter.) These schools plan the basic content for each term, building up resource centres. This careful planning and anticipation of what pupils and teachers will need at each stage contributes to the success of the schemes.

Classroom organization

An operational approach – you learn to argue a case, solve a problem, write a poem or story by doing it – puts the pupil at the heart of the learning situation. It is the pupil who must get into new information and relate it to existing networks of ideas, the pupil's standpoint which must be the springboard to progress. The teacher creates the contexts for the learning and is a crucial part of the learning environment, but he is no longer the only source of wisdom. Sometimes the teacher will be dominant, he will want to address the class as a group and give formal talks and general instructions and guidance. In most projects, at primary or secondary level, there is a common core of information all the pupils need to encounter.

Then there are class discussions; in sharing anecdotes and views in Context 9 the teacher leads a discussion about a story he has read. But pupils can also learn from their peers in small discussion groups.[9] Some teachers doubt that their pupils would be able to work well in this way but we think that given a favourable environment pupils can over a period of time achieve the sort of dialogue that the group in Context 10 enjoy, where they ruminate so fruitfully on their own poems and stories. Clearly, this is not a question of short-term strategy, but it is the likely outcome where teachers work together over the long term to create the right kind of conditions for learning, and this includes creating a climate in which pupil–teacher interaction is mutually sympathetic and constructive. Some learning situations cannot come into being if the teacher feels he must always be dominant. He needs to see himself, too, as mediator between pupils and print, a guide, a provider of possibilities and a sympathetic audience to ideas in development. The tone of the letter from teacher to class in Context 4, commenting on the term's work suggests a partnership and promises the possibility of a dialogue between pupils and teacher. (Occasionally we found teachers writing for pupils, and the response of pupils was encouraging – it seems much more balanced that writing and talk should be a two-way activity in school.) In Chapter III (pages 148–60) we find teachers approaching learners skilfully and sensitively, avoiding a premature pressing of information, but by no means abdicating their role as teachers. Not all small-group talk situations yield immediate good results; pupils sometimes get entangled in circular arguments when left to their own devices and need the teacher's help in finding direction again. We note a teacher trying to help groups with difficulties in Context 12.

Small-group talk with or without a teacher is one approach with potential for making the remote accessible. Another way is through improvised drama. A look at Context 6 and the latter part of Chapter III should banish the myth that this kind of work degenerates into 'free expression', for here pupils and teacher are seen working with keen concentration and commitment.

It is a great pity that the outings, visits and practical work, so strong and wise a feature of the primary school, fall off or disappear completely in the secondary years. Keeping in touch with the outside environment lessens the gap which so many pupils perceive between school work and 'real life'. We find the young pupils in Context 2 talking to residents of the village they are studying. Some secondary schools encourage this way of learning and the results are promising. Pupils are more willing to organize, assess and share information they have had such an immediate part in collecting. It is the way to come to understand that certain kinds of information are best presented in an economical way, giving each fact its relevant status. Naturally, for older pupils out of classroom ventures would herald more focused work. Collecting work in the field also creates the perfect context for different groups and individuals to report back to the others, answer questions, proffer theories and modify them in the light of a teacher's or pupil's comment. While making progress in systematic study, pupils can write their personal accounts and impressions alongside the impersonal. These are complementary ways of understanding at any level. Indeed we have not always managed to help student teachers get a personal foothold in the theoretical knowledge which should inform practice. There has sometimes been the same splitting off of personal approaches that we regret at school level. We need to relate the observations they bring back from their forays into the classroom to the theories which seem helpful, and we should welcome a tentative, speculative approach.[10]

The primary school

The eight-year-old is at home with many forms of the spoken language and will hopefully have made some headway in learning to read. Most pupils will be able to get some of their thoughts down in writing. These early efforts will resemble talk, they will be expressive in that they will serve the needs of the learner, setting down his developing notions, rather than those either of the reader, or of the objective demands of the topic.

In the junior-school years we hope the pupil will take a firmer hold on his environment and use his talk and writing both to learn and to share what he has learned. Experience and activities in the participant role will mingle with spectator-role activities. 'They mingle because experiences, individual or communal, may be followed up in either role, and because activity in one role may spark off activity in the other.'[11]

This intermingling may be found in the project work characteristic of the primary school. In Context 2 we find expressive accounts in the participant role (how the ladies in the kippering yard prepare the fish), and a wealth of writing in the spectator role (Michael's reconstruction of a battle in the castle not far from the village). Everything is to be gained from this fluidity between ways of looking which comes naturally where teachers have responsibility for all areas of learning.

The primary school provides such a good opportunity for harmony and unity in learning that it is a pity that some schools tend to cut off some elements, often 'creative', 'intensive' or 'imaginative' writing, from the rest of the programme, with the consequent danger of contrivance and the engineering of starting-points away from meaning and interest (see earlier in this chapter and Chapter IV, pages 171–81). Far more promising is the idea some schools are adopting, of preserving a stretch of time in which spectator-role activities run together.

Connie and Harold Rosen point to the potential of the primary school as a bridge between the pre-school years and the secondary stage, and the difficulties in recommending any particular way of organizing the curriculum.

It is the scale of most primary schools which is potentially their greatest advantage. They can be almost domestic in their ways of living and so become a very satisfactory transition from private to public for young children. For its own purposes the primary school can have the best of both worlds, both the warm intimacy and also the promise of new explorations, both the welcoming acceptance and also the wider circle of others. To say that a school has an integrated day tells us nothing about this. At any rate it tells us very little about the particular world being established, how the people in it talk to one another, the messages they send and how they are received, and what is distinctive about the adult's voice when it enters the conversation.[12]

We have tried to capture something of the atmosphere of the primary schools we observed in Chapter I. We agree that there is no blueprint for practice and that it is the quality of the relationships between people in a school which counts most. We can, however, make some general comments about what seems to us promising practice. For instance, it is not helpful for teachers or schools to think of their approach as 'formal' or 'progressive'. It seems much more constructive to consider and plan each learning situation according to our understanding of how pupils learn. Sometimes a structured situation will be needed, the teacher will rightly want to impart knowledge in a formal talk to the whole class, or to give careful guidance on the content or structure of an enterprise. Punctuation and spelling need to be tackled in a direct way but not given an unjustified emphasis. On other occasions the pupil benefits from having the initiative in deciding what he wants to do. In the last resort the pupil has to do the learning – and we have to convince him of the point of doing so. Learning and teaching are co-operative activities and the onus is on the primary school to make a good beginning. If pupils feel that English work is about mastering the conventions – then our emphasis has been wrong. The main achievement of the primary school is surely to send pupils forward with confidence in their ability to learn and make sense, to their own satisfaction, of what confronts them, to feel that their everyday language and thought are valid tools for learning.

The secondary school

The pupil entering a subject-based secondary school, with the emphasis on what is to be taught rather than on how the learner fares, may perceive a break in continuity in his learning. There are many different patterns of organization but there is a broad division between the subject-divided curriculum allotting short periods of about thirty-five minutes to each of eight lessons a day with some double periods, and an integrated programme, particularly for the lower-school pupils, in which several specialist teachers combine to study with the pupils a broad-based topic drawing on several areas of knowledge. Some schools integrate the creative arts – English, art, music, drama, dance and craft. Others combine English with social studies, history, geography and perhaps science. What are the implications of the different organizations for English and language work?

The main strength of the subject-centred curriculum for English is that the spectator-role activities are safeguarded. Time is set aside so that the pupils have opportunity for the talking, writing, reading and listening that make up an English diet. English lessons are freed from the bonds of a topic which may have been chosen for its potential in other subject areas in an integrated programme. However, one danger in a subject-centred programme is the tendency to split off the different aspects of English, so that literature, composition and so on are spread round the school week. A generous block of time for English makes it possible to harmonize all the spectator-role activities. Also, in a subject-centred curriculum, the role of language in all learning is often not recognized. English is frequently regarded as a 'service' subject for all departments on the assumption that the English specialist teaches language abilities which the pupils are then able to apply in other lessons. We believe, on the contrary, that talk and writing are a part of every subject and that every teacher needs to take some responsibility for their development.

In the lower-secondary school, pupils are increasingly offered an integrated programme of study in which specialists in history, geography and perhaps the social sciences, join with the English teacher to take a broad look at a theme or topic. It is difficult to generalize about these interdisciplinary programmes because they vary so greatly in their aims, teaching methods and achievements. Some pupils seem still to be doing conventional history and geography, and so on, and the only integrating factor is the topic itself. In other schemes the specialists, while being available for consultation on their subjects, teach every aspect at class and group level. The English element in such programmes lies in sanctioning expressive language on the grounds that it is the best way of tackling new learning, selecting poems and stories with some bearing on the general theme, and encouraging pupils to write their own stories, poems and personal narratives. By definition, integrated programmes offer the likelihood that teachers will get together and discuss the provision of a rich and varied programme of language and learning situations. There is, potentially, more hope of securing a language policy across all subjects. The informed English teacher at least gets the chance to explain the uses of personal language in learning. In Contexts 11 and 12 we see these ideas being interpreted in a promising way.

The main difficulty with this sort of programme is that the story writing and the personal writing may be too firmly controlled – too much limited to the topic in hand. English lessons are the setting for hearing about things that have happened outside school, in the home, with friends or in the imagination. Children will talk and write about their experiences to savour and share them. Sometimes they need to go back over disturbing experiences to come to terms with them. Such needs may be impossible to meet in an integrated programme, no matter how good. Organizers of integrated schemes should consider reserving a generous block of time for English lessons as such.

The middle school

Most pupils become able to deal with a differentiated curriculum towards the upper end of the middle years, and potentially the middle school offers the ideal situation for continuity through that period of transition. In favourable circumstances a child would arrive at eight from a first school where much of the work has been experience-based to find that topic work and practical activity continued in the early years of the middle school, while the later years paved the way for more differentiated work, more stress on books and the objective demands of subjects. If primary and secondary schools worked together the same welcome continuity of programme could be achieved, but the middle school makes such co-operation easier and more likely. There are often feelings of separation and misunderstanding between primary and secondary teachers. On the one hand, secondary teachers sometimes complain that the primary school has not 'prepared' the pupils properly for the senior school. On the other hand, many primary-school teachers feel that the positive attitudes they have nurtured in their pupils will be lost in a secondary school which insists on pupils taking over styles of thinking and language which are beyond them. One of the greatest contributions of the informed middle school is its capacity to offer a programme in which pupils move gradually towards the more systematic and differentiated work. It is perhaps not insignificant that the child has an extra year in the infant school in which to get a firmer foothold in reading and writing. The larger size of the middle school makes more likely a generous provision of facilities, including a good library. We have, however, seen a great number of primary schools without elaborate facilities, offering an environment rich in experience, the intimate atmosphere more difficult to achieve in a larger school, and with a strong propensity to make imaginative use of whatever resources the school or the environment could offer. People make schools and much depends on the quality of the working relationship which pupils and teachers build together.

Patterns of language work in six schools

Each of the schools described is working, in its own way, towards the provision of a promising programme of language and learning. Our comments are based on our impressions at the time of our visits; we recognize that there will have been changes and developments since then.

Example 1 *An open-plan primary school providing an integrated curriculum made cohesive by teachers working as a team to plan and carry through each day's learning.*

This open-plan primary school caters for 280 infant and junior children. The children's families have a particularly rich and varied range of occupations, interests and life-styles. A close link is preserved between home and school by encouraging parents to come into school. Although they are free to walk around watching the various activities, they are also encouraged to assist in the work of the school by, for example, giving special help to small groups or to individual children, by providing extra practical help on school outings and by helping with the library or repairing books and equipment.

The design of the school, with its small 'home-bases' for each class opening out into larger shared 'resource' areas, creates a physical environment particularly conducive to the mingling of children and adults who are able, in the words of the headmaster in his account of the school for parents and visitors, 'to flow through the building with the minimum of fuss and noise'. Part of the day is spent with the class teacher in the 'home-base' or classroom. The furniture there is moveable and often dual-purpose so that, for example, there might be a display area, bookshelves and cupboards on one side of a unit and a chalkboard on the other. This provides considerable flexibility in how the home-base may be used – small bays can be created for group work and small areas curtained off if children want to read alone or hear a story read by the teacher. The contents of the home-base are frequently moved about the room to serve the changing needs of the children and teacher. While the children benefit greatly from their freedom to use all the space in the school, their teachers are aware of the need for a special place and particular adult to whom they can return at various points in the day. The headmaster comments in his account of the school: 'The one thing I have found it necessary to preserve – especially for the younger children – is the linking (at the beginning and ending of each day) of teachers to a particular group of children in a particular teaching space. We call this the home-base. It is here that a child begins his school day moving out from the security given by a trusted adult into the greater challenge of the school community. It is to this group that the child returns to listen to a story at home-time or perhaps to discuss the activities which will be attempted next day.'

Much of the day, however, is spent in the three large resource areas, one of which is the library, where the staff operate in teams, sharing their particular knowledge, skills and experience and making available to all the children in the school, rather than just to those who might be in their class, their particular strengths and interests. Where children are spread over several working areas, teachers are not tied to one age-group but can take a group of children who share an interest or who need special help. Teachers have noted that in exploring the school, children have become aware of what others can do, 'the ways materials behave, how books and equipment are handled, how facts and information can be recorded'. Although children have one teacher who cares for them the child–pupil ratio tends to be thought of as 2:80 or 3:120 rather than 1:40. From time to time the headmaster, peripatetic and part-time teachers and parents join the teaching teams, making the formation of relatively small groups with an adult possible when this is useful.

As might be expected, a school working on this basis has no formal time-table. A flexible structure for each day is planned by the teachers at a lunch-time meeting. The forecast for the following day is written down by each member of staff, and at the end of the day when her own group return to the home-base she discusses the plans with them. In assessing this way of working the headmaster says: 'These forecasts are invaluable. They mean that we are continually thinking in practical terms of the learning situations we are trying to create. We communicate . . . the curriculum is not written down but grows and develops daily.' (See the sample forecast sheet, Fig. 1.)

The forecast gives many clues about the way the school works and what its priorities are. There are no set break-times and the time of the following day's assembly is decided the previous day to fit in with the children's activities. Special thought is given to the needs of students who come into the school to work with the children as we see from the provision of a special column. There are broad headings such as 'Activities' for the early part of the morning, and 'Undifferentiated programme' which takes up the

DATE: 25 April	FORECAST	STUDENTS
ACTIVITIES Tutankhamun outing Prepare assembly Maths, stories and topics Assembly at 10.30		8.50–10.30
UNDIFFERENTIATED PROGRAMME		10.30–12.20
3rd year maths – Jeanne Bring candle	City girls – netball 4th and 3rd year groups – Rita Dragon pictures and story	Verna David W. Sarah Pat Jane Keith Julian Stephen Russell
Lorraine – movement? 1.30 Ring Davis Coaches	Roger – maths Jeanne's 3rd year maths Rita's Tuesday maths	1.40–3.15
DISCUSSIONS, STORY, POETRY Deborah Jane reading Jaques showing picture, reading Keith – reporter Darryl – picture Katy's poem Paul's writing Deborah – 'How the world began'		3.15–3.40

Fig. 1. A sample forecast sheet.
Planning sheets like this are used by each teacher daily. The main headings: 'Activities', 'Undifferentiated programme' and 'Discussions, story, poetry' are constant.

time until the lunch-break, and gives the broad sweep of time which allows for the free flowing of activities one into another. There is room for stories, poems and talk, the spectator-role activities which often, but not exclusively, take place at the end of the day when a class meet together. There are two things to point out here. First, it seems appropriate that children should be with the teacher who knows them best for these activities which so much depend on a sympathetic atmosphere. Secondly, it is interesting that this area of learning should be singled out. Could it be that these are the activities which are most in danger of being lost if special provision is not made for them?

An outline of what has been said and agreed at the planning meetings is recorded in a diary, but detailed notes on the development of teaching groups are not found to be a practical proposition. However, two ways of monitoring what is happening are encouraged: periodic checks of reading progress (Holborn scale); and preparing individual folders for the children each term containing typical samples of work – writing, number and art-work. These are date-stamped and can contribute to building up an educational history.

Here then is a primary school committed to the daily planning of activities for the children, activities which link from one day to the next in a sequence meaningful to both teachers and children. There is no feeling that any particular content must be explored in the junior-school years. The quality of work and the enthusiasm and involvement which accompany it are the priorities. Talk and writing arise out of the experiences of the day. The walls display pupils' writing and although poems and stories do arise out of project work, children also have the opportunity to write where the topic is not so firmly controlled. In this way an interesting and balanced programme is achieved.

Example 2 *A rural village primary school, providing large blocks of time for class, group and individual activities in which both individual interests and general themes may be explored.*

This small village school has ninety pupils from varied family backgrounds. There are three classes, the first for infants, the second for seven- and eight-year-olds and a third class for the nine-, ten- and eleven-year-old children. Apart from the three classrooms there is a hall, a garden and a small playground. Maximum advantage is taken of the school's natural surroundings which include a park, a lake and a wood, and the children spend a good deal of time outdoors. Many activities arise out of outings and nature walks, and much of the language work is based on these first-hand experiences. It is the third class which contains children in our age-range and most attention has been focused here. It is interesting to see how a class with almost three years between youngest and oldest can be catered for together. The teacher chooses themes and topics which can be followed up at many different levels. By offering the opportunity for individual work within a framework, there is scope both for the slower nine-year-old and the forward eleven-year-old. The teacher comments on how the varied learning situations are generated:

I find a sort of rhythm has developed itself running in four- to six-week periods. There is a period of stimulation, perhaps a day or two, perhaps a week, when certain experiences are provided – outside expeditions, or reading from books or watching films, talking or drama work, or most usually a combination of some or all of these. Then there is a discussion among us all, perhaps as one big unit, perhaps in smaller units, of the work that could arise to cover all aspects of the curriculum. Now that the children are accustomed to working in this way I find my role is not so much to supply the initial ideas, but rather to help them turn their own ideas to really good use and follow through and see extensions. What generally seems to happen is that the first follow-up work tends to be done in groups initiated by children or by me, but in any case supervised by me. After that it tends to go off into individual channels, or the groups re-sort themselves. During the day there is a definite flow – sometimes all the class will be together, then move out to groups of individual tasks, come together again, move away and so on.

Although the teacher arrives each day with a flexible plan, she doubts whether she has ever completed a day exactly as planned. To observe her is to understand this, for she works very much from what the children bring to the classroom.

The variety of classroom grouping gives many varied opportunities for talking. Often children will talk over new ideas in a group situation and then come together as a class, the teacher at this stage taking the opportunity to point out any possibilities that might otherwise be missed. A great deal of expressive, free-moving talk accompanies the many outings, and often when the children return they are quite ready to commit to paper some of the ideas and responses their experiences have thrown up. Experience is at the heart of this learning programme, and the experience is structured and ordered through talking, writing and art. The mechanical aspects find a place, and the children have a spelling test on a Friday. The words to be tested are, of course, those which have been a problem during the week. The teacher rightly believes that children must be helped to make their written language conform to accepted public standards, although she would agree that the mechanical aspects are not at the heart of the language programme. This is very much a 'talking' classroom and, as we note in Context 1, the teacher does not press the children to write but when they do their response is often lively.

As in the case of the school in Example 1, there is no formal timetable although times of radio programmes the children want to hear and times when the hall is free are noted. A retrospective account of a typical day is given in Fig. 2. The teacher felt that the very act of writing it down, for the purpose of this report, tends to give the impression that the learning activities are less integrated than actually they are.

This is an example of a primary school, very different from the first in terms of its situation and in the facilities it is able to offer, which manages to provide a sympathetic milieu for the learning of young children. It offers full and imaginative use of a particularly attractive and interesting environment rather than a roomy building with good facilities. Language and experience are firmly intertwined. Poems and stories arise frequently from outings but, as in the school in Example 1, the end of the day is often a time for teacher and children to enjoy a story together, or to read each other their own stories and poems (sometimes the teacher's), or perhaps to share

9.00 am	Registration (children may read or make corrections in their written work)
9.10 am	Assembly
9.38 am	Maths groups until about 10.10 Drift to: individual group activities reading groups Some children leave their groups a little early to make a start on their baking
10.25–10.40 am	Break
	Nature trail broadcast Follow-up of broadcast Drift to individual and group activities
11.56–1.15 pm	Lunch
	Time available for short visits to wood or lake Individual and group activities – some children go to another classroom for recorder practice
2.30–2.45 pm	Break
3.45 pm	Individual activities may continue, but the end part of the day if often the time when children and teacher together enjoy poems and stories, their own and other people's

Fig. 2. Account of a typical day.
Times are only approximate. Children may prefer to continue their activities during break.

an experience. There is no school library but the teacher has created a reading area in the classroom and made sure that books are displayed there. The children have a particularly rich and varied diet of literature and poetry, carefully selected to appeal to different interests and preoccupations. Often there are displays, drawing attention to books which link with some of the topics and activities of the week.

There seems to be a happy balance between pupil and teacher contributions, and between class, group and individual work, the teacher providing the broad framework and the pupils taking advantage of the considerable scope for individual initiative and personal choice.

Example 3 *A Midland middle school, making a gradual change from an undifferentiated curriculum for the younger children to a more structured curriculum for the older children.*

This seven-year-old open-plan building has operated as a middle school for 700 nine- to thirteen-year-old children for three years. Most of the children come from economically comfortable backgrounds. The primary schools from which they are drawn are in many cases rather formal in their approach, and it seems that the children must make some adjustment to the freer environment offered by the middle school. The twenty-five teachers were chosen by the headmaster when the school began, as people who could work together within the framework of the school. Most were previously either grammar-school or primary-school teachers

Each class of children has a home-base which opens out into larger working areas where resources are available and where the help of teachers other than the class or home-base teacher is available. (In this respect the school is not unlike the school in Example 1.) In addition there is a large library, a drama studio, music centre, a hall, gymnasium, French room, art room and science laboratories.

The children in the first two years, those who would otherwise have been in a primary school, follow an undifferentiated curriculum, while the older children work in a rather more structured way, tackling what are called 'bands' of study.

In the first two years the children work largely in the home-bases and the year units. The home-bases have 'corners', 'bays' and 'areas' for quiet reading and writing, craft, mathematics, library and display. The class teacher spends most of the time with her class, and at the beginning of the day she guides and advises each child in following his or her individual programme of work. The headteacher comments as follows in the school prospectus:

> Subjects and interest are integrated quite naturally as children work out their individual ideas. A child has time to follow a line of individual study in depth, even though it may take several days. He or she will explore mathematics, science, English, art, craft, music, geography, history, religion and social education without recognising the artificial barriers adults often mount. The form teacher will ensure that the child has a balanced diet. The timetable is interpreted very broadly, so that learning is a continuous process and not interrupted too frequently by artificial breaks.

Whether or not the barriers of which the headmaster speaks are artificial is a matter of continuing debate, but certainly it seems sound that the younger children should set off from this broad base, gradually being helped to see what might be appropriate in different subject areas.

Some work is done under the supervision of the class teacher alone, but much is done in conjunction with the other classes in the year-group (there are five in the first year and four in the second year), and here teams of teachers, each with a special expertise, help the children. As the work is planned on a day-to-day basis no timetable is available at the younger end of the school. However, it has been necessary to note times when each class may visit the hall, gymnasium and so on. The headmaster feels that one of the strongest features of the curriculum pattern he has implemented is that the entire building with all its facilities and adults with their various specialisms and interests are available most of the time to all of the pupils.

This integrated approach allows for individual choice and makes it more likely that the younger children will have the advantages they would have enjoyed in a good primary school, together with the added benefits of the wider range of facilities found in the middle school. This kind of curriculum organization has considerable potential for implementing good practice, but ultimately it depends on how far individual teachers are able to help children take up and extend the opportunities offered. Much depends on how teachers see their role in helping children's learning – whether they know how to allow for children's choice yet make sure the pupils understand the full possibilities involved in their choices, how to give opportunity for small-group talk yet know at what point intervention might be helpful, and how to mediate between pupils and the secondary sources which are so often a part of topic work. Where experienced and less experienced teachers work in teams there are good opportunities for teachers to learn from each other and a child is not restricted to one adult.

In this school the writing arising out of science and mathematics has a special vitality and this seems connected with the staff's appreciation that children must be allowed to explore such areas of knowledge expressively before they can achieve more distanced ways of looking. However, the humanities project work often seems to depend rather heavily on secondary sources. Sometimes the personal, expressive element seems lacking. This is not a problem peculiar to this school, it faces all schools giving pupils the opportunity to do their own research. It may be that a substantial part of the work of children under the age of twelve should arise out of first-hand experience. Where a topic can only be explored through secondary sources it seems that most pupils need to talk over the concepts in groups and with the teacher if they are to be able to evaluate and use what they find.

The staff feel some concern about what they call the 'creative' writing element in the children's work. Where broad-based topic work is the centre of the curriculum it does seem that reading and writing stories and poems often figures less strongly. The staff have tried to make available short periods for creative writing, but the danger of this arrangement, as pointed out earlier, lies in the risk of a rather contrived atmosphere. A better solution is that adopted by the two previous schools – providing a generous block of time for spectator-role activities, so that talking, reading and writing can flow together.

In the third year the children are faced by a rather more structured daily pattern, although the routine is very much less differentiated than many secondary schools. In both third and fourth years the children are divided into four unstreamed forms. Four major bands of study are followed – humanities, mathematics and science, creative arts and crafts and physical education. Each band has a team of teachers associated with the work of two forms. In the humanities band a broad theme is introduced and teacher and children discuss possible starting points, pupils choosing for themselves the way into the topic that appeals to them most. Each child discusses his expected work pattern with a member of the team before branching out on his own. Many resources – cine films, tape-recordings, books and so on – are available to the pupils, and teachers suggest these where they think they would be helpful. Some themes have led to interviewing people in the school or the neighbourhood with a specialist knowledge. When work on one of these major themes (the one just ending when the school was visited had focused on various aspects of the nineteenth century) comes to an end, the children usually make a display for the rest of the school. They also have an opportunity to tell others what they have found and read out to other groups pieces of writing of particular interest. These disseminatory activities give added point to the children's writing activity.

Unlike the younger forms, the third and fourth years follow a timetable. A typical day of a third-year class is shown in the timetable, Fig. 3. This shows how the older children are following a pattern somewhere between an undifferentiated and a subject-centred curriculum. Thus the children are able to prepare gradually for the subject-centred orientation of the secondary school which they join at thirteen, while continuing to enjoy the scope of broad-based work. The problem of dealing with secondary sources arises here as well as in the lower school, although by thirteen a child is rather more able to structure information from secondary sources than he was at nine. How to include the full range of spectator-role activity is not yet solved in the upper school although teachers seem aware of the difficulties and anxious to overcome them.

This is a school which has made a start on implementing a promising

Classes and class teacher	Morning break	Lunch break			
3 MN	Mathematics BS DR UD	Humanities MA MD MN	Art and craft periods 5 and 6 MN period 7 HD GE		
3 AR			PD		
3 PD	Physical education GT	Humanities JE PD	Mathematics BS DR NS	French AS	Humanities JE
3 UD	MN			Humanities AR JE	French AS

Fig. 3. A typical day for the third-year classes. (The initials show the teachers responsible for the classes and different areas of work.)

programme. Improvements are constantly being made as head and teachers get together to discuss problems and imperfections in the curriculum. The overall organization promises well for language opportunities, across the curriculum, and a minor adjustment in allocating a block of time for the less controlled aspects of spectator-role activity should safeguard the personal side of the pupils' development.

Example 4 *An inner-city secondary school, providing an integrated studies programme, safeguarding spectator-role activities which are not tied to the current themes and topics.*

The lower school of this large urban comprehensive school offers an integrated World Studies programme combining English, geography and history, and planned by the teachers involved. The other normal curriculum subjects are studied as self-contained units.

There are eight classes of first-year children (eleven- to twelve-year-olds) and eight classes of second-year children (twelve- to thirteen-year-olds), with about thirty pupils in each class. Together the two year-groups form the junior part of the school, the older children are housed in a separate building. Each year-group is divided into groups of four classes for the World Studies lectures given in the hall throughout Monday. Follow-up work spreads out over the week, mainly in individual classes. Since the four classes who share the Monday lectures are timetabled for follow-up work at the same time there is, theoretically, time for combined activities. Here staff are somewhat restricted because of the limitations of the building. Nevertheless, this is very much a team-teaching situation.

The organizing theme of the World Studies programme is 'Man and his environment'. This is broadly concerned with how man lives in widely differing geographical conditions in different parts of the world, and which factors are most potent in deciding how a people develops. The relatively formal lectures when the subject-matter for the week is provided by one teacher, are followed by the more intimate classroom lessons when teacher and pupils explore the ideas and information. Work-cards are used to give children a framework for some of their writing, and when the information is difficult for the children to understand, teachers spend a long time discussing with them how the ideas relate and how they might be best explained in a written account. Each teacher is free to conduct the follow-up work as he wishes, but there is general concern that teachers should mediate between the pupils and some of the more difficult concepts and ideas which the broad inquiry generates. Frequently it is suggested that pupils write a first-person account about people in a particular situation or predicament. Subject English ways of looking are seen as a way of helping pupils make sense of the work.

English is not restricted to the themes taken up in the World Studies programme. The staff appreciate that children will not always want to write poems, stories and personal accounts tied to these themes. Time is given for the reading, writing and expressive talk that is at the heart of English work. If a teacher wishes to spend some time on English work unrelated to the Monday lecture he has a substantial session in which to do so as the timetable shows in Fig. 4. It is not necessary to split the English activities into self-contained boxes as would be the case if a 35-minute period had been allocated. A workshop atmosphere can be organized, children moving easily from talking groups to individual writing and reading, the whole class meeting together at some stage to share what has been achieved. Often a group of children will tape-record a discussion, and play to the rest of the class what they consider to be the most interesting parts.

In many ways this is a most satisfactory way of organizing the timetable, for children benefit from the English element in the language across the curriculum activities, and get their fair share of less controlled spectator-role activity. Children passing from a modern primary school to a school operating this kind of curriculum suffer little feeling of discontinuity. Perhaps the most vulnerable element is the formal lecture which introduces the week's work. This way into a topic may discourage the less able children.

World Studies: four of the second-year classes meet with their class teachers in the hall for a lecture by one member of staff.
World Studies: each class returns to the classroom for follow-up work organized by each class teacher. Part of the time may be used for English work – poetry appreciation or talking and writing – which has no connexion with the theme of the World Studies work.
Lunch break
Art and craft Mathematics Library period

Fig. 4. A typical day for a second-year class.

Example 5 *A purpose-built country comprehensive school integrating English with history and geography to form a humanities programme, and with music and drama as 'expressive arts', both as parts of a common-core curriculum.* This new comprehensive with about seven hundred children draws on a mixed catchment area and misses the special problems often faced by the inner-city schools. In addition to the humanities and the expressive arts, there are five other common-core areas which the head and staff call 'faculties' – mathematics, creative activities, physical activities, science and languages. A wide range of subjects not included in the common core, for example, cookery, Latin and typing, are offered as options.

The school is of particular interest because of the two ways in which English contributes to other areas of the curriculum: English is intermeshed with history and geography to provide a humanities programme; and it is seen as having a central role in enriching, and being enriched by, the expressive arts. Many schools integrate English in one of these ways, fewer choose to operate both kinds of organization. In Context 11 there is a detailed analysis of the language work resulting from the two integrated programmes. Here we briefly explore some of the implications.

The humanities programme
Our main interest was in the work of the first- and second-year groups. Here the specialist teachers plan a coherent and consecutive course. The work is content-centred on the grounds that pupils need to be helped to get a foothold in the areas of knowledge that have evolved over the centuries. Thus the specialists are at pains to ensure that the content they regard as being important to historical or geographical understanding is included. Context 11 gives a detailed account of how the programme is operated, but the themes for each term are set out below to indicate the areas selected for a foundation course in the humanities.

1 Prehistory and the creation myths
2 Prehistoric Britain; how man survives; language and communication
3 The medieval world
4 Ancient civilizations; Greece and Rome
5 The Renaissance and exploration
6 Agricultural and village life.

Common ground is covered by each pupil and while there is scope for the development of individual interest at every point, there is particular opportunity for specializing in the second term.

The basic working unit is the small group, particularly appropriate in view of the wide range of ability. The groups change but care is taken that as far as possible they have completed the intended job before moving on. The usual pattern is discussion followed by written work, maps, wall charts and paintings as appropriate.

The first unit, on prehistory and the creation myths, is designed by the English specialist. The focus is on movement, drama, music, reading and writing as ways of getting into the ancient myths. The English contribution goes beyond this, however, and although all the teachers concern themselves with the children's reading and writing in all the units, the availability of the English specialist for help, particularly in finding the way through an extensive reading list, is fully recognized. The English specialist is also favourably placed to help pupils in getting a grip on unfamiliar material. In particular, he is aware of the role of all the teachers in mediating between the pupils and the information they are trying to extract from books and films, and so on. Context 11 gives examples of the copious written work the pupils do which develops from their own initial framework. Of particular interest is Kim's work (see page 103).

The expressive arts

The humanities programme is content-based. The expressive arts programme is much more centred on the English activities of reading, writing,

		10.20–		11.55–		14.15–		15.30
8.45	1	10.45	2	12.55	3	14.20	4	Notes
Mon	Expressive arts	Humanities		Humanities		Games		
Tues	Expressive arts	Science		Humanities		Mathematics		
Wed	Science	French		Mathematics		Creative activities		
Thurs	Humanities	PE		Expressive arts		Mathematics		
Fri	Creative activities	Creative activities		French		Humanities		

Name: First-year class

Fig. 5. First-year class timetable.

listening and discussing, rather as in a specialist English programme. Here, however, they may arise from and be developed and extended by the other specialisms. Music, drama and English are mutually supportive in exploring feeling and ideas. Context 11 includes the writing of a first-year group as part of a programme of improvised movement and their own music about the animal world. The quality of this work crystallizes the benefits of mingling English with other creative subjects as a way to explore the world.

Here then is an organization that seems to work well in terms of the very wide scope it provides for satisfying language work. A good organizational pattern needs to be operated by a good team, and here this happy combination produces some unusually satisfying results.

Example 6 *An open-plan mixed-ability, co-educational secondary school, in the process of becoming a senior high school. The English department is seen here in development against a general background of an attempt to promote new kinds of person interaction.*

One feature which makes the school of special interest is the attempt to forge new responsibility relationships. Traditionally the headteacher is responsible for school policy, but in this institution the warden joins the whole staff at a weekly meeting where, under a voluntary chairman, they have the brief to decide collectively on policy. The head acts in an executive capacity only. Such an arrangement would not necessarily preclude the head working behind the scenes to achieve his own policy, but there was no evidence of this happening during the visit there. The children, too, have their own meeting, a pupil's council, which appeared to have open access in discussion to matters of policy, although in general they would not have power to alter pedagogical decisions. In other ways, also, the school is unusual. All members of the community are on first-name terms; there are no clothes restrictions for pupils or teachers; all eat together in a common dining-room; there are no explicit rules, or punishments, or overt sanctions. All these things contribute to a distinctive atmosphere in the school, an atmosphere which permeates breaks as well as lesson time. Institutionally, the school is committed to a base-line development of the individual, offering maximum choice on the grounds that choice must be seen in operation, before it can be consciously operated.

The curriculum is organized in seven departments: science, mathematics, art and its manifestations, languages, the individual and the group (IG), the creative and expressive use of words, music and movement (CW), and physical education. The two humanities departments have built-in integration. First, there is an overlap of staff, out of five in CW and six in IG, two work in both departments. They can call on a movement specialist from the physical education department, and on the music teacher. The music teacher is responsible for all music in the school and all pupils have lessons with him. He also offers some time for individual tuition. Thus there is considerable potential for work across departments. Secondly, within departments a team of three teachers is responsible for thirty pupils. Although most pupils are taught in groups of thirty there are possibilities for teaching groups of different sizes as staff see ways of exploiting the open-plan environment.

Subject English is incorporated into the CW department, but members of the department are raising basic questions about their role. As answers emerge, the timetable alters to keep pace. Discussions have centred on how far the department should resemble the conventional English department, how far it must take responsibility for the development of basic literacy, and how the particular qualities and abilities of the teachers in the department can be best used. They have also asked questions about where the drama specialist fits into the pattern, how can X's special capacity for promoting good writing, and Y's facility in using films and other visual aids be fully used so that as many pupils as possible benefit from these particular strong points? It is worth noting the three prevailing views:

1 Teaching should continue on a class basis – one teacher to thirty pupils.
2 Some move should be made to allow members of the department each to learn from the strong points of the others to widen the range of what an individual teacher has to offer – this could be a very real contribution to a teacher's development.
3 The curriculum should be changed so that those who have particular specialisms can operate them with as many children as possible.

The first two could be implemented within the existing organization, the third would necessitate considerable reorganization.

There remain questions which will continue to exercise many schools. Does the need to provide basic literacy promote the class unit? Should other priorities override this – will, for example, the drama specialist be seen as offering a core that is the province of all education for all pupils?

How do you reconcile the relative merits of music, movement, drama, literacy, literature and the creative use of words?

Here a team of teachers are rethinking the school curriculum, challenging basic assumptions, trying out new approaches and being prepared to change what does not seem to be working. The stress is on finding ways to involve pupils in the work they do in school, to change the emphasis from imposed tasks to work and activities which seem of value to the pupil, and create a framework in which this type of work predominates. The efforts to change the pattern of interpersonal relationships in the school aim to make a contribution to this and must also have implications for the English work done by the CW department. English work flourishes where pupils can enter into a dialogue with fellow pupils and teacher, a dialogue that has little to do with being competitive or being assessed. The teacher must sometimes assess, but this is not his only role and perhaps not his major one. This school has made a start on the road towards real communication and co-operation between the adults and pupils within its walls, and the benefits for language work are clear.

References and notes

1. For a detailed discussion of the role of reading in learning across the curriculum, see Department of Education and Science, *A Language for Life*, Report of Committee of Inquiry appointed by Secretary of State for Education and Science under Chairmanship of Sir Alan Bullock. [Bullock Report] (HMSO, 1975), pp. 118–20 paras 8.10, 8.11, 8.12 and 8.13.

2. L. S. VYGOTSKY, *Thought and Language* (MIT Press, 1962), pp. 108–9.

3. Ibid., see pp. 83 and 84, where Vygotsky gives Tolstoy's description of how we acquire concepts from a general linguistic context.

4. For a convincing account of the necessity of engaging the feelings as well as the thoughts in learning, see M. R. JONES, *Fantasy and Feeling in Education* (Penguin Books, 1970).

5. Some of our thinking originates from a paper by JAMES BRITTON and B. NEWSOME 'What is learnt in English lessons?', *Journal of Curriculum Studies*, 1 (November 1968), 68–78.

6. See DOUGLAS BARNES, et al., *Language, the Learner and the School* (Penguin Education, 1969), part 3.

7. L. STENHOUSE, *Culture and Education* (Nelson, 1967).

8. J. S. BRUNER, *The Process of Education* (Vintage Books, Random House, New York, 1960), p. 52. See also J. S. BRUNER, *Toward a Theory of Instruction* (Harvard University Press, Cambridge, Mass., 1966).

9. For an interesting account of small-group discussions of a novel at secondary level, see the work of DOUGLAS BARNES, et al., in 'Group talk and literary response', *English in Education*, 5 (Winter 1971), 63–76.

10. See 'Language in the initial training of the primary-school teacher' in A. JONES and J. MULFORD, eds., *Children Using Language* (Oxford University Press, 1971).

11. JAMES BRITTON, *Language and Learning* (Allen Lane, Penguin Press, 1970), p. 152.

12. CONNIE and HAROLD ROSEN, *The Language of Primary School Children* (Penguin Education, 1973), pp. 23 and 24.

Bibliography

Allen, J. *Drama*. Department of Education and Science, Education Survey 2. HMSO, 1967.

Barnes, D., ed. *Drama in the English Classroom*. National Council of Teachers of English, Illinois, 1968.

ed. *Language, the Learner and the School*. Penguin Books, 1969.

Barnes, D., Churley, P. and Thompson, C. 'Group talk and literary response', *English in Education*, **5**, Winter 1971, 63–76.

Bernstein, B. B. 'A critique of the concept of "compensatory education" ', in *Education for Democracy*, ed. D. Rubenstein and C. Stoneman. Penguin Books, 1970, pp. 120–1.

'Education cannot compensate for society', in *School and Society*, Routledge & Kegan Paul in association with Open University Press, 1971.

Blackie, J. *Inside the Primary School*. HMSO, 1969.

Brearley, M. and Hitchfield, E. *A Teacher's Guide to Reading Piaget*. Routledge & Kegan Paul, 1966.

Britton, J. N. *Language and Learning*. Allen Lane, Penguin Press, 1971.

'The role of fantasy', *English in Education*, **5**, Winter 1971, 39–44.

'What's the use – a schematic account of language function', *Birmingham Education Review*, **23**, June 1971, 205–19.

Britton, J. N., ed. *Talking and Writing*. Methuen, 1967.

Britton, J. N. and Newsome, B. 'What is learnt in English lessons?', *Journal of Curriculum Studies*, **1**, November 1968, 68–78.

Brown, R. W. *Words and Things: Introduction to Language*, Free Press, New York, 1958.

Bruner, J. S. 'The course of cognitive growth', in *Readings in the Psychology of Human Growth and Development*, ed. W. R. Baller. Holt, Rinehart & Winston, 1962.

Toward a Theory of Instruction. Harvard University Press, 1966.

Bruner, J. S., et al. *Studies in Cognitive Growth*. John Wiley, New York, 1966.

Burgess, C., et al. *Understanding Children Writing*. Penguin Education, 1973.

Cass, J. *Literature and the Young Child*. Longmans, 1967.

Cassirer, E. *An Essay on Man.* Yale University Press, 1944.

Central Advisory Council for Education. *Children and their Primary Schools.* [Plowden Report.] HMSO, 1967.

Chomsky, N. 'Review of B. F. Skinner's *Verbal Behaviour*', *Language*, **35**, January–March 1959, 26–58.

Clegg, A. B., ed. *The Excitement of Writing.* Chatto & Windus, 1964.

Cook, E. *The Ordinary and the Fabulous.* Cambridge University Press, 1969.

Cosin, B., ed. *School and Society.* Routledge & Kegan Paul in association with Open University Press, 1971.

D'Arcy, Pat, *Reading for Meaning*, Vol. 1, Learning to Read, Vol. 2, The Reader's Response. Hutchinson Educational for Schools Council, 1973.

Department of Education and Science. *A Language for Life.* Report of Committee of Inquiry appointed by Secretary of State for Education and Science under Chairmanship of Sir Alan Bullock. [Bullock Report.] HMSO, 1975.

Dixon, J. *Growth Through English: Report based on the Dartmouth Seminar, 1966.* Oxford University Press, 1969.

Erikson, E. H. *Childhood and Society.* Hogarth Press, 1964 and Penguin Books, 1969.

Identity: Youth and Crisis. Faber, 1971.

'Youth and the life cycle', in *Readings in the Psychology of Human Growth and Development*, ed. W. R. Baller. Holt, Rinehart & Winston, 1962.

Flower, F. D. *Language and Education.* Longmans, 1966.

Friedlander, Kate. 'Children's books and their function in latency and prepuberty', *New Era*, **39**, 1958, 77–83.

Gardner, D. E. M. *Susan Isaacs.* Methuen Educational, 1969.

Goodenough, E., Pitcher, E. G. and Prelinger, E. *Children Tell Stories.* International Universities Press, New York, 1963.

Hannam, C., Smyth, P. and Stephenson, N. *Young Teachers and Reluctant Learners.* Penguin Books, 1971.

Harding, D. W. *Experience into Words.* Chatto & Windus, 1963.

'Psychological processes in the reading of fiction', *British Journal of Aesthetics*, **II**, 1962, 133–47.

'The role of the onlooker', *Scrutiny*, **VI**, 1937, 247–58.

Heathcote, D. 'Improvisation', *English in Education*, **1**, Autumn 1967, 27–30.

Holbrook, D. *The Secret Places.* Cambridge University Press, 1964.

English for the Rejected. Cambridge University Press, 1964.

Hourd, M. L. *The Education of the Poetic Spirit.* Heinemann, 1949.

Isaacs, S. *Intellectual Growth in Young Children.* Routledge & Kegan Paul, 1930.

Social Development in Young Children. Routledge & Kegan Paul, 1950.

Jersild, A. T. 'Self understanding in childhood and adolescence', in *Readings in the Psychology of Human Growth and Development,* ed. W. R. Baller. Holt, Rinehart & Winston, 1962.

Jones, A. and Buttrey, J. *Children and Stories.* Blackwell, 1970.

Jones, A. and Mulford, J., eds. *Children Using Language: An Approach to English in the Primary School.* Oxford University Press, 1972.

Jones, R. M. *Fantasy and Feeling in Education.* Penguin Books, 1972.

Kelly, G. A. *A Theory of Personality.* Norton, New York, 1963.

Labov, W. L. 'The logic of non-standard English', in *Language and Poverty: Perspectives on a Theme,* ed. F. Williams. Markham, Chicago, 1970, chapter 9, pp. 153–87.

Langer, S. K. *Feeling and Form.* Routledge & Kegan Paul, 1953.

Philosophy in a New Key. Harvard University Press, Cambridge, Mass., 1960.

Mind: an Essay on Human Feeling. Johns Hopkins Press, Baltimore, 1967.

Lawton, D. *Social Class, Language and Education.* Routledge & Kegan Paul, 1969.

Class, Culture and the Curriculum. Routledge & Kegan Paul, 1975.

Lawton, D., Campbell, J. and Burkitt, V. *Social Studies 8–13.* Schools Council Working Paper 39, Evans/Methuen Educational, 1971.

Lewis, M. M. *Language and the Child.* National Foundation for Educational Research in England and Wales, Slough, 1969.

Language, Thought and Personality in Infancy and Childhood. Harrap, 1963.

Luria, A. R. *The Role of Speech in the Regulation of Normal and Abnormal Behaviour.* Pergamon Press, Oxford, 1961.

Luria, A. R. and Yudovitch, F. *Speech and the Development of the Mental Processes of the Child.* Staples Press, 1960; Penguin, 1971.

Lyons, J. *Chomsky.* Fontana, 1970.

Mackay, D., Thompson, B. and Schaub, P. *The Theory and Practice of Teaching Initial Reading and Writing,* Breakthrough to Literacy, Teacher's Manual. Longmans for Schools Council, 1970.

McCandless, B. *Children: their Behaviour and Development.* Holt, Rinehart & Winston, 1967.

Maier, H. W. *Three Theories of Child Development.* Harper & Row, 1969.

Mallett, M. 'English in projects', *English in Education,* 8, Spring 1974, 13–23.

'Improvised drama and writing', *Speech and Drama,* 25, Autumn 1976, 15–20.

Marsh, L. G. *Alongside the Child in the Primary School.* Black, 1970.

Marshall, S. *Adventure in Creative Education.* Pergamon Press, Oxford, 1968.

Martin, N. 'Children and stories: their own and other people's', *English in Education,* 6, Summer 1972, 43–54.

Medway, P. *From Information to Understanding.* Ward Lock Educational, 1976.

Melnik, A. P. and Merritt, J., eds. *The Reading Curriculum: Readings.* University of London Press with Open University Press, 1972.

Moffett, J. *Teaching the Universe of Discourse*. Houghton Mifflin, Boston, 1968.
A Student-centred Language Arts Curriculum, Grades 11–13. A Handbook for Teachers. Houghton Mifflin, Boston, 1968.

Newsome, B. 'The nature of English and the strategies and priorities within it', *English in Australia*, **19**, February 1972, 41–61.

Opie, I. and Opie, P. *The Lore and Language of Schoolchildren*. Oxford University Press, 1959.

Peel, E. A. 'Intellectual growth during adolescence', *Birmingham Education Review*, **17**, June 1965, 169–80

Piaget, J. *Play, Dreams and Initiation in Childhood*. Routledge & Kegan Paul, 1951.
Six Psychological Studies. University of London Press, 1964.
Comments on Vygotsky's Critical Remarks concerning the Language and Thought of the Child, and Judgement and Reasoning in the Child. MIT Press, 1962.

Piaget, J. and Inhelder, B. *The Growth of Logical Thinking: from Childhood to Adolescence*. Trans. A. Parsons and S. Milgram. Routledge & Kegan Paul, 1958.

Polanyi, M. *The Study of Man*. Routledge & Kegan Paul, 1959.

Postman, N. and Weingartner, C. *Teaching as a Subversive Activity*. Penguin Books, 1971.

Read, H. *Education Through Art*. Faber, 1943.

Reiner, E. *School is Dead*. Penguin Books, 1971.

Rogers, Carl P. *On Becoming a Person: A Therapist's View of Psycho-therapy*. Constable, 1967.
'Towards becoming a fully functioning person', in *Readings in the Psychology of Human Growth and Development*, ed. W. R. Baller. Holt, Rinehart & Winston, 1962.

Rosen, C. 'Living language', *Primary English*, NATE Bulletin, **III**, Winter 1966, 2–10.

Rosen, C. and Rosen, H. *The Language of Primary School Children*. Penguin Books, 1974.

Sapir, E. *Language, an Introduction to the Study of Speech*. Hart-Davis, 1963.
Culture, Language and Personality, ed. David G. Mandelbaum. University of California Press, Berkeley and Los Angeles, 1949.

Schutz, A. *The Phenomenology of the Social World*. Trans. G. Walsh and F. Lehnert. Heinemann Educational Books, 1972.

Squire, J. R., ed. *Response to Literature*. National Council of Teachers of English, Illinois, 1968.

Stenhouse, L. *Culture and Education*. Nelson, 1967.

Stratta, L., Dixon, J. and Wilkinson, A. *Patterns of Language: Explorations of the Teaching of English*. Heinemann Educational Books, 1973.

Vygotsky, L. S. *Thought and Language*. MIT Press, 1962.

Waldon, J. *Oral Language and Reading*. National Council of Teachers of English, Illinois, 1967.

Walsh, J. A. *Teaching English*. Heinemann Educational Books, 1965.

White, D. M. *Books Before Five*. Cambridge University Press for New Zealand Council for Educational Research, 1956.

Whitehead, F. *The Disappearing Dais*. Chatto Educational, 1971.

Wilkinson, A. *The Foundation of Language: Talking and Reading in Young Children*. Oxford University Press, 1971.

Winnicott, D. W. *Playing and Reality*. Tavistock Publications, 1971.

The Child, the Family and the Outside World. Penguin Books, 1964.

Young, M. F. D. *Knowledge and Control: New Directions in the Sociology of Education*. Collier–Macmillan, 1971.

Project staff, consultative committee and schools involved

Project staff

Bernard Newsome (*Director*)
Margaret Mallett (*Research Officer*)

Consultative committee

James Britton (*Chairman*)	Professor of Education, Goldsmiths' College, University of London
Miss J. Braithwaite	Schools Council Field Officer
J. Coe	Senior Adviser, Oxfordshire Local Education Authority
J. Holland	Vice Principal, Dunmurray County Secondary School, Dunmurray, County Antrim
J. Eryl Jones	Headmaster, Flint Mountain County Primary School, Flint
Miss Nancy Martin	Head of English Department, University of London Institute of Education
T. M. McCutcheon	Principal, Ballymacash Primary School, Lisburn, County Antrim
Peter Medway	Head of English Department, Walworth Lower School, London
B. Morton	Headmaster, Woodseats Boys' Primary School, Sheffield
D. Oldfield	Senior Tutor and Lecturer in English, University of Sussex
†Mrs C. Rosen	Director, Schools Council Language Development in the Primary School Project, Goldsmiths' College, University of London (till 1971); then Senior Lecturer, Trent Park College, Middlesex
T. Woolly	Headmaster, East Preston County Primary School, East Preston, Sussex
M. Young	Lecturer in Sociology, University of London Institute of Education

Schools involved in the project

We gratefully acknowledge the contribution the following schools have made to our thinking:

Alnwick R. C. Primary School, Alnwick, Northumberland
Balliol County Middle School, Newcastle-upon-Tyne 12
Ballymacash Primary School, County Antrim, Northern Ireland
Bladon C of E Primary School, Woodstock, Oxford
Brierly Grimethorpe, Milefield Middle School, Barnsley, South Yorkshire
Brindley Heath Primary School, Kinver, West Midlands
Burradon First School, Dudley, West Midlands
Clissold Park Secondary School, London N16
Countesthorpe College, Leicestershire
Crofton Junior School, Blyth, Northumberland
Croydon High School for Girls, Surrey
Crown Woods Comprehensive School, Eltham, London SE9
Dickson Country Primary School, Portavogie, Lurgan, Northern Ireland
Doe Bank Primary School, Great Barr, West Midlands
Ducklington Primary School, Oxford
Dundonald Girls School, Dundonald, Country Down, Northern Ireland
Dunmurray County Secondary School, County Antrim, Northern Ireland
Felkirk Middle School, Barnsley, South Yorkshire
Gordano School, Bristol, Avon
Greeneway Middle School, Royston, Hertfordshire
Holy Rosary Primary School, Belfast, Northern Ireland
Kingsley Primary School, Hartlepool, Cleveland
Morpeth Girls School, Morpeth, Northumberland
Newbiggin-by-the-Sea West County Junior School, Newbiggin, Northumber-
land
Orangefield Boys School, Belfast, Northern Ireland
Poverest Junior School, Orpington, London Borough of Bromley
Prior Weston Primary School, London EC1
Primrose Hill Primary School, London NW1
Ravenhill Primary School, Rugeley, Staffordshire
Settle High School, Settle, North Yorkshire
Sheredes School, Hoddesdon, Hertfordshire
Shiremoor County Middle School, Shiremoor, North Tyneside
St Roses School, Belfast, Northern Ireland
Sullivan Preparatory School, Belfast, Northern Ireland
South Elmsall Middle School, West Yorkshire
Sudbury Girls High School, Suffolk

Tidemill Primary School, Deptford, Wiltshire
Wandsworth Comprehensive School, London SW18
Walworth Lower School, London SE17
William Tyndale Primary School, London N1
Woodhall County Primary School, Suffolk
Wylam Primary School, Northumberland

WESTMINSTER COLLEGE

VIRTUTE · ET · FIDE

LIBRARY